Adobe
Premiere Pro CC
A Tutorial Approach

CADCIM Technologies

525 St. Andrews Drive
Schererville, IN 46375, USA
(www.cadcim.com)

Contributing Author

Sham Tickoo
Professor
Purdue University Calumet
Hammond, Indiana, USA

CADCIM Technologies

Adobe Premiere Pro CC: A Tutorial Approach
Sham Tickoo

Published by CADCIM Technologies, 525 St Andrews Drive, Schererville, IN 46375 USA.

ISBN 978-1-936646-63-0

NOTICE TO THE READER

www.cadcim.com

DEDICATION

*To teachers, who make it possible to disseminate knowledge
to enlighten the young and curious minds
of our future generations*

*To students, who are dedicated to learning new technologies
and making the world a better place to live in*

THANKS

To employees of CADCIM Technologies for their valuable help

Online Training Program Offered by CADCIM Technologies

CADCIM Technologies provides effective and affordable virtual online training on various software packages including Computer Aided Design and Manufacturing (CAD/CAM), computer programming languages, animation, architecture, and GIS. The training is delivered 'live' via Internet at any time, any place, and at any pace to individuals as well as students of colleges, universities, and CAD/CAM training centers. The main features of this program are:

Training for Students and Companies in a Class Room Setting

Highly experienced instructors and qualified engineers at CADCIM Technologies conduct the classes under the guidance of Prof. Sham Tickoo of Purdue University Calumet, USA. This team has authored several textbooks that are rated "one of the best" in their categories and are used in various colleges, universities, and training centers in North America, Europe, and in other parts of the world.

Training for Individuals

CADCIM Technologies with its cost effective and time saving initiative strives to deliver the training in the comfort of your home or work place, thereby relieving you from the hassles of traveling to training centers.

Training Offered on Software Packages

CADCIM provides basic and advanced training on the following software packages:

CAD/CAM/CAE: CATIA, Pro/ENGINEER Wildfire, SolidWorks, Autodesk Inventor, Solid Edge, NX, AutoCAD, AutoCAD LT, Customizing AutoCAD, EdgeCAM, and ANSYS

Computer Programming: C++, VB.NET, Oracle, AJAX, and Java

Animation and Styling: Autodesk 3ds Max, Autodesk 3ds Max Design, Autodesk Maya, eyeon Fusion, Adobe Flash, and Autodesk Alias Design

Architecture, Civil, and GIS: Autodesk Revit Architecture, AutoCAD Civil 3D, Autodesk Revit Structure, and AutoCAD Map 3D

For more information, please visit the following link:

www.cadcim.com

NOTE

If you are a faculty member, you can register by clicking on the following link to access the teaching resources: **www.cadcim.com/Registration.aspx**. The student resources are available at **www.cadcim.com**. We also provide **Live Virtual Online Training** on various software packages. For more information, write us at **sales@cadcim.com**.

Table of Contents

Preface

Adobe Premiere Pro CC

Adobe Premiere Pro CC is one of the most powerful real-time professional grade video editing applications. It has flexible, precise, and reliable editing tools. You can use the roundtrip audio workflow with the Adobe Audition CC application. In addition, you can render a high quality video for computers, TV, smart phones, films, and tablets by using Adobe Media Encoder CC.

Adobe Premiere Pro CC: A Tutorial Approach textbook has been written to enable the readers to use the video editing power of Premiere Pro CC effectively. The textbook caters to the needs of both video and audio editors.

This textbook will help users learn to apply video and audio effects. The textbook will help the learners transform their imagination into reality with ease. Also, it takes the users across a wide spectrum of video editing through progressive examples, numerous illustrations, and relevant exercises. In totality, this book covers each and every concept of the software with the help of progressive examples and numerous illustrations.

The main features of this textbook are as follows:

- **Tutorial Approach**

    The author has adopted the tutorial point-of-view and the learn-by-doing theme throughout the textbook. This approach helps the users through the process of editing videos in the tutorials.

- **Tips and Notes**

    Additional information related to various topics is provided to the users in the form of tips and notes.

- **Learning Objectives**

    The first page of every chapter summarizes the topics that will be covered in that chapter. This will help the users to easily refer to a topic.

- **Self-Evaluation Test, Review Questions, and Exercises**

    Every chapter ends with Self-Evaluation Test so that the users can assess their knowledge of the chapter. The answers to the Self-Evaluation Test are given at the end of the chapter. Also, the Review Questions and Exercises are given at the end of each chapter and they can be used by the Instructors as test questions and exercises.

Formatting Conventions Used in the Text

Please refer to the following list for the formatting conventions used in this textbook.

- Names of tools, buttons, panels, and tabs are written in boldface.

  Example: The **Razor Tool**, the **Mark In** button, the **Color** tab, the **Tools** panel, the **Sequence1** tab, and so on.

- Names of dialog boxes, windows, drop-down lists, and check boxes are written in boldface.

  Example: The **Open Project** dialog box, the Titler window, the **Captured Video** drop-down list, the **Uniform Scale** check box, and so on.

- Values entered in edit boxes are written in boldface.

  Example: Enter the value **0.02** in the **Position** edit box.

- Names of the files saved are italicized.

  Example: *chapter03.prproj*.

Naming Conventions Used in the Text

Button

The item in the dialog box that has a rectangular shape is termed as **Button**. For example: **OK** button, **Cancel** button, and **Browse** button.

Dialog Box

In this textbook, different terms are used to indicate various options in a dialog box. Refer to Figure 1 for terminologies used in a dialog box.

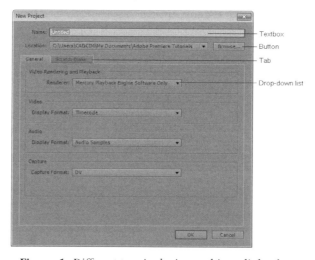

Figure 1 *Different terminologies used in a dialog box*

Drop-down List

A drop-down list is the one in which a set of options are grouped together. You can identify a drop-down list with a down arrow on it. These drop-down lists are given a name based on the tools grouped in them. For example, **Display Format** drop-down list, refer to Figure 1.

Flyout

A flyout is a menu which is displayed on choosing a button/item. Figure 2 shows a flyout displayed on choosing the **New Item** button from the **Project** panel.

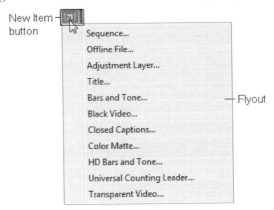

*Figure 2 The flyout displayed on choosing the **New Item** button*

Free Companion Website

It has been our constant endeavor to provide you the best textbooks and services at affordable price. In this endeavor, we have come out with a Free Companion website that will facilitate the process of teaching and learning of Adobe Premiere Pro CC. If you purchase this textbook, you will get access to the files on the companion website.

The following resources are available for the faculty and students in this website:

Faculty Resources
• **Technical Support**
    You can get online technical support by contacting *techsupport@cadcim.com*.

• **Instructor Guide**
    Solutions to all review questions in the textbook are provided in this guide to help the faculty members test the skills of the students.

• **PowerPoint Presentations**
    The contents of the book are arranged in PowerPoint slides that can be used by the faculty for their lectures.

• **Premiere Projects**
    The premiere projects created in tutorials are available for free download.

- **Rendered Images and Media Files**

    Rendered images of all tutorials are provided in the CADCIM website. You can use these images to compare with your rendered images.

- **Colored Images**

    You can download the PDF file containing color images of the screenshots used in this textbook from CADCIM website.

Student Resources
- **Technical Support**

    You can get online technical support by contacting *techsupport@cadcim.com*.

- **Premiere Projects**

    The premiere projects used in tutorials are available for free download.

- **Rendered Images and Media Files**

    Rendered images of all tutorials are provided in the CADCIM website. You can use these images to compare with your rendered images.

- **Colored Images**

    You can download the PDF file containing color images of the screenshots used in this textbook from CADCIM website.

Stay Connected

You can now stay connected with us through Facebook, Linkedin, Pinterest, and Twitter to get the latest information about our textbooks, videos, and teaching/learning resources. To stay informed of such updates, follow us on Facebook *(www.facebook.com/cadcim)*, Linkedin *(http://in.linkedin.com/in/Cadcim)*, Pinterest *(www.pinterest.com/cadcimtech)*, and Twitter *(@cadcimtech)*. You can also subscribe to our YouTube channel *(www.youtube.com/cadcimtech)* to get the information about our latest video tutorials.

If you face any problem in accessing these files, please contact the publisher at *sales@cadcim.com* or the author at *stickoo@purduecal.edu* or *tickoo525@gmail.com*.

Chapter *1*

Introduction to Adobe Premiere Pro CC

Learning Objectives

After completing this chapter, you will be able to:

- *Work with panels*
- *Work with the Workspace*
- *Understand the Source Monitor and the Program Monitor*
- *Customize preferences*
- *Customize keyboard shortcuts*

INTRODUCTION

Adobe Premiere Pro CC is a part of the Adobe Creative Cloud. With Creative Cloud, you have access to every Adobe creative tool and service. It also has a library of video tutorials that will make the learning process fast. In addition, you have access to Sync services, 20GB of online storage, access to Behance Community Hub, and updates (the moment they are released) to all programs.

Adobe Premiere Pro is one of the most powerful real-time professional grade video editing applications. It has flexible, precise, and reliable editing tools. It is a non-linear video editing software that allows you to place, replace, reorder, and modify video elements in the timeline. Adobe Premiere Pro supports latest technologies and cameras. It supports a wide range of video formats including AVCHD, XDCAM, Cannon XF, and QuickTime to name a few.

In this chapter, you will create a new project with required settings, and learn to work with the interface of Adobe Premiere CC. You will also learn how to work with the workspace, navigate through panels, and customize keyboard shortcuts.

Downloading Files

Download the *c01_premiere_cc_tut.zip* and *media.zip* files from *www.cadcim.com*. The path of the files is as follows: *Textbooks > Animation and Visual Effects > Premiere Pro > Adobe Premiere Pro CC: A Tutorial Approach*

Next, navigate to the *Documents* folder and create a new folder with the name *Adobe Premiere Tutorials* and then extract the contents of the zipped files to *\Documents\Adobe Premiere Tutorials*.

Note
1. The path mentioned above for extracting the zip files depends on the operating system being used.

2. The media.zip file contains all media files that are used in this book. Therefore, before proceeding, you need to download the media.zip file at least once.

Starting Adobe Premiere Pro CC and a New Project

After installing Adobe Premiere Pro CC on your computer, follow the steps given below to start Adobe Premiere Pro CC.

1. Choose the **Start** button on the taskbar to display the **Start** menu. Choose **All Programs > Adobe Premiere Pro CC** from the **Start** menu, as shown in Figure 1-1; the screen is displayed along with **Welcome to Adobe Premiere Pro** dialog box, as shown in Figure 1-2.

2. Choose the **New Project** button in the **Welcome to Adobe Premiere Pro** dialog box; the **New Project** dialog box is displayed, as shown in Figure 1-3.

Note
*If you want to open the previously saved projects, choose the **Open Project** button in the **Welcome to Adobe Premiere Pro** dialog box. You can also open the recently saved projects by choosing them from the **Open a Recent Item** list in this dialog box.*

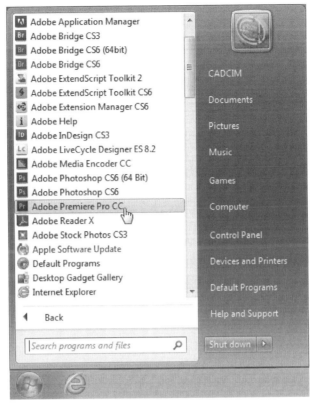

*Figure 1-1 Starting Adobe Premiere Pro CC using the **Start** menu*

*Figure 1-2 The **Welcome to Adobe Premiere Pro** dialog box*

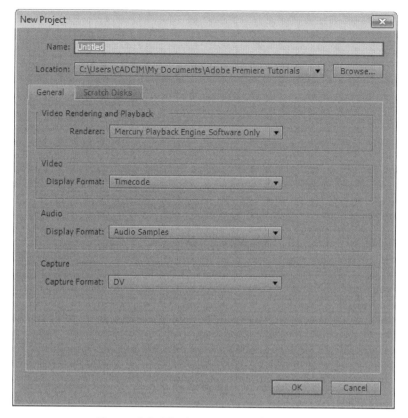

Figure 1-3 *The **New Project** dialog box*

3. In the **General** tab of the **New Project** dialog box, accept the default settings in the **Video Rendering and Playback**, **Video**, **Audio**, and **Capture** areas.

4. Choose the **Scratch Disks** tab from the **New Project** dialog box. The options in this tab are shown in Figure 1-4.

    The options in the **Scratch Disks** tab are used to specify the location of the scratch disks. By default, the files are saved at *\Documents\Adobe\Premiere Pro\7.0*. When you edit a project, Premiere uses the disk space to store files required by your project. Premiere stores captured video and audio files, preview files, and conformed audio files in the scratch disks. It is the best practice to assign a different disk to each asset type. It ensures real-time editing, optimized performance, and 32-bit floating point quality.

5. Choose the **Browse** button on the right of the **Location** drop-down list to specify the location of the new project; the **Please select the destination path for your new project** dialog box is displayed. Next, browse to the location *\Documents\Adobe Premiere Tutorials* and then choose the **Select Folder** button.

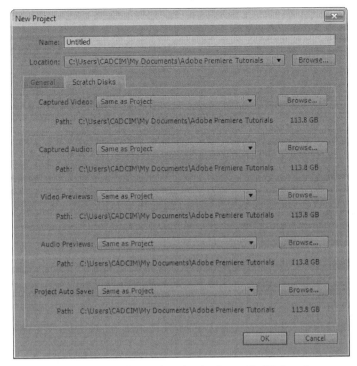

Figure 1-4 *The options in the* **Scratch Disks** *tab*

6. Type the name of the project as **Chapter01** in the **Name** text box in the **New Project** dialog box and then choose the **OK** button; a new project screen with the new sequence is displayed, as shown in Figure 1-5. The new project screen consists of various panels. These panels are discussed in the next section.

Panels

Adobe Premiere Pro CC interface consists of various panels such as the **Project** panel, the **Timeline** panel, the **Media Browser** panel, and so on, refer to Figure 1-5. Some of these panels are discussed next.

Project Panel

The **Project** panel is used to import all media files such as videos, audios, and stills that you will use in the project. By default, the **List View** button is chosen at the bottom of the **Project** panel. As a result, the media files are displayed as a list.

1. Choose **File > Open Project** from the menu bar; the **Open Project** dialog box is displayed. In this dialog box, navigate to *\Documents\Adobe Premiere Tutorials* and select the **chapter01_general** file that you have downloaded from the CADCIM website and choose the **Open** button to close the dialog box.

2. Choose **File > Save As** from the menu bar; the **Save Project** dialog box is displayed. Browse to *\Documents\Adobe Premiere Tutorials*. Type the name **chapter01_general_02** in the **File name** text box and choose the **Save** button; the opened file is saved with the specified name, refer to Figure 1-6.

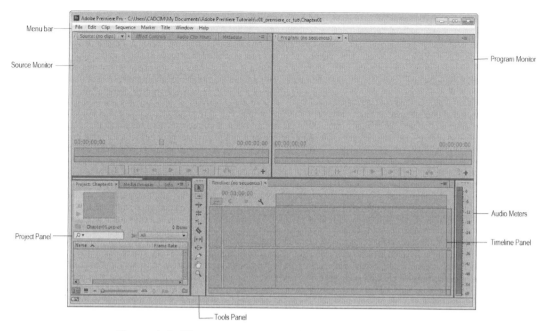

Figure 1-5 *The new project screen displaying various panels*

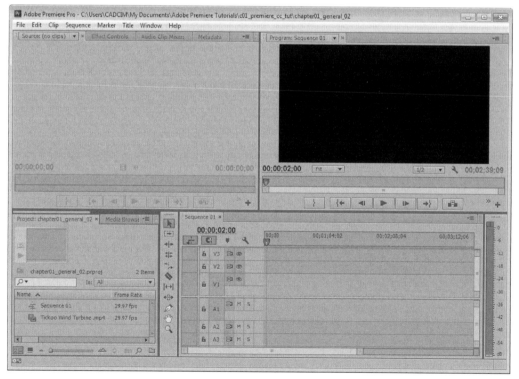

Figure 1-6 *The chapter01_general_02 file displayed in the Premiere Pro interface*

Note
*The Tickoo Wind Turbine file is already imported and saved in the **Project** panel. You will learn more about importing media files in Chapter 2.*

3. Choose the **Icon View** button at the bottom of the **Project** panel, refer to Figure 1-7; the *Tickoo Wind Turbine* file and the **Sequence 01** are displayed as icons.

    When the **Icon View** button is chosen, you can arrange clips in the **Project** panel in a storyboard style. It helps you in quickly visualizing and assembling the sequence. Then, you can use the **Automate to Sequence** button on the lower right of the **Project** panel to move the assembled storyboard to a sequence in the **Timeline** panel.

4. Choose the **List View** button from the **Project** panel and then select the **Tickoo Wind Turbine** media file in the **Project** panel; its preview is displayed at the top of the **Project** panel. Also, the details of the media file are displayed on the right of the preview thumbnail, refer to Figure 1-7. You can choose the **Play-Stop Toggle (Space)** button to view the preview of the selected video clip.

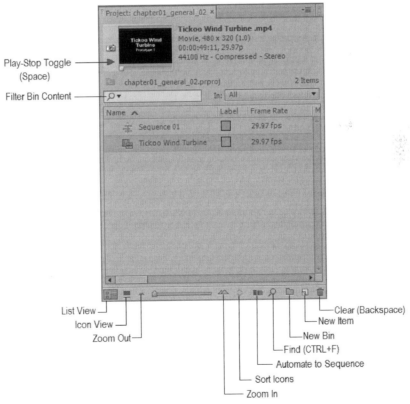

*Figure 1-7 The **Project** panel with various buttons*

To view full details of the media files in the **Project** panel, you need to drag the slider located at the bottom of the **Project** panel. Alternatively, you can increase the size of the **Project** panel to view the details.

Tip: *You can expand a panel to display it in the full screen mode. To do so, hover the cursor over the panel and press the accent key (` ). The accent key is also referred to as back quote key or the tilde key. Alternatively, select the panel by clicking on it and then choose* **Window > Maximize Frame** *from the Menu bar or press SHIFT + `.*

To delete a media file from the **Project** panel, select the file and then choose the **Clear** button. If you have a number of media files in the **Project** panel and you want to delete a specific media file, use the **Filter Bin Content** search field to search the required media file from the list. To do so, type few characters of the required media file in the **Filter Bin Content** search field; a list of files having the typed characters in their names will be displayed, refer to Figure 1-8. Next, select the required option from the list and choose the **Close** button to displayed on the right of the **Filter Bin Content** search field; the required media files will be displayed in the **Project** panel.

5. Choose the **New Bin** button; a new folder (Bin01) is created in the **Project** panel.

Folders are used to organize media files in the **Project** panel. You can rename the newly created folder as per your requirement.

6. Choose the **New Item** button; a flyout is displayed, as shown in Figure 1-9. You can create a new sequence, a new title, and so on by using the options in this flyout.

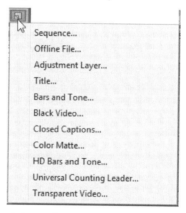

Figure 1-8   *The list showing searched media file*

Figure 1-9   *A flyout displayed on choosing the* **New Item** *button*

A small arrow on the right of the **Name** column header in the **Project** panel indicates that the media files or assets in the **Name** column header are displayed in the alphabetical order. Click on the **Name** column header; the alphabetical order of the assets in the **Project** panel as well as the arrow will be reversed. Next, click on the **Label** column header; a small arrow is displayed on its right and the assets will be sorted according to the **Label** column header.

In Premiere Pro, the **Label** color swatch helps you identify and associate the assets in the **Project** panel.

Next, you will learn how to assign a label to a media file.

7. Select the **Tickoo Wind Turbine** file in the **Project** panel. Choose **Edit > Label** from the menu bar; a cascading menu is displayed, as shown in Figure 1-10.

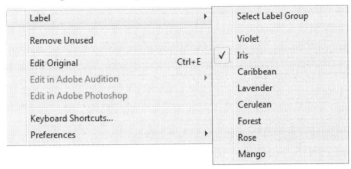

Figure 1-10 *The cascading menu displayed on choosing the* **Label** *option*

8. Choose a color of your choice from the cascading menu; the chosen label color is assigned to the selected clip.

    You can also select all media files having the same label color in the **Project** panel. To do so, select one of the media files. Next, choose **Edit > Label** from the menu bar; a cascading menu is displayed. Now, choose the **Select Label Group** option from the cascading menu; the media file having the same color as that of the selected file will be selected.

    In the following steps, you will learn to modify the name and color of the labels.

9. Choose **Edit > Preferences** from the menu bar; a cascading menu is displayed. Next, choose **Label Colors** from it; the **Preferences** dialog box is displayed with the **Label Colors** option selected in it, refer to Figure 1-11.

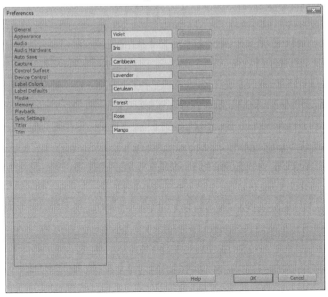

Figure 1-11 *The* **Preferences** *dialog box with the* **Label Colors** *option selected*

Note that the default label colors and their names are displayed on the right, refer to Figure 1-11.

10. Choose the required color swatch; the **Color Picker** dialog box is displayed. Next, select the color of your choice and then choose the **OK** button; the selected color is displayed on the chosen color swatch.

11. Specify a new name for the new color in the text box corresponding to that color in the left of the color swatch. Choose the **OK** button in the **Preferences** dialog box to save the changes made.

    Also, you can move a column to reposition the other column header.

    Next, you will learn how to customize the column header in the **Project** panel.

12. Drag the slider at the bottom of the **Project** panel and move the cursor over the **Media Duration** column header.

13. Press and hold the left mouse button on the **Media Duration** column header and drag the cursor to the left of the **Label** column header; the **Media Duration** column header is now placed on the left of the **Label** column header, refer to Figure 1-12.

14. Choose the button on the top right of the **Project** panel; a flyout is displayed, as shown in Figure 1-13.

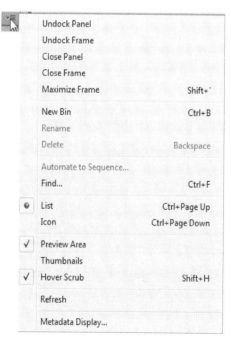

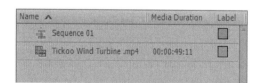

Figure 1-12 *The* **Media Duration** *column header moved to the left of the* **Label** *column header*

Figure 1-13 *The flyout displayed*

15. Choose the **Metadata Display** option from the flyout; the **Metadata Display** dialog box is displayed.

16. Click on the arrow on the left of the **Premiere Pro Project Metadata** node to expand it; a list of all column headers available in this node is displayed, as shown in Figure 1-14.

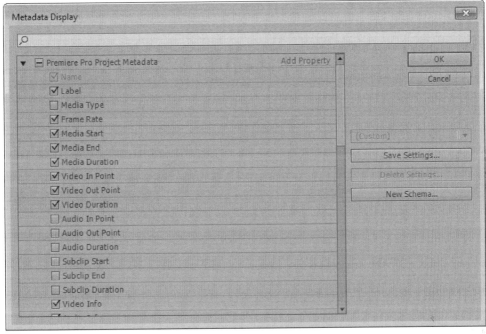

*Figure 1-14 The **Metadata Display** dialog box with the **Premiere Pro Project Metadata** node expanded*

17. Select the check boxes on the left of the column names that you need to display in the **Project** panel. Also, clear the check boxes for the column headers that you do not need to display in the **Project** panel.

18. Choose the **OK** button; the selected column headers are displayed in the **Project** panel.

Media Browser Panel

The **Media Browser** panel is used to navigate to the media files such as video, audio, and stills on your hard drive. When you navigate to the media folder, all media files inside that folder are displayed on the right of the panel, as shown in Figure 1-15.

Info Panel

The **Info** panel displays the details of the media file selected in the **Project** panel, refer to Figure 1-16.

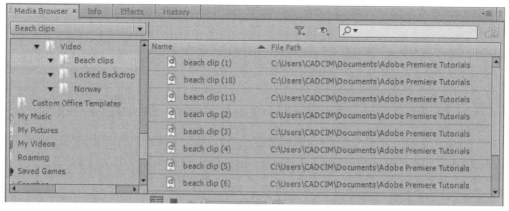

Figure 1-15 The media files displayed in the **Media Browser** panel

Effects Panel

Adobe Premiere Pro CC has a variety of audio and video effects that can be used to make a project more appealing. All these effects are contained in the **Effects** panel and are divided into several categories such as **Presets**, **Audio Effects**, **Audio Transitions**, **Video Effects**, **Video Transitions**, and **Lumetri Looks**, refer to Figure 1-17.

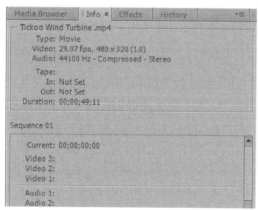

Figure 1-16 The **Info** panel

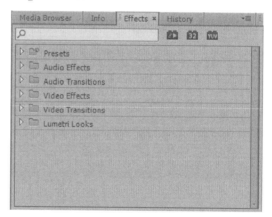

Figure 1-17 The **Effects** panel

History Panel

The **History** panel displays the records of all the actions performed on the project. It is used to jump to any previous state of the project. Each time you make a change to the project, the new state of the project is added to the **History** panel, refer to Figure 1-18.

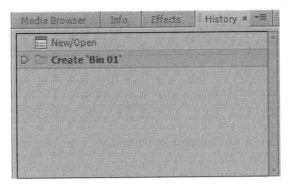

*Figure 1-18 The **History** panel*

Timeline Panel

The **Timeline** panel is located on the lower middle portion of the Premiere Pro interface. You need to drag the media file from the **Project** panel and drop it on the **Timeline** panel, refer to Figure 1-19. Every Premiere Pro project may contain one or more sequences. You can assemble and rearrange sequences in one or more **Timeline** panels. You can open a specific sequence on a tab in the **Timeline** panel or assign a separate **Timeline** panel for it.

Note
*While dragging the clip from the **Project** panel to the **Timeline** panel, if the **Clip Mismatch Warning** message box is displayed, then you need to choose the **Change Sequence Settings** button.*

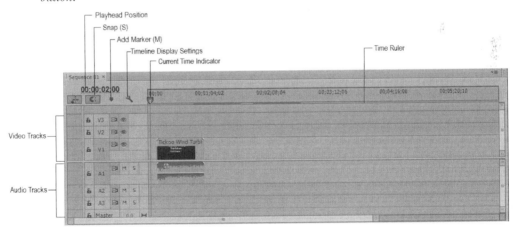

*Figure 1-19 The **Timeline** panel*

The **Playhead Position** shows the timecode for the current frame in the **Timeline** panel, refer to Figure 1-19. To move the CTI (Current Time Indicator) to a different position in the **Timeline**, click on the **Playhead Position**; it will get converted into an edit box. Now, enter a new time. Alternatively, place the cursor over the **Playhead Position**; the shape of the cursor will change. Now, drag the cursor to a new time.

The **Time ruler** is used to measure sequence time horizontally. It also displays icons for markers and the In and Out points of the sequence. You will learn more about these points and markers in the later chapters.

The **Work area bar** is located at the bottom of the **Time ruler**. It specifies the duration of the sequence that you need to preview or export.

The video and audio tracks are located below the **Work area bar**. It displays the video and audio clips in the sequence. You can add, delete, or rename a track using the options displayed in the shortcut menu which is displayed on right-clicking on the track name.

Tools Panel

This panel is located on the lower right of the interface. The tools in the **Tools** panel are used to select, trim, and edit the clips of a sequence, refer to Figure 1-20. You will learn to edit the clips using these tools in the later chapters.

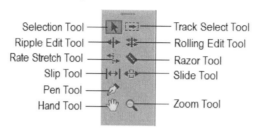

Selection Tool ———— ———— Track Select Tool
Ripple Edit Tool ———— ———— Rolling Edit Tool
Rate Stretch Tool ———— ———— Razor Tool
Slip Tool ———— ———— Slide Tool
Pen Tool ————
Hand Tool ———— ———— Zoom Tool

*Figure 1-20 Tools in the **Tools** panel*

Working with the Workspace

In Premiere Pro interface, a workspace is an area where various panels of different sizes are located.

1.   Choose **Window > Workspace** from the menu bar; a cascading menu is displayed, as shown in Figure 1-21.

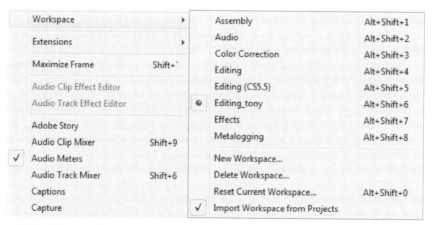

*Figure 1-21 The cascading menu displayed on choosing **Workspace** from the **Window** menu*

By default, the **Editing** workspace is selected for the new project. You can change your workspace to **Audio**, **Color Correction**, **Effects**, **Metalogging**, and so on, based on your requirement.

Note

In this textbook, all the tutorials are performed in a customized workspace. To work in the customized workspace, save the UserWorkspace3.xml file to \Documents\Adobe\Premiere Pro\7.0\Profile-user\Layouts. The xml file is in c01_premiere_cc_tut.zip file that you have downloaded.

You can also modify the current workspace by moving the panels and changing their size, based on your requirement. Now, you will learn how to change the location of the panels and modify their size.

2. Move the cursor over the top-left point of any panel label, refer to Figure 1-22. Now, click and drag it to the location where you want to place it; a light blue colored highlight is displayed to show the preview of the area where the panel will be placed. Release the mouse button to move the panel to the highlighted location.

Figure 1-22 The cursor placed to move the panel

If a rectangular highlight is displayed while dragging the panel, as shown in Figure 1-23, then after releasing the mouse button, the panel will become an additional tab to the set of panels, refer to Figure 1-24. If a trapezoid highlight is displayed at the time of dragging the panel, as shown in Figure 1-25, then the panel will be displayed in between the existing panels.

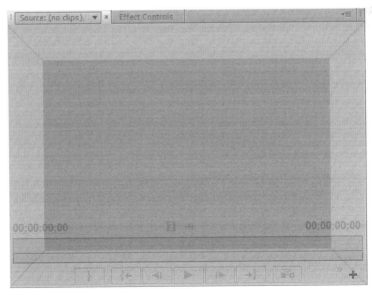

Figure 1-23 A rectangular highlight displayed while dragging

Figure 1-24 *The panel displayed as an additional tab*

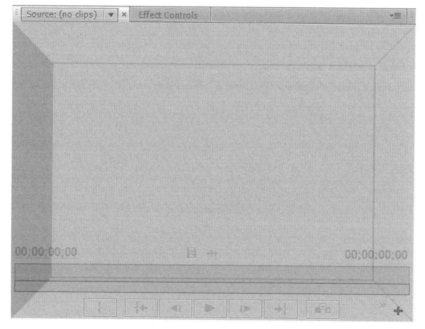

Figure 1-25 *A trapezoid highlight displayed*

3. Choose **Window > Workspace** from the menu bar; a cascading menu is displayed. Next, choose the **Reset Current Workspace** option from the cascading menu; the **Reset Workspace** message box is displayed. Choose the **Yes** button; the current workspace is displayed with the default layout.

    To display the additional panels, select them from the **Window** menu in the menu bar. To close a panel, choose the **Close** button located on the right of the panel label. To resize the panel, move the cursor over the boundary of the panel; the shape of the cursor gets changed, as shown in Figure 1-26. Now, drag the mouse button to resize the panel based on your requirement and release the mouse button.

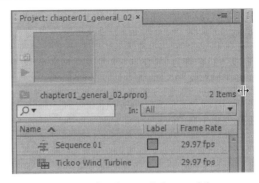

Figure 1-26 The changed shape of the cursor

4. Choose **Window > Workspace > New Workspace** from the menu bar to save your own workspace; the **New Workspace** dialog box is displayed, as shown in Figure 1-27. Type the name of the workspace and then choose the **OK** button; the new workspace is added to the **Window** menu with the specified name.

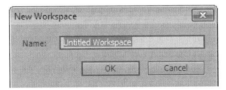

Figure 1-27 The New Workspace dialog box

Source Monitor and Program Monitor

By default, the Source Monitor is located at the top middle of the Premiere Pro interface, refer to Figure 1-28. It is used to edit the video and audio clips that you want to use in the sequence. It plays back individual clips that you will use in the sequence. In the Source Monitor, you can set the In and Out points for a clip (audio or video), insert clip markers based on your requirement, and add the clip to the sequence. You can also specify the video or audio track of the clip in the Source Monitor. You will learn more about these features in the later chapters.

The Program Monitor is placed on the top right portion of the Premiere Pro screen, refer to Figure 1-29. It plays back the sequence of clips that had been assembled in the **Timeline** panel.

Figure 1-28 *The Source Monitor*

The Source and Program Monitors have playback controls at their bottom. These playback controls are used to playback and cue the current frame of the source clip or sequence. To change the magnification settings of the clip displayed in the Source or Program Monitor, click on the arrow on the right of the **Select Zoom Level** button; a drop-down list is displayed, as shown in Figure 1-30. Next, select the magnification based on your requirement.

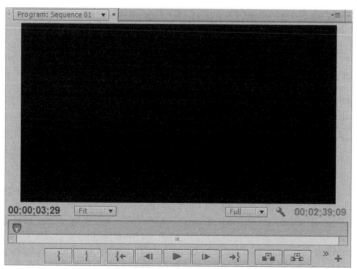

Figure 1-29 *The Program Monitor*

Figure 1-30 *The drop-down list displayed on choosing the* ***Select Zoom Level*** *button*

Customizing Preferences

In Premiere Pro, you can customize the preferences such as appearance of the interface, audio settings, capture, and so on. Next, you will adjust the brightness of the Premiere interface.

1. Choose **Edit > Preferences** from the menu bar; a cascading menu is displayed, as shown in Figure 1-31.

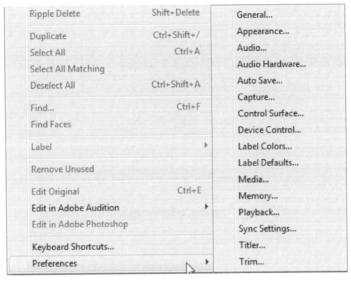

Ripple Delete	Shift+Delete	General...
Duplicate	Ctrl+Shift+/	Appearance...
Select All	Ctrl+A	Audio...
Select All Matching		Audio Hardware...
Deselect All	Ctrl+Shift+A	Auto Save...
		Capture...
Find...	Ctrl+F	Control Surface...
Find Faces		Device Control...
Label	▶	Label Colors...
		Label Defaults...
Remove Unused		Media...
		Memory...
Edit Original	Ctrl+E	Playback...
Edit in Adobe Audition	▶	Sync Settings...
Edit in Adobe Photoshop		Titler...
Keyboard Shortcuts...		Trim...
Preferences	▶	

Figure 1-31 The cascading menu displayed on choosing the Preferences option from the Edit menu

2. Choose the **Appearance** option from the cascading menu; the **Preferences** dialog box is displayed, refer to Figure 1-32.

3. In the **Brightness** area, drag the slider; the brightness of the Premiere Pro interface is changed, as shown in Figure 1-32.

    You can choose the **Default** button to restore the appearance of the Premiere Pro interface to default.

4. After specifying the settings for appearance, choose the **OK** button to save the changes made.

Customizing Keyboard Shortcuts

In this section, you will understand how to customize keyboard shortcuts. When you move the cursor over a button or tool; the name of the button or tool with its keyboard shortcut is displayed on the tool tip, as shown in Figure 1-33.

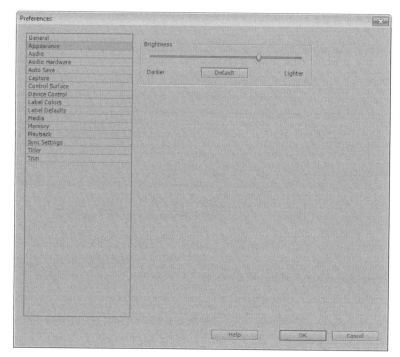

Figure 1-32 The **Preferences** *dialog box*

Figure 1-33 The tool tip showing the name and shortcut key

You can view the shortcuts of buttons, panels, and commands from menus. Figure 1-34 displays the shortcut commands for some of the options.

Next, you will change the shortcut of the **Capture** command.

1. Choose **Edit > Keyboard Shortcuts** from the menu bar; the **Keyboard Shortcuts** dialog box is displayed. By default, the **Application** option is selected in the drop-down list located below the **Keyboard Layout Preset** drop-down list. Also, all commands related to the **Application** option are displayed in the **Command** column.

2. Click on the arrow on the left of the **Window** command in the **Command** column; various options under the **Window** node are displayed.

3. Select the **Capture** row; it is highlighted, as shown in Figure 1-35. Next, choose the **Edit** button.

*Figure 1-34 Partial view of the **Window** menu displaying different options and their shortcuts*

*Figure 1-35 The **Capture** row highlighted*

4. Now, press the J key on the keyboard; a warning message "**The Shortcut J was already in use by the Application > Shuttle Left command. That command will no longer have a keyboard shortcut**" is displayed at the bottom of the dialog box.

5. Make sure the edit mode is enabled for the **Capture** row. Next, press the CTRL+SHIFT+J keys. Now, choose the **OK** button from the **Keyboard Shortcuts** dialog box; the CTRL+SHIFT+J key combination is assigned to the **Capture** command.

    You can reset the default keyboard shortcut settings by choosing **Adobe Premiere Pro Default** from the **Keyboard Layout Preset** drop-down list from the **Keyboard Shortcuts** dialog box.

Self-Evaluation Test

Answer the following questions and then compare them to those given at the end of this chapter:

1. Which of the following buttons in the **Welcome to Adobe Premiere Pro** dialog box is used to create a new project?

    (a) **Open Project**   (b) **Help**
    (c) **New Project**   (d) All of the above

2. Which of the following panels is used to import all media files such as videos, audios, and stills to your project?

    (a) **Project**   (b) **Info**
    (c) **Effects**   (d) **Timeline**

3. Which of the following panels is used to navigate through the media files such as video, audio, and stills on your hard disk?

    (a) **Project**   (b) **Effects**
    (c) **Info**   (d) **Media Browser**

4. Which of the following panels is used to select, trim, and edit the clips in a sequence?

    (a) **Project**   (b) **Tools**
    (c) **Info**   (d) **Media Browser**

5. The options in the _____ tab in the **New Project** dialog box are used to specify the location of various types of files in Adobe Premiere Pro CC.

6. The _____ button in the **Project** panel is used to display the preview of the selected video clip.

7. The **New Bin** button is used to create a new folder in the **Project** panel to organize files or assets. (T/F)

8. You can open an existing project by choosing the **Open Project** button in the **Welcome to Adobe Premiere Pro** dialog box. (T/F)

9. The **Timeline** panel is placed in the lower middle portion of the Adobe Premiere Pro CC screen. (T/F)

10. The **Current time indicator** (CTI) is used to specify the current frame displayed in the Source Monitor. (T/F)

Review Questions

Answer the following questions:

1. Which of the following buttons in the **Welcome to Adobe Premiere Pro** dialog box is used to open the online help?

   (a) **Open Project**   (b) **Resources**
   (c) **New Project**   (d) All of the above

2. Which of the following monitors is used to playback the sequence of clips that you have assembled in the **Timeline** panel?

   (a) Source Monitor   (b) Reference Monitor
   (c) Program Monitor   (d) None of the above

3. Which of the following panels has a variety of audio and video effects that you can use in a project?

   (a) **Effects**   (b) **Info**
   (c) **Media Browser**   (d) **History**

4. Which of the following options in the **Edit** menu of the menu bar is used to customize the preferences of Adobe Premiere Pro CC?

   (a) **Preferences**   (b) **Keyboard shortcuts**
   (c) **Label**   (d) None of these

5. Which of the following options in the **Preferences** dialog box is used to set the brightness of the Adobe Premiere Pro CC interface?

   (a) **General**   (b) **Media**
   (c) **Appearance**   (d) **Capture**

6. The _____ is used to measure the sequence time horizontally.

7. The _____ is located at the bottom of the time ruler and is used to specify the area of the sequence that you need to preview or export.

8. The Source Monitor is used to playback and prepare the video and audio clips that you need to use in your sequence. (T/F)

EXERCISE

Exercise 1

Create a new project in Adobe Premiere CC as per the specifications of your video clip. Try to create your own workspace by dragging the panel boundaries to modify their sizes and to change their location. Create a new sequence in the same project.

Chapter 2

Importing Media Files

Learning Objectives

After completing this chapter, you will be able to:

- *Import media files using the import option*
- *Import media files using the Media Browser panel*
- *Import multiple media files*
- *Import still images and layered Photoshop files*
- *Import a saved Premiere project into the opened project*

INTRODUCTION

In this chapter, you will learn to open the project file and import various types of media files using different methods. You will also learn to import single layered and multi-layered Photoshop files. Moreover, you will learn to import a saved Premiere project into an opened project.

Before you start this chapter, you need to download the *c02_premiere_cc_tut.zip* from *www.cadcim.com*. The path of the file is as follows: *Textbooks > Animation and Visual Effects > Premiere Pro > Adobe Premiere Pro CC: A Tutorial Approach*

Next, extract the contents of the zip file at *\Documents\Adobe Premiere Tutorials*.

OPENING THE PROJECT FILE

In this section, you will open the project file.

1. Start Premiere as discussed in Chapter 1; the **Welcome to Adobe Premiere Pro** dialog box is displayed along with the Premiere screen.

2. Choose the **Open Project** button in this dialog box; the **Open Project** dialog box is displayed, refer to Figure 2-1.

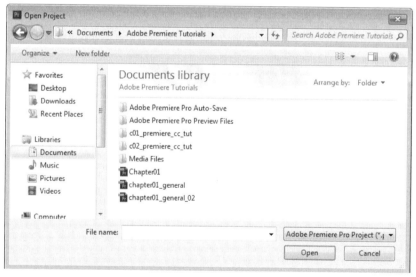

*Figure 2-1 The **Open Project** dialog box*

3. In this dialog box, browse to the location *\Documents\Adobe Premiere Tutorials\ c02_premiere_cc_tut*. Next, select the **chapter02** file and then choose the **Open** button; the *chapter02* file is opened.

4. Choose **File > Save As** from the menu bar; the **Save Project** dialog box is displayed, refer to Figure 2-2. Type the name **chapter02_02** in the **File name** text box and choose the **Save** button; the opened file is saved with the specified name.

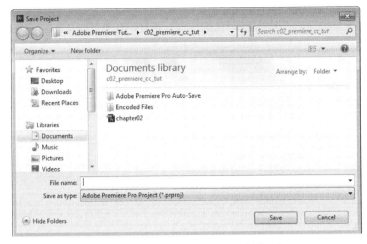

*Figure 2-2 The **Save Project** dialog box*

IMPORTING FILES

You can import video, audio, still images, and Photoshop files to the Premiere project. In this process, you can import a single file, multiple files, or an entire folder. Next, you will learn to import various types of files.

Importing Files Using the Import Option

In this section, you will import files by using the **Import** option from the **File** menu.

1. Choose **File > Import** from the menu bar; the **Import** dialog box is displayed, as shown in Figure 2-3. Alternatively, press CTRL+I to invoke the **Import** dialog box.

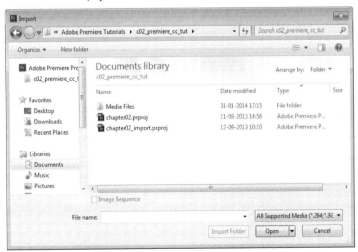

*Figure 2-3 The **Import** dialog box*

2. In this dialog box, browse to \Documents\Adobe Premiere Tutorials\02_premiere_cc_tut\Media Files\Video and then select **Tickoo Wind Turbine.mp4**. Next, choose the **Open** button; the selected file is imported and displayed in the **Project** panel, as shown in Figure 2-4.

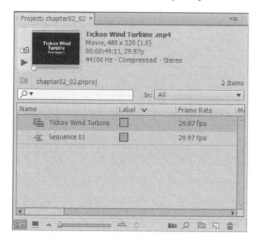

*Figure 2-4 The **Tickoo Wind Turbine** file displayed in the **Project** panel after importing*

Next, you will import multiple media files.

3. Double-click on an empty area in the **Project** panel; the **Import** dialog box is displayed.

4. In this dialog box, browse to \Documents\Adobe Premiere Tutorials\c02_premiere_cc_tut\Media Files\Video. Next, select all media files except the *Tickoo Wind Turbine.mp4*, *beach clips*, *Locked Backdrop*, and *Norway* folders.

5. Choose the **Open** button; all the selected media files in the *Video* folder are imported and displayed in the **Project** panel, as shown in Figure 2-5.

6. Select all the media files in the **Project** panel except *Tickoo Wind Turbine* and then press DELETE; the selected media files are deleted from the **Project** panel.

Next, you will import a folder containing the media files.

7. Press CTRL+I; the **Import** dialog box is displayed.

8. In this dialog box, browse to \Documents\Adobe Premiere Tutorials\c02_premiere_cc_tut\Media Files\Video. Now, select the **Beach clips** folder; the **Import Folder** button is activated. Choose this button; the entire folder is displayed in the **Project** panel, as shown in Figure 2-6.

9. In the **Project** panel, click on the arrow on the left of the folder label to view all the files inside the folder.

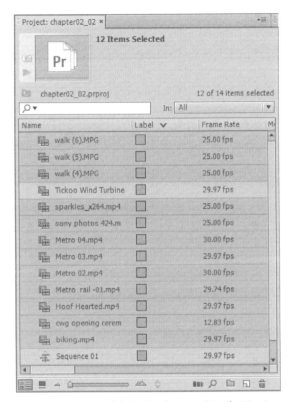

Figure 2-5 *Multiple files imported in the **Project** panel*

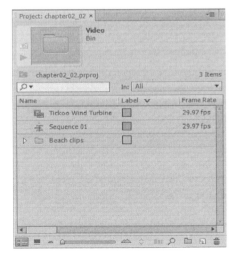

Figure 2-6 *An entire folder imported in the **Project** panel*

Note

*If you have deleted any recently imported file from the **Project** panel, you can easily reimport that file. To do so, choose **File > Import Recent File** from the menu bar; a cascading menu is displayed showing all the recently imported files, refer to Figure 2-7. Now, you can choose the required file from the cascading menu.*

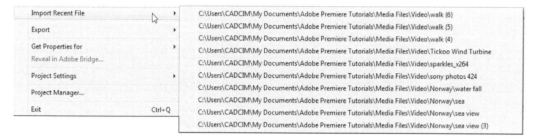

Figure 2-7 The recently imported files displayed in the cascading menu

Importing Files Using the Media Browser Panel

In this section, you will import the files using the **Media Browser** panel.

1. Choose the **Media Browser** panel, if it is not already chosen; all the drives are listed on the left of this panel, as shown in Figure 2-8.

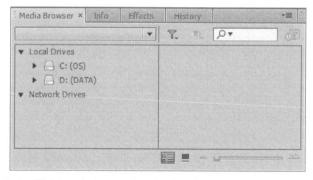

*Figure 2-8 All drives in hard drive displayed in the **Media Browser** panel*

2. In this panel, navigate to the *\Documents\Adobe Premiere Tutorials\c02_premiere_cc_tut\Media Files* folder. Now, double-click on the *Video* folder in the right pane of the **Media Browser** panel; all the files inside the *Video* folder are displayed on the right of the **Media Browser** panel, as shown in Figure 2-9.

3. Right-click on the file name that you want to import; a shortcut menu is displayed, refer to Figure 2-10.

4. Choose the **Import** option from the shortcut menu; the selected media file is imported and displayed in the **Project** panel.

    Alternatively, drag the required file from the **Media Browser** panel to the **Project** panel to import it.

*Figure 2-9 All files inside the **Video** folder displayed in the **Media Browser** panel*

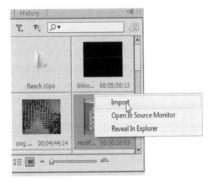

Figure 2-10 The shortcut menu displayed after right-clicking on a file

Importing Still Image in Adobe Premiere Pro CC

In this section, you will import the still image.

1. Double-click on empty area in the **Project** panel; the **Import** dialog box is displayed.

2. In this dialog box, browse to *\Documents\Adobe Premiere Tutorials\c02_premiere_cc_tut\Media Files\Stills* and then select **sea beach.JPG.** Next, choose the **Open** button; the selected image is imported and displayed in the **Project** panel. The thumbnail preview and description of the imported image is displayed at the top of the **Project** panel, as shown in Figure 2-11.

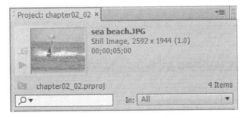

Figure 2-11 The thumbnail preview and description of the image displayed

As per the description, the default duration of the imported image is 5 seconds. However, you can change the default duration of the still image as per your requirement. To change the default duration, follow the steps given next.

3. Choose **Edit > Preferences > General** from the menu bar; the **Preferences** dialog box is displayed.

4. In this dialog box, enter **120** in the **Still Image Default Duration** edit box and then choose the **OK** button to close the dialog box.

5. Import another still image in the **Project** panel. Now, you will notice that the duration of the image is 4 seconds.

Note
It is recommended to change the default duration of the still images based on your requirement before importing them.

Importing Layered Photoshop Files

You can import the stills created in Photoshop using one of the methods discussed earlier in this tutorial. In this section, you will import a layered Photoshop file in Premiere Pro.

1. Double-click on empty area in the **Project** panel; the **Import** dialog box is displayed.

2. Browse to the *\Documents\Adobe Premiere Tutorials\c02_premiere_cc_tut\Media Files\psd* folder that you have downloaded from CADCIM website. Now, select the **Photoshop** option from the drop-down list located on the right of the **File name** text box; the Photoshop files are displayed in the **Import** dialog box, refer to Figure 2-12.

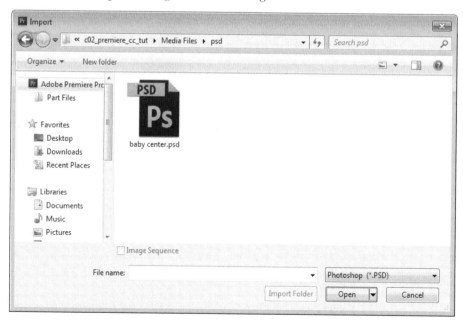

*Figure 2-12 The Photoshop files displayed in the **Import** dialog box*

3. Select the **baby center** file and then choose the **Open** button; the **Import Layered File: baby center** dialog box is displayed, as shown in Figure 2-13.

*Figure 2-13 The **Import Layered File: baby center** dialog box*

By default, the **Merge All Layers** option is selected in the **Import As** drop-down list in this dialog box. This option is used to import the entire *psd* file as a single flattened PSD clip. On selecting the **Individual Layers** option, only the selected layers will be imported. Next, you will import an individual layer from the PSD file.

4. Select the **Individual Layers** option from the **Import As** drop-down list and then choose the **Select None** button; all the layers are deselected.

5. Select the **Home Page Support** check box to select this layer and then choose the **OK** button; the selected individual layer is imported and displayed in the **Project** panel, as shown in Figure 2-14.

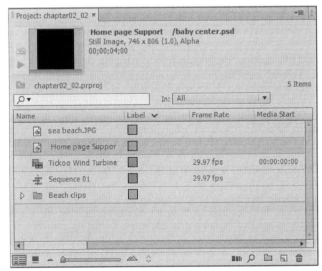

*Figure 2-14 The individual layer imported and displayed in the **Project** panel*

Next, you will import the individual layers according to the footage dimensions.

6. Repeat steps 1 to 4 discussed above.

7. Select the **Funny nanny** check box and make sure that the **Document Size** option is selected in the **Footage Dimensions** drop-down list. Now, choose the **OK** button; the selected layer is imported and displayed in the **Project** panel.

8. In the **Project** panel, double-click on the imported **Funny nanny** layer icon; it is displayed in the Source Monitor, as shown in Figure 2-15.

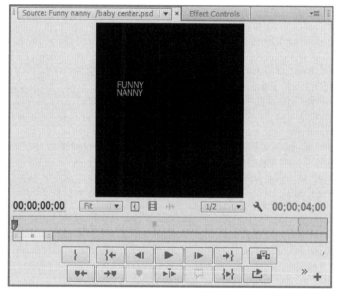

Figure 2-15 *The **Funny nanny** layer displayed in the Source Monitor*

9. Repeat steps 1 to 4 and select the **Funny nanny** check box.

10. In the **Footage Dimensions** drop-down list, select the **Layer Size** option and choose the **OK** button; the individual selected layer is imported.

11. In the **Project** panel, double-click on the imported **Funny nanny** layer icon; it is displayed in the Source Monitor, as shown in Figure 2-16.

Next, you will import the layered Photoshop file as a sequence.

12. Press the CTRL+ I; the **Import** dialog box is displayed.

13. Select the **baby center** file and choose the **Open** button; the **Import Layered File: baby center** dialog box is displayed.

Figure 2-16 The Funny nanny layer displayed in the Source Monitor

14. Select the **Sequence** option from the **Import As** drop-down list and choose the **OK** button; a new bin (folder) with the name **baby center** is created in the **Project** panel. Expand the **baby center** folder, if not already expanded. Notice all the layers and the sequence created are displayed in the **Project** panel, refer to Figure 2-17.

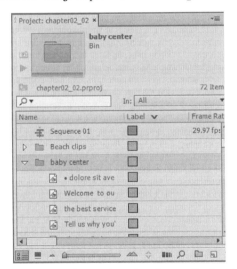

Figure 2-17 All Photoshop layers displayed in the baby center bin in the Project panel

15. Drag the vertical slider in the **Project** panel to view the new **baby center** sequence and then double-click on it; the sequence is displayed in the **Timeline** panel as well as in the Program Monitor, as shown in Figures 2-18 and 2-19. You need to press the backslash (\) key to properly view the Photoshop layers in the **Timeline** panel, refer to Figure 2-18. Also, drag the slider in the **Timeline** panel to view all the video tracks. Press CTRL+S to save the file.

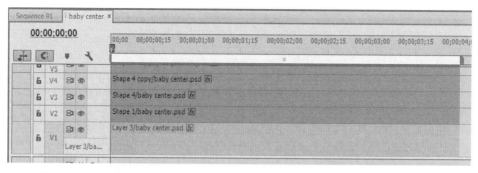

Figure 2-18 *The* ***baby center*** *sequence displayed in the* ***Timeline*** *panel*

Figure 2-19 *The new sequence displayed in the Program Monitor*

Importing the Saved Premiere Projects

You can import the saved Premiere projects into the opened Premiere project. This is the only way to transfer the complete sequence and clip information of a project into another project. In this section, you will learn to import a saved Premiere project into the opened project.

1. Open the file *chapter02_import.prproj* that you have downloaded from the CADCIM website.

2. Choose **File > Save As** from the menu bar; the **Save Project** dialog box is displayed. Type the name **chapter02_import_02** in the **File name** text box and choose the **Save** button; the opened file is saved with the specified name, refer to Figure 2-20.

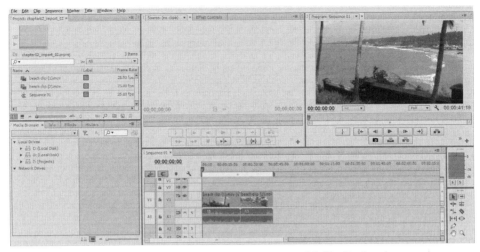

*Figure 2-20 The **chapter02_import_02** file displayed*

3. Delete the beach clips from the **Project** panel by selecting them and then pressing DELETE. On pressing DELETE; the **Adobe Premiere Pro** message box is displayed, as shown in Figure 2-21. Choose the **Yes** button from the message box.

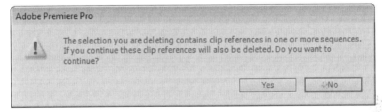

*Figure 2-21 The **Adobe Premiere Pro** message box*

4. Double-click on empty area in the **Project** panel; the **Import** dialog box is displayed.

5. In the **Import** dialog box, select **Adobe Premiere Pro Projects** from the drop-down list located at the bottom right corner of the dialog box. Next, browse to the location *\Documents\Adobe Premiere Tutorials\c02_premiere_cc_tut*. Then, select the **chapter02_import** file and choose the **Open** button; the **Import Project: chapter02_import** dialog box is displayed, as shown in Figure 2-22.

*Figure 2-22 The **Import Project: chapter02_import** dialog box*

In the **Import Project: chapter02_import** dialog box, the **Import Entire Project** radio button is selected by default. This radio button is used to import the entire project with all its sequences and media assets. The **Import Selected Sequences** radio button in this dialog box is used to import the selected sequences from the project.

6. Make sure the **Import Entire Project** radio button is selected in the **Import Project: chapter02_import** dialog box and then choose the **OK** button; the **chapter02_import** file is imported and displayed in the **Project** panel as a folder. You can expand the bin to view its sequence and files, refer to Figure 2-23.

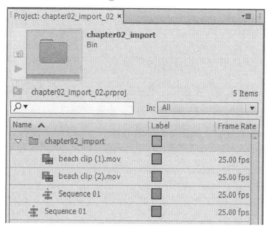

Figure 2-23 *Partial view of the* **chapter02_import** *folder in the* **Project** *panel*

Self-Evaluation Test

Answer the following questions and then compare them to those given at the end of this chapter:

1. Which of the following shortcut keys is used to invoke the **Import** dialog box?

    (a) CTRL+I   (b) ALT+CTRL+I
    (c) ALT+I   (d) SHIFT+I

2. Which of the following panels is used to import the media files in Premiere project?

    (a) **Media Browser**   (b) **Info**
    (c) **Effects Controls**   (d) **Effects**

3. To search files on your computer hard drive, you can use the _____ panel.

4. You cannot import an entire folder into Adobe Premiere Pro. (T/F)

5. You can import the saved Premiere Pro projects into your current opened project. (T/F)

Review Questions

Answer the following questions:

1. Which of the following shortcut keys is used to select a range of files to import them in Adobe Premiere Pro?

    (a) CTRL   (b) SHIFT
    (c) CTRL+ALT   (d) ALT

2. Which of the following media files can be imported into the Premiere project?

    (a) Video clips   (b) Photoshop files
    (c) Audio clips   (d) All of these

3. Before importing a file, you can preview in the _____ to decide whether to import or not.

4. You can double-click on empty area in the **Project** panel to invoke the **Import** dialog box. (T/F)

EXERCISE

Exercise 1

Create a new project in Premiere as per the specifications of a video clip. Try to import various types of files using different options in Premiere.

Answers to Self-Evaluation Test
1. a, **2.** a, **3.** Media Browser, **4.** F, **5.** T

Chapter 3

Assembling Sequences in the Timeline

Learning Objectives

After completing this chapter, you will be able to:

- *Organize video clips in the Project panel*
- *Create a new sequence based on the specifications of a clip*
- *View clips in the Source Monitor*
- *Set the Source In and Source Out points*
- *Add clips to a sequence*
- *Perform the Overlay and Insert edits*
- *Use the Toggle Sync Lock and Toggle Track Lock buttons*
- *Perform the three-point Overlay and Insert edits*

INTRODUCTION

In this chapter, you will learn to view clips in the Source Monitor, assemble a sequence by dragging clips in the **Timeline** panel, set markers, set the In and Out points, and perform Overlay and Insert edits. In addition, you will learn three-point editing with monitor controls.

TUTORIALS

Before you start the tutorials, you need to download the *c03_premiere_cc_tut.zip* file from *www.cadcim.com*. The path of the file is as follows: *Textbooks > Animation and Visual Effects > Premiere Pro > Premiere Pro CC: A Tutorial Approach*

Next, extract the contents of the zip file to *\Documents\Adobe Premiere Tutorials*.

Tutorial 1

In this tutorial, you will import a video clip, organize multiple clips, set markers on them and create a sequence. In addition, you will set the In and Out points in the Source Monitor and add clips to the sequence. The output of the sequence at frame 00:00:09:00 is shown in Figure 3-1.

(Expected Time: 30 min)

Figure 3-1 *The output of the sequence at frame 00:00:09:00*

The following steps are required to complete this tutorial:

a. Create a new project.
b. Import video clips.
c. Organize video clips in the **Project** panel.
d. Create a new sequence based on the specifications of a clip.
e. View clips in the Source Monitor.
f. Set Markers.
g. Set the In and Out points in the Source Monitor.
h. Add clips.

i.   Save the file.
j.   Render the sequence.

Creating a New Project
In this section, you will create a new project.

1.   Start Premiere; the **Welcome to Adobe Premiere Pro** dialog box is displayed.

2.   Choose the **New Project** option; the **New Project** dialog box is displayed.

3.   In the **General** tab of the **New Project** dialog box, type **chapter03** in the **Name** text box.

4.   Choose the **Browse** button corresponding to the **Location** drop-down list; the **Please select the destination path for your new project** dialog box is displayed. In this dialog box, browse to *\Documents\Adobe Premiere Tutorials\c03_premiere_cc_tut* and choose the **Select Folder** button.

5.   Choose the **Scratch Disks** tab. In the **Captured Video**, **Captured Audio**, **Video Previews**, **Audio Previews**, and **Project Auto Save** drop-down lists, select the **Same as Project** option.

6.   Choose the **OK** button; a new project is displayed. Also, the file is saved with the name *chapter03.prproj*, as shown in Figure 3-2.

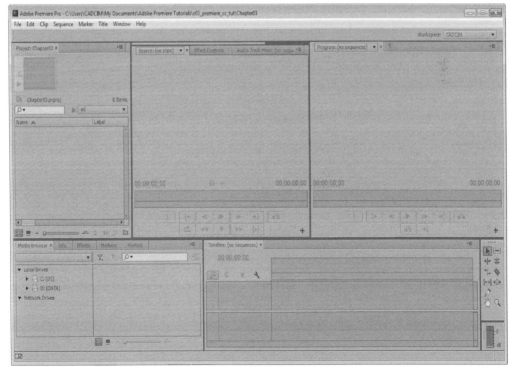

Figure 3-2 *The chapter03 file displayed*

Importing Video Clips

In this section, you will import video clips.

1. Press the CTRL+I keys; the **Import** dialog box is displayed.

2. Browse to *\Documents\Adobe Premiere Tutorials\c03_premiere_cc_tut\Media Files* and then select the **road drive (1).AVI** clip from it. Next, choose the **Open** button; the selected file is imported and displayed in the **Project** panel.

    Next, you will import multiple media files.

3. Double-click on the empty area in the **Project** panel; the **Import** dialog box is displayed.

4. Browse to *\Documents\Adobe Premiere Tutorials\c03_premiere_cc_tut\Media Files*. Press CTRL + A to select all media files. Next, press and hold the CTRL key and then click on the **road drive (1).AVI** clip to deselect it.

5. Choose the **Open** button; all selected media files in the *Media Files* folder are imported and displayed in the **Project** panel, as shown in Figure 3-3.

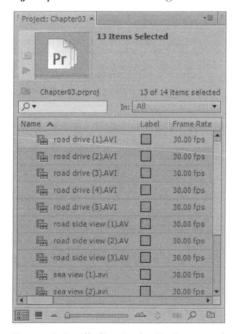

Figure 3-3 *All clips in the **Project** panel*

Organizing Video Clips in the Project Panel

In this section, you will organize video clips in the **Project** panel.

1. Choose the **New Bin** button at the bottom of the **Project** panel; a new bin with the name **Bin 01** is created in the **Project** panel. Modify its name to **sea clips**.

2. Select all sea clips in the **Project** panel by using the CTRL key and then drag them to the **sea clips** bin; all selected files are moved into the **sea clips** bin.

3. Click on the empty area in the **Project** panel to deselect the files.

4. Create a new bin with the name **road clips** and select all road clips and then move them to **road clips** bin. All clips are organized in the **Project** panel, as shown in Figure 3-4.

Figure 3-4 *All clips arranged in bins in the* **Project** *panel*

Creating a New Sequence Based on the Specifications of a Clip

In this section, you will create a new sequence based on the settings of your clips or footage in the **Project** panel.

1. Select **water fall.AVI** in the **Project** panel; the thumbnail preview of the clip and its specifications are displayed on the top of the **Project** panel, as shown in Figure 3-5.

2. Choose the **New Item** button at the bottom of the **Project** panel; a flyout is displayed. Choose the **Sequence** option from the flyout; the **New Sequence** dialog box is displayed.

Figure 3-5 *The thumbnail preview and settings of the selected clip*

3. Accept the default settings in the **Sequence Presets** tab.

4. Choose the **Tracks** tab from the dialog box; all areas in this tab are displayed. In the **Audio** area, select the **Mono** option from the **Master** drop-down list.

5. In the **Sequence Name** text box, make sure that the **Sequence 01** is displayed, and then choose the **OK** button; the **Sequence 01** is displayed in the **Timeline** and **Project** panels.

Viewing Clips in the Source Monitor

In this section, you will view the imported clips in the Source Monitor.

1. Double-click on the **sea.AVI** clip in the **Project** panel; the clip is displayed in the Source Monitor, as shown in Figure 3-6.

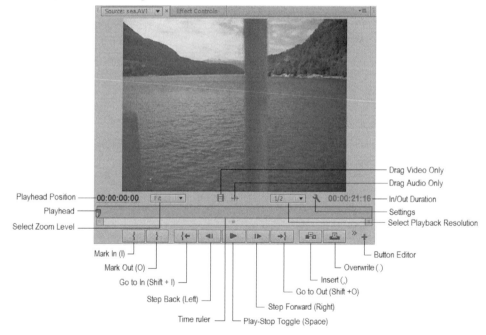

Figure 3-6 *The **sea.AVI** clip in the Source Monitor*

Note
In Figure 3-6, the shorcut for choosing the buttons are shown inside parentheses.

In the Source Monitor, you can preview the clip, control the playback of the clip, specify edit points, trim the audio and video clips, and specify some more viewing options. In other words, the Source Monitor allows you to preview the audio and video clips and decide whether you need the entire footage or only a part of it to add to the **Timeline** panel.

2. Choose the **Play-Stop Toggle** button from the Source Monitor; the video clip starts playing in the Source Monitor. Choose the **Play-Stop Toggle** button again to stop the video clip. You can also press the SPACEBAR key on the keyboard to play and stop the video clip.

3. Choose the **Step Forward** or **Step Back** button to move the video clip one frame forward or one frame backward, respectively. Alternatively, press the right arrow key on the keyboard to move the video clip one frame forward and press the left arrow key to move the video clip one frame backward.

   Press the HOME key to move the Playhead to the beginning of the clip and press the END key to move the Playhead to the end of the clip. If you want to play the clip forward, press the L key. You can stop the playback by pressing the K key. If you want to play the clip backward, press the J key. Press the SHIFT+L keys to play the clip forward in slow motion. Similarly, press the SHIFT+J keys to play the clip backward in slow motion.

   The total duration of the video clip is displayed on the top right of the time ruler. Also, the current frame time is displayed on the top left of the time ruler, refer to Figure 3-6.

4. Drag the Playhead on the time ruler to set the current frame to another time.

5. Move the cursor over the end of the time navigator bar, refer to Figure 3-7, and drag it to zoom in the time ruler to view it in more detail.

Figure 3-7 *The time navigator bar dragged*

6. Move the cursor over the **Playhead Position** in the Source Monitor; the cursor changes to a hand symbol, as shown in Figure 3-8. Next, click on the **Playhead Position**; it is converted into an edit box, as shown in Figure 3-9. Now, type **3.00** and press the ENTER key; the Playhead moves to the specified frame, refer to Figure 3-10.

Figure 3-8 *The cursor changed into a hand symbol*

Figure 3-9 *The current time display changed to an edit box*

Figure 3-10 *The Playhead moved to another frame*

7. Enter **3.25** in the **Playhead Position** edit box; the Playhead moves 25 frames forward, at 00:00:03:25, refer to Figure 3-11. Similarly, type **2.25** in the **Playhead Position** edit box; the Playhead moves 30 frames backward, at 00:00:02:25.

Figure 3-11 *The CTI moved to 25 frames forward*

8. Click on the down arrow next to the Source label, as shown in Figure 3-12; a drop-down list is displayed with the names of all the recently opened clips in the Source Monitor.

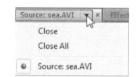

You can use the required option from the drop-down list to reopen clip in the Source Monitor. You can select the **Close** option to close the currently opened clip. You can also select the **Close All** option to close all clips and clear the Source Monitor.

Figure 3-12 *Clicking the down arrow on the right of the Source label*

9. In the **Project** panel, select multiple video clips simultaneously using the SHIFT key. Next, drag and drop them in the Source Monitor; the selected clips are listed in the drop-down list at the top-left corner of the Source Monitor. Using this list, you can quickly switch to the required clip and view it in the Source Monitor.

10. Click on the down arrow on the right of the **Select Zoom Level** option; a drop-down list is displayed, as shown in Figure 3-13. Now, select the required option to zoom the view of the clip in the Source Monitor.

11. In the Source Monitor, choose the **Settings** button; a flyout is displayed. By default, the **Composite Video** option is chosen in this flyout. Choose the **Audio Waveform** option; the audio waveform of the video clip is displayed in the Source Monitor, refer to Figure 3-14.

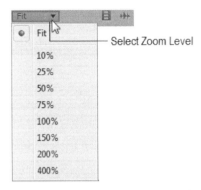

Figure 3-13 *Various zooming options in the drop-down list*

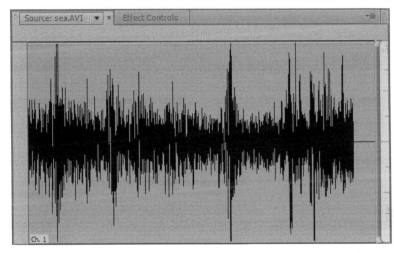

Figure 3-14 *The audio waveform displayed in the Source Monitor*

Setting Markers

In Premiere, you can set clip markers as well as sequence markers. Markers are used to mark specific frame of a clip. In this section, you will set the clip markers on the important frames in a video clip for further reference.

1. In the **Project** panel, double-click on **sea view (1).AVI**; it is displayed in the Source Monitor.

2. Press the L key; the clip starts playing in the Source Monitor. Now, press the K key at 00:00:03:03 frame. Alternatively, you can type **3.03** in the **Playhead Position** edit box and then press the ENTER key to jump to that frame, as shown in Figure 3-15.

3. Choose the **Button Editor** button from the lower right corner of the Source Monitor; the **Button Editor** dialog box is displayed. Next, click-drag the **Add Marker** button to the playback controls area and choose the **OK** button to close the dialog box. As a result, the **Marker** button is added in the playback controls area of the Source Monitor. Choose the **Add Marker** button in the playback controls area of the Source Monitor; a clip marker is set to that frame. Also, an icon is displayed above the time ruler, refer to Figure 3-16.

Figure 3-15 *The view at 00:00:03:03 frame*

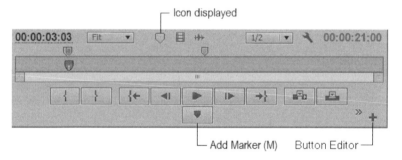

Figure 3-16 *The icon displayed above the time ruler*

Note

1. To view the marker, you need to move the Playhead.

*2. To show the marker in the Source Monitor, choose the **Settings** button; a flyout is displayed. Next, choose the **Show Markers** option from it.*

4. Again press the L key to play the clip and press the K key at 00:00:12:17 frame; the clip is paused.

5. Make sure the **Show Markers** option is selected. Next, choose the **Add Marker (M)** button in the playback controls area of the Source Monitor.

6. Similarly, set the markers at 00:00:18:01 and 00:00:20:28 frames.

7. Move the cursor over the video clip in the Source Monitor. Next, press and hold the left mouse button over the clip and drag the clip to the **V1** track in the **Timeline** panel. If the **Clip Mismatch Warning** message box is displayed then clear the **Always ask** check box and also choose the **Keep existing settings** button in this message box; the markers are displayed on the tracks, as shown in Figure 3-17.

Figure 3-17 *The markers displayed in the V1 track*

Note
If the markers are not visible on the track, you can expand the track to view the markers.

Setting the In and Out Points in the Source Monitor

If you want to use only a part of the video clip in your sequence, then you trim the part that is not needed. The first frame of the trimmed clip is known as the In point and the last frame of the trimmed clip is known as the Out point. In this section, you will set the In and Out points in the Source Monitor to use a particular part of the clip in the sequence.

1. Make sure that the **sea view (1).avi** clip is opened in the Source Monitor. Note that the markers have already been set in the clip and displayed on the time ruler. Choose the **Go To In** button to move the Playhead to the start of the video.

2. Press the L key; the clip starts playing in the Source Monitor. Next, press the K key at the 00:00:03:03 frame; the clip is paused.

3. Choose the **Mark In** button from the playback controls of the Source Monitor; an icon similar to the open bracket is displayed on the time ruler to specify the In point. You need to move the Playhead to view the icon.

4. Choose the **Button Editor** button from the lower right corner of the Source Monitor; the **Button Editor** dialog box is displayed. Next, click-drag the **Go to Next Marker**, **Go to Previous Marker**, **Loop**, and **Play In to Out** buttons in the playback controls area and choose the **OK** button to close the dialog box.

5. Choose the **Go to Next Marker** button; the CTI is moved to the next marker at 00:00:10:27 frame. Next, choose the **Mark Out** button; another icon is created similar to the closed bracket on the time ruler to specify the Out point. The area between the In and Out points is highlighted, as shown in Figure 3-18. Also, the total duration of the trimmed clip (00:00:07:25) is displayed on the top right of the time ruler, refer to Figure 3-18.

Tip. *You can also use the I or O key to set the In or Out point, respectively in the Source Monitor.*

Figure 3-18 *The trimmed clip highlighted*

Choose the **Play In to Out** button to play the trimmed clip in the Source Monitor.
To play the trimmed clip in a loop, choose the **Loop** button and then choose
the **Play In to Out** button. To move the Playhead to the In or Out point, choose
the **Go to In** or **Go to Out** button, respectively.

 Tip: *Press the SHIFT+I keys to move the Playhead to the In point and SHIFT+O keys*
to move to the Out point.

If you need to change the In or Out point, then move the Playhead to the required frame
and choose the **Mark In** or **Mark Out** button again. To remove the In point, press the
ALT key and choose the **Mark In** button. Similarly, to remove the Out point, press the
ALT key and choose the **Mark Out** button.

Adding Clips to the Sequence

Once you have viewed and trimmed the required part of the video clip by specifying the In
and Out points, you need to add the trimmed clip to the sequence.

1. Make sure the clip is selected in the **Timeline** panel and then press the DELETE key to
   delete the clip. Next, make sure that the **sea view (1).avi** clip is opened in the Source
   Monitor. Also, the In and Out points are set earlier in the clip.

2. Move the cursor over the Source Monitor. Press and hold the left mouse button and drag
   the clip from the Source Monitor to the **V1** track in the **Timeline** panel. Next, release
   the left mouse button at the beginning of the **Timeline** panel; the clip is placed in the
   sequence. Also, it is displayed in the Program Monitor, refer to Figure 3-19. Since this
   video clip has both audio and video components, the video is placed on the video track
   and the audio is placed on the corresponding audio track.

3. In the **Project** panel, double-click on the **road drive (5).AVI** clip; the clip is displayed in
   the Source Monitor, as shown in Figure 3-20.

4. Press the L key to play the clip and press the K key when the Playhead reaches the
   00:00:02:28 frame; the clip pauses at that frame.

5. Choose the **Mark In** button at 00:00:02:28 frame; an icon similar to open bracket is
   displayed, which specifies the In point.

6. Again press the L key to play the clip and press the K key when the Playhead reaches the
   00:00:14:11 frame; the clip pauses at this frame.

Figure 3-19 *The clip placed in the sequence and displayed in the Program Monitor*

Figure 3-20 *The **road drive (5).AVI** clip in the Source Monitor*

7. Choose the **Mark Out** button at 00:00:14:11 frame; an icon similar to close bracket is displayed, which specifies the Out point. Also, the area between the In and Out points is highlighted, which specifies the trimmed clip, refer to Figure 3-21. The total duration of the trimmed clip is 00:00:21:19.

Figure 3-21   *The trimmed clip highlighted*

Next, you need to add this clip just after the first clip in the **Timeline** panel.

8. Move the cursor over the clip in the Source Monitor. Press and hold the left mouse button and drag the clip from the Source Monitor to the **Timeline** panel just after the first clip. When you drag the clip, its edges snap to the first clip. Also, its edges get aligned with that of the first clip, refer to Figure 3-22. Next, release the left mouse button; the second clip is placed just after the first clip in the sequence.

Figure 3-22   *The second clip placed next to the first clip*

 Note
*By default, the **Snap** button available on the top left of the **Timeline** is chosen. As a result, the snap feature will be available. You can deactivate this button to make the snap feature unavailable.*

When you drag the video clip from the Source Monitor to the **Timeline** for assembling a sequence, the video and audio get linked together and both are displayed on the corresponding tracks. If you need to add only the video or the audio to the sequence, you need to follow the steps given below.

To add only the video of the clip, move the cursor over the **Drag Video Only** button in the Source Monitor and drag it to the **Timeline** on the video track; only the video of the clip is added to the sequence.

To add only the audio of the clip, move the cursor over the **Drag Audio Only** button in the Source Monitor and drag it to the **Timeline** on the audio track; only the audio of the clip is added to the sequence.

9. Press CTRL+S to save the file.

Rendering the Sequence

In this section, you will render the sequence.

1. Make sure the **Timeline** panel is active. Next, press the HOME key to move the CTI to the beginning of the sequence.

2. Press the ENTER key; the progress of rendering begins and the output are displayed in the Program Monitor after the completion of the rendering.

   The output of the sequence displayed at frame 00:00:09:00 is shown in Figure 3-23.

Figure 3-23 *The output of the sequence at frame 00:00:09:00*

Tutorial 2

In this tutorial, you will add clips over the existing clips or between the clips in a sequence using the Overlay and Insert edits. Also, you will protect one or more tracks from being moved during insert edits using the **Toggle Sync Lock** and **Toggle Track Lock** buttons. The output of the sequence at a frame is shown in Figure 3-24.   **(Expected Time: 20 min)**

The following steps are required to complete this tutorial:

a. Open the project.
b. Perform the Overlay edit.
c. Perform the Insert edit.
d. Protects tracks by using the **Toggle Sync Lock** and **Toggle Track Lock** buttons.

Figure 3-24 *The output of the sequence at a frame*

Opening the Project

In this section, you will open the project.

1. First, open the *chapter03_overlay_insert_edits.prproj* file that you have downloaded from the CADCIM website. Two clips are already placed in the sequence.

2. Choose **File > Save As** from the menu bar; the **Save Project** dialog box is displayed. Browse to *\Documents\Adobe Premiere Tutorials\c03_premiere_cc_tut*. Type **chapter03_overlay_insert_2** in the **File name** text box and choose the **Save** button; the opened file is saved with the specified name.

Performing the Overlay Edit

In the Overlay edit, without shifting the frames in the tracks, the new clip overlaps the existing clips in the **Timeline** panel. Also, the Overlay edit does not change the total duration of the sequence. However, it changes the duration of any clip in the **Timeline** panel, if it gets overlapped by the new clip. In this section, you will perform the Overlay edit.

1. In the **Project** panel, double-click on the **road side view (3).AVI** clip; it is displayed in the Source Monitor.

2. Set the In and Out points in the Source Monitor at **00:00:7:27** and **00:00:12:10** frames respectively, as discussed in Tutorial 1.

3. Press and hold the left mouse button over the Source Monitor and drag the clip to the track in the **Timeline** panel to the edit point of the first and second clips, which are already placed in the **Timeline** panel. Note that while dragging the clip to the **Timeline** panel, the Program Monitor displays the current duration and view of the first and second clips, as shown in Figure 3-25. Next, release the left mouse button; the new clip is placed in the **Timeline** panel. Also, the duration of the first and second clips is reduced according to the overlapping area, Figure 3-26. However, the total duration of the sequence is not changed.

4. Press CTRL+Z to undo the last step. Now, you will perform the Insert Edit.

Figure 3-25 The current duration of the first and second clips in the Program Monitor

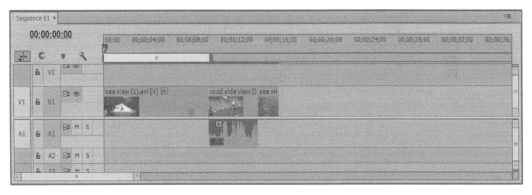

*Figure 3-26 The **road side view (3).avi** clip dragged to the edit point of the first and second clips*

Performing the Insert Edit

In the Insert edit, the new clip shifts the already placed clips on the track to make room for itself. Also, the Insert edit changes the total duration of the sequence but it does not change the duration of any clip in the **Timeline** panel. In this section, you will perform the Insert edit.

1. In the **Project** panel, double-click on the **road drive (5).AVI** clip; the clip opens in the Source Monitor.

2. Set the In and Out points, as discussed earlier.

3. Press and hold the left mouse button over the Source Monitor and drag the clip between the first and second clips in the **Timeline** panel; the shape of the cursor changes, as shown in Figure 3-27. Next, press the CTRL key; a vertical line is displayed with forward arrows on it, as shown in Figure 3-28. These arrows indicate the direction in which the clips will be shifted in the **Timeline** panel. Now, release the left mouse button; all clips after the insertion point shift forward to make room for the new clip. Also, the new clip is placed between the first and second clips, refer to Figure 3-29. Note that the total duration of the sequence increases in this process.

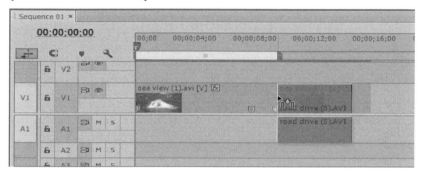

Figure 3-27 The changed shape of the cursor after placing the cursor between the clips

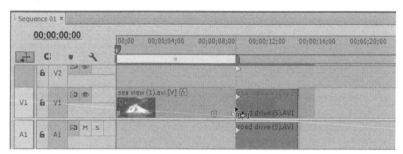

Figure 3-28 The vertical line with forward arrows

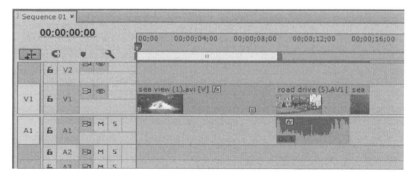

Figure 3-29 The new clip placed between the two clips

4. Press the SPACEBAR key to view the sequence; the clip starts playing in the Program Monitor.

You can also split an existing clip by using the new clips. To do so, you need to follow the steps given below:

5. In the **Project** panel, double-click on the **road drive (2).AVI** clip; it is opened in the Source Monitor.

6. Set the In and Out points based on your requirement.

7. Press and hold the left mouse button over the Source Monitor and drag the clip in the middle of the **sea view.AVI** clip in the **Timeline** panel. Next, press the CTRL key; a vertical line is displayed with forward arrows on it, as shown in Figure 3-30. Next, release the left mouse button; the **sea view.AVI** clip is split into two parts and the second part is shifted forward in the **Timeline** panel. Also, the new clip is placed in the middle of the two parts, refer to Figure 3-31.

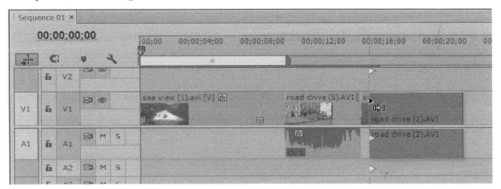

Figure 3-30 *The vertical line displayed with forward arrows*

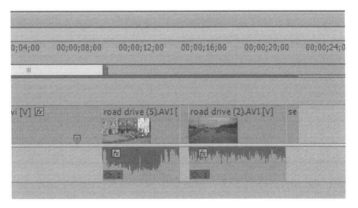

Figure 3-31 *The new clip placed in the middle of the two parts*

8. Press the SPACEBAR key to view the sequence; the clip starts playing in the Program Monitor.

Protecting Tracks by Using the Toggle Sync Lock and Toggle Track Lock Buttons

In a typical video editing project, you may have multiple tracks of video and audio clips in the **Timeline** panel. While performing the Insert or Ripple edits, if one track shifts, all other tracks will also shift. However, sometimes you do not want to shift a particular track. In such a case, you can protect one or more tracks from being moved by using the **Toggle Sync Lock** and **Toggle Track Lock** buttons. In this section, you will use these buttons to protect tracks.

1. In the **Project** panel, double-click on the **water fall.AVI** clip; the clip opens in the Source Monitor.

2. Set the In and Out points based on your requirement.

3. Move the cursor over the **Drag Video Only** button in the Source Monitor and drag it to the **Timeline** panel in the **V2** track; the video portion of the clip is displayed on the **V2** track, as shown in Figure 3-32.

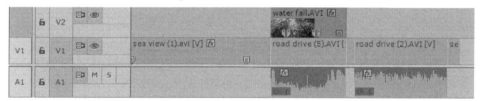

Figure 3-32 V1 and V2 tracks

Next, you need to insert a new clip in the **V1** track in such a way that the clip in the **V2** track is not affected by the Insert edit.

4. In the **Project** panel, double-click on the **sea view (2).AVI** clip; the clip opens in the Source Monitor.

5. Set the In and Out points based on your requirement.

6. In the **V2** track, choose the **Toggle Sync Lock** button; the button gets deactivated.

7. Move the cursor over the **Drag Video Only** button in the Source Monitor and drag it to the **Timeline** in the **V1** track in the middle of the **sea view (1).AVI** clip and the **road drive(5). AVI**, refer to Figure 3-33. Next, press the CTRL key; a vertical line is displayed with forward arrows on it, refer to Figure 3-34. Next, release the left mouse button; the new clip shifts the other clips forward in the **Timeline** and it is placed in the middle of the **sea view (1).AVI** clip and the **road drive(5). AVI** in the **V1** track, refer to Figure 3-35. However, the clip in the **V2** track is not affected by the Insert edit.

Figure 3-33 *The cursor in the middle of the **sea view (1)** clip and the **road drive(5).AVI** in the **V1** track*

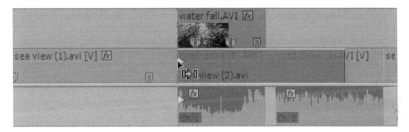

Figure 3-34 *The vertical line with arrows displayed on pressing the CTRL key*

Figure 3-35 *The new clip inserted in the **V1** track*

8. In the **V1** track, choose the **Toggle Track Lock** button; this button is active now. Also, diagonal lines are displayed in the **V1** track, as shown in Figure 3-36. Next, insert a new clip in the **V1** track. You will notice that you cannot perform any action in the **V1** track as you choose the button.

Figure 3-36 *Diagonal lines in the **V1** track*

9. Press CTRL+S to save the file. Next, press the ENTER key to view the output of the sequence in the Program Monitor. The output of the sequence at a given frame is shown in Figure 3-37.

Figure 3-37 *The output of the sequence at a given frame*

Tutorial 3

In this tutorial, you will perform the Three-Point Overlay and Insert edits using the editing buttons available in the Source Monitor. The output of the sequence at frame 00:00:09:12 is shown in Figure 3-38.   **(Expected Time: 20 min)**

Figure 3-38 *The output of the sequence at frame 00:00:09:12*

The following steps are required to complete this tutorial:

a.   Open the project.
b.   Perform the Three-Point Overlay and Insert Edits.

Opening the Project

In this section, you will open the project.

1. First, open the *chapter03_overlay_insert_edits.prproj* file that you have downloaded from the CADCIM website. Two clips are already placed in the sequence.

2. Choose **File > Save As** from the menu bar; the **Save Project** dialog box is displayed. Browse to *\Documents\Adobe Premiere Tutorials*. Type the name **chapter03_three_point_edit** in the **File name** text box and choose the **Save** button; the opened file is saved with the specified name.

Performing the Three-Point Overlay and Insert Edits

In this section, you will perform the three-point Overlay and Insert edits.

1. In the **Project** panel, double-click on the **sea view (2).AVI** clip; the clip opens in the Source Monitor.

2. Set the In and Out points based on your requirement.

3. In the **Timeline** panel, set the CTI at a position where you want to set the starting point of the new clip, refer to Figure 3-39.

4. Choose the **Overwrite** button in the playback controls area of the Source Monitor to perform the Overlay edit; the new clip is placed in the sequence. Also, the CTI is moved to the end of the new clip, as shown in Figure 3-40.

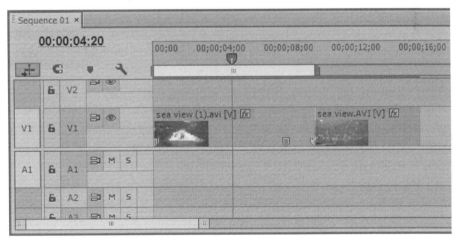

Figure 3-39 The CTI set over the clip

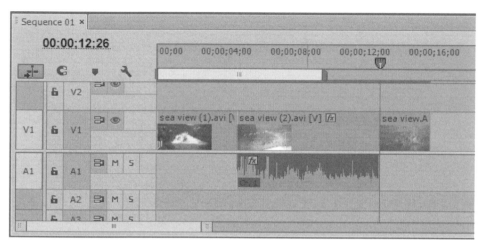

Figure 3-40 *The CTI placed at the end of the new clip*

Next, you will perform the Insert edit using the editing buttons.

5. Move the CTI to the end of the first clip and at the starting point of the second clip, refer to Figure 3-41.

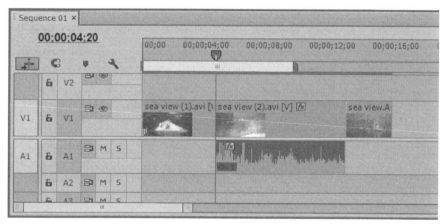

Figure 3-41 *The CTI set in the **Timeline***

6. In the **Project** panel, double-click on the **sea.AVI** clip; the clip opens in the Source Monitor.

7. Set the In and Out points based on your requirement.

8. Choose the **Insert** button in the playback controls area of the Source Monitor; the new clip is inserted, shifting the other clips forward in the **Timeline**, refer to Figure 3-42.

Note
You can also press the period (.) key for performing the Overlay edit and the comma (,) key for performing the Insert edit.

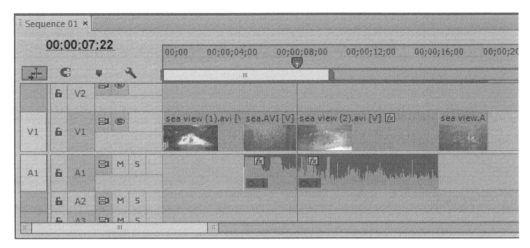

Figure 3-42 The new clip inserted

9. Press CTRL+S to save the file. Next, press the ENTER key to view the output of the sequence in the Program Monitor. The output of the sequence at frame 00:00:09:12 is shown in Figure 3-43.

Figure 3-43 The output of the sequence at frame 00:00:09:12

Self-Evaluation Test

Answer the following questions and then compare them to those given at the end of this chapter:

1. Which of the following shortcut keys is used to invoke the **Import** dialog box?

   (a) I   (b) CTRL + I
   (c) SHIFT + I   (d) CTRL + SHIFT + I

2. Which of the following buttons is used to create a new bin in the **Project** panel?

   (a) **New Item**   (b) **Icon view**
   (c) **New Bin**   (d) None of these

3. Which of the following shortcut keys is used to perform the Overlay edit?

   (a) Period (.)   (b) Comma (,)
   (c) I   (d) O

4. Which of the following shortcut keys is used to perform the Insert edit?

   (a) Period (.)   (b) Comma (,)
   (c) I   (d) O

5. _____ is used to set the In point and _____ is used to set the Out point.

6. You can remove the In points by first pressing the ALT key and then choosing the _____ button.

7. To view the marker in the Source Monitor, you need to choose the **Button Editor** button. (T/F)

8. The **Drag Video Only** button in the Source Monitor is used to add only the video of the clip to the **Timeline** panel. (T/F)

9. In the Overlay edit, the new clip overlaps the already placed clips in the **Timeline** panel and it shifts the frames in the tracks. (T/F)

10. The Insert edit changes the total duration of the sequence, but it does not change the duration of any clip in the **Timeline** panel. (T/F)

Review Questions

Answer the following questions:

1. Which of the following buttons is used to protect one or more tracks from being moved while performing the Insert edit?

   (a) **Toggle Track Lock**   (b) **Toggle Sync Lock**
   (c) **Toggle Track Output**   (d) None of these

2. Which of the following buttons is used to protect one or more tracks from being moved in the Timeline panel?

   (a) **Toggle Track Lock**   (b) **Toggle Sync Lock**
   (c) **Toggle Track Output**   (d) All

3. Which of the following buttons in the Source Monitor is used to perform the Overlay edit?

   (a) **Insert**   (b) **Overwrite**
   (c) **Set In Point**   (d) **Set Out Point**

4. Press the _____ key to move the clip forward in Source Monitor and Program Monitor. Press the _____ key to move the clip backward in Source Monitor and Program Monitor and press the _____ key to pause the clip.

5. In the Source Monitor, you can play the clip, specify edit points, trim the audio and video clips, and specify some more viewing options. (T/F)

6. The Overlay edit does not change the total duration of the sequence, but it changes the duration of any clip in the **Timeline** panel. (T/F)

EXERCISE

Exercise 1

Create a new project in Premiere based on the settings of your video clip. Next, import the video clips in the **Project** panel. Try to set the In and Out points of the clips in the Source Monitor. Also, perform the Insert and Overlay edits using the shortcut keys.

Answers to Self-Evaluation Test
1. b, **2.** c, **3.** a, **4.** b, **5. Mark In, Mark Out**, **6. Mark In**, **7.** F, **8.** T, **9.** F, **10.** T

Chapter 4

Editing Clips in the Timeline

Learning Objectives

After completing this chapter, you will be able to:

- *Navigate a sequence in the Timeline panel*
- *Work with tracks*
- *Select clips using the Selection Tool*
- *Select clips using the Track Select Tool*
- *Use the Lift and Extract Tools*
- *Trim a clip using the Selection and Ripple Edit Tools*
- *Use the Rolling Edit Tool*
- *Use the Rate Stretch Tool*
- *Split and cut clips using the Razor Tool*
- *Perform the Slip and Slide Edits*

INTRODUCTION

In this chapter, you will learn to navigate a sequence in the **Timeline** panel, work with the tracks, select clips using the **Selection Tool**, and use various tools in the **Tools** panel to edit clips in a sequence.

NAVIGATING A SEQUENCE IN THE TIMELINE PANEL

To navigate a sequence in the **Timeline** panel, you can follow any one of the following methods:

(a) Drag the CTI in the **Timeline** panel.
(b) Click on the time ruler.
(c) Use the **Playhead Position** edit box.
(d) Use the playback controls in the Program Monitor.
(e) Press the left and right arrow keys on the keyboard.

The CTI indicates the current frame in the sequence which is also displayed in the Program Monitor. Also, the CTI in the **Timeline** panel and Program Monitor is always positioned at the same frame. The playback controls of the Program Monitor are same as that of the Source Monitor. These controls have already been discussed in Chapter 3. To snap the CTI to the clips edges and the markers in the sequence, press and hold the SHIFT key and then drag the CTI towards the edge or marker.

You can press the EQUAL (=) key to zoom in the sequence, the MINUS (-) key to zoom out the sequence, and the BACKSLASH (\) key to fit all clips of the sequence in the **Timeline** panel.

WORKING WITH TRACKS IN THE TIMELINE PANEL

To add, edit, or arrange clips and to add effects to them, you need to add them to the video and audio tracks in the **Timeline** panel.

Excluding and Renaming Tracks

To exclude a video track from previewing and exporting, choose the **Toggle Track Output** button in the video track, refer to Figure 4-1. You can also mute an audio track by choosing the **Mute Track** button from the audio track, refer to Figure 4-2.

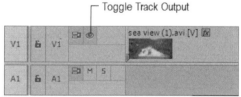 

*Figure 4-1 The **Toggle Track Output** button in the video track*   *Figure 4-2 The **Mute Track** button in the audio track*

To rename a track, expand the **V1** track by double-clicking on the blank area at the right side of the **Toggle Track Output** button. Next, right-click on **Video 1**; a shortcut menu will be displayed. Next, choose the **Rename** option from the shortcut menu; the **Video 1** label is changed into an edit box, as shown in Figure 4-3. Now, type a new name in the **Clip Name** text box.

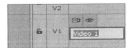

*Figure 4-3 The **Video 1** label changed into edit box*

Adding Tracks

The **Add Tracks** option is used to add multiple new tracks at a time in the **Timeline** panel. To add a new track, right-click on the track; a shortcut menu will be displayed. Now, choose the **Add Tracks** option from the shortcut menu, as shown in Figure 4-4; the **Add Tracks** dialog box will be displayed, as shown in Figure 4-5. Enter the number of tracks in the **Add** text box of the respective track area. Also, select the required option from the **Placement** drop-down list. Next, choose the **OK** button; a new track will be added to the **Timeline** panel.

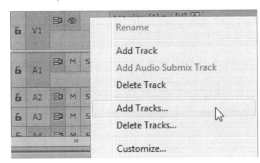

*Figure 4-4 Choosing the **Add Tracks** option from the shortcut menu*

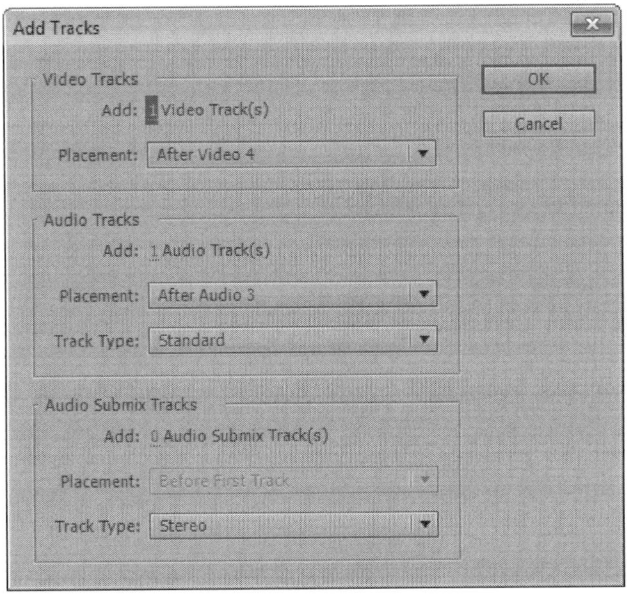

*Figure 4-5 The **Add Tracks** dialog box*

Deleting Tracks

The **Delete Tracks** option is used to delete multiple tracks at a time in the **Timeline** panel. To delete an existing track, right-click on the track; a shortcut menu will be displayed. Now, choose the **Delete Tracks** option from the shortcut menu; the **Delete Tracks** dialog box will be displayed, as shown in Figure 4-6. Next, select the check box in the **Video Tracks** or **Audio Tracks** area to delete the corresponding tracks. Also, select the tracks to be deleted in the drop-down lists in these areas. Now, choose the **OK** button; the selected tracks will be deleted.

Figure 4-6 The **Delete Tracks** dialog box

SELECTING AND EDITING CLIPS IN TIMELINE PANEL

In this section, you will learn to edit clips in **Timeline** panel using the tools available in the **Tools** panel. Also, you will learn to use the **Lift** and **Extract** tools.

Selecting Clips Using the Selection Tool

To perform an action that will affect the entire clip such as deleting a clip, moving a clip, or applying an effect to a clip, you first need to select the clip. To do so, choose the **Selection Tool** from the **Tools** panel. To select a single clip in the **Timeline** panel, click on it. Note that if a clip has both the audio and video components, then on selecting either one, both the components will get selected. To deselect a clip, just click on the empty area in the **Timeline** panel.

To select multiple clips, press and hold the SHIFT key and click on the clips one by one to select all of them. If you need to deselect any clip from the selection, then press and hold the SHIFT key and click on the clip that you need to deselect. To select a range of clips, press and hold the left mouse button and drag rectangular marquee selection around the range of clips that you need to select, refer to Figure 4-7.

To select only the audio or video portion of a clip, press and hold the ALT key and click on the audio or video portion of the clip.

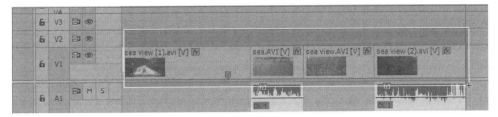

Figure 4-7 *A range of clips selected in the* **Timeline** *panel*

Selecting Clips Using the Track Select Tool

The **Track Select Tool** is used to select all the clips on the right of the cursor in the
Timeline panel. To do so, choose the **Track Select Tool** from the **Tools** panel. Move
the cursor on the clip whose right side clips need to be selected. Next, click on the clip;
all the clips on the right of the cursor will be selected, refer to Figure 4-8.

Figure 4-8 *The clips selected on the right of the cursor*

TUTORIALS

Before you start the tutorials, you need to download the *c04_premiere_cc_tut.zip* file from
www.cadcim.com. The path of the file is as follows: *Textbooks > Animation and Visual Effects >
Premiere Pro > Adobe Premiere Pro CC: A Tutorial Approach*

Next, extract the contents of the zip file to */Documents/Adobe Premiere Tutorials*.

Tutorial 1

In this tutorial, you will create a new section based on the settings of the clips in the project.
The output of the sequence at frame 00:00:05:23 is shown in Figure 4-9.

(Expected Time: 20 min)

The following steps are required to complete this tutorial:

a.   Create a new project.
b.   Import video clips.
c.   Create a new sequence for the current project.

Figure 4-9 *The output of the sequence at frame 00:00:05:23*

Creating a New Project

In this section, you will create a new project.

1. Start Adobe Premiere Pro CC; the **Welcome to Adobe Premiere Pro** dialog box is displayed.

2. Choose the **New Project** button; the **New Project** dialog box is displayed.

3. In the **General** tab, type **chapter04** in the **Name** text box.

4. Choose the **Browse** button corresponding to the **Location** drop-down list; the **Please select the destination path for your new project** dialog box is displayed. In this dialog box, browse to the location *\Documents\Adobe Premiere Tutorials\c04_premiere_cc_tut* and choose the **Select Folder** button.

5. Choose the **Scratch Disks** tab and make sure the **Same as Project** option is selected from the **Captured Video**, **Captured Audio**, **Video Previews**, and **Audio Previews** drop-down lists.

6. Choose the **OK** button in the **New Project** dialog box; a new project screen without any sequence is displayed, as shown in Figure 4-10. Also, the file is saved with the name *chapter04.prproj*.

Note
You will create a sequence based on the settings of the clips in your project in the later section.

Importing Video Clips

In this section, you will import video clips.

1. Choose the **Media Browser** panel, if not already chosen. This panel is located in the lower left corner of the screen.

2.   Browse to *\Documents\Adobe Premiere Tutorials\c04_premiere_cc_tut* and then select the *Media Files* folder; all clips in this folder are displayed on right in the **Media Browser** panel, as shown in Figure 4-11.

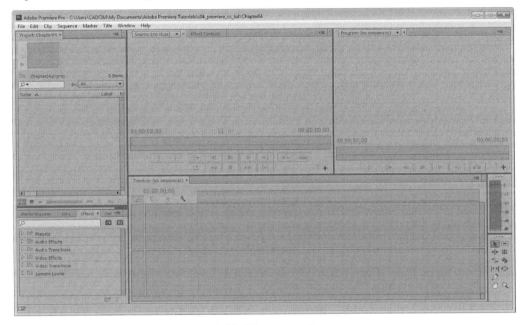

Figure 4-10 *The new project screen*

Figure 4-11 *All clips displayed in the **Media Browser** panel*

 Note
*You may need to adjust the size of the **Media Browser** panel to view clips properly.*

3.   Select all clips using the **SHIFT** key in the *Media Files* folder and then right-click on them; a shortcut menu is displayed, as shown in Figure 4-12.

4.   Choose the **Import** option from the shortcut menu; all the files are imported and displayed in the **Project** panel.

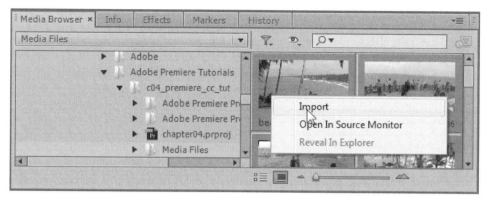

Figure 4-12 *The shortcut menu displayed*

Creating a New Sequence for the Current Project

In this section, you will create a new sequence based on the settings of your clips in the project.

1. Select one of the clips in the **Project** panel; the preview of the clip and its specifications are displayed in the **Project** panel, as shown in Figure 4-13.

2. Choose the **New Item** button located at the bottom of the **Project** panel; a flyout is displayed. Choose the **Sequence** option from the flyout; the **New Sequence** dialog box is displayed.

    Next, you need to select one of the presets from the **Available Presets** area that has the same settings as that of the selected clip.

3. In the **Available Presets** area of the **Sequence Presets** tab, expand the **DV - PAL** node, if it is not already expanded. Select the **Widescreen 48kHz** preset. The settings of this preset are displayed on the right in the **Preset Description** area, as shown in Figure 4-14.

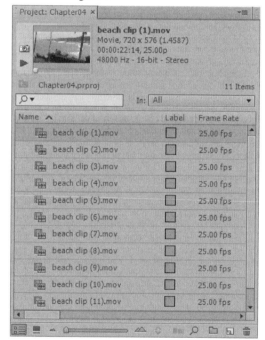

Figure 4-13 *The preview and settings of the selected clip in the **Project** panel*

Note that the frame size settings of the **Widescreen 48 kHz** preset are exactly the same as that of the clips in the **Project** panel.

4. In the **New Sequence** dialog box, make sure that the **Sequence 01** is displayed in the **Sequence Name** text box. Next, choose the **OK** button in this dialog box; the **Sequence 01** is displayed in the **Timeline** and **Project** panels, as shown in Figure 4-15.

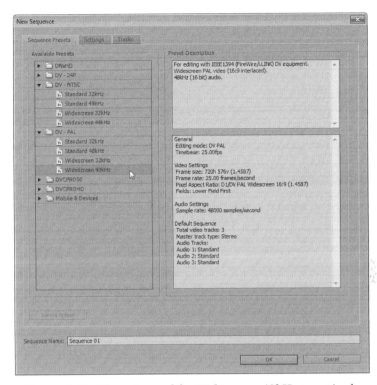

Figure 4-14 *The settings of the* **Widescreen 48kHz** *preset in the*
Preset Description *area*

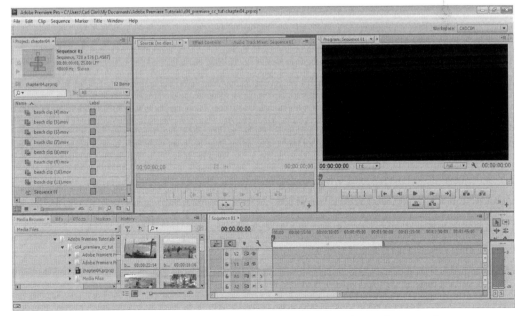

Figure 4-15 *The* **Sequence 01** *in the* **Project** *and* **Timeline** *panels*

Now, you have a new sequence that has the same settings as that of the clips in your project. Next, you will place these clips in the **Timeline** panel.

5. Select a clip in the **Project** panel and then press CTRL+A; all the clips are selected in the **Project** panel. Next, press CTRL and then click on the **Sequence 01** in the **Project** panel to remove it from the selection.

6. Make sure that the CTI is positioned at the extreme left of the panel. Next, press and hold the left mouse button on the selected clips in the **Project** panel and drag the cursor to the **V1** track in the **Timeline** panel. Now, release the left mouse button; the **Clip Mismatch Warning** message box is displayed. Clear the **Always ask** check box and choose the **Keep existing settings** button in this message box; the clips are placed in the **Timeline** panel, as shown in Figure 4-16.

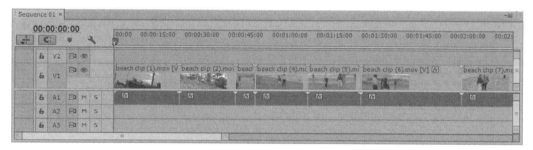

*Figure 4-16 The clips placed in the **Timeline** panel*

7. Press the BACKSLASH (\) key; all the clips become visible in the **Timeline** panel, as shown in Figure 4-17.

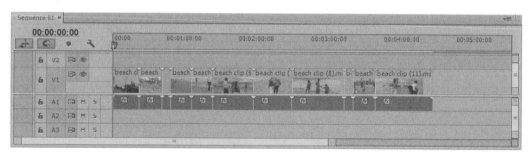

*Figure 4-17 All clips visible in the **Timeline** panel*

8. Press CTRL+S keys to save the file. Next, press the ENTER key to view the output of the sequence in the Program Monitor. The output of the sequence at frame 00:00:05:23 is shown in Figure 4-18.

Figure 4-18 The output of the sequence at frame 00:00:05:23

Tutorial 2

In this tutorial, you will trim clips using the **Selection Tool**, the **Ripple Edit Tool**, and the **Rolling Edit Tool**. The output of the sequence at frame -00:00:00:20 is shown in Figure 4-19.

(Expected Time: 20 min)

Figure 4-19 Output of the clips displayed while dragging the clip

The following steps are required to complete this tutorial:

a. Open the project.
b. Remove a range of frames from the Timeline by using the **Lift** and **Extract** tools.
c. Trim a clip using the **Selection Tool**.
d. Trim the In and Out points using the **Ripple Edit Tool**.
e. Perform rolling edit on the clips using the **Rolling Edit Tool**.

Opening the Project

In this section, you will open the project.

1. Open the file *chapter04_02.prproj* that you have downloaded from the CADCIM website.

2. Choose **File > Save As** from the menu bar; the **Save Project** dialog box is displayed. Browse to *\Documents\Adobe Premiere Tutorials\c04_premiere_cc_tut*. Type the name **chapter04_02_edit** in the **File name** text box and choose the **Save** button; the opened file is saved at the specified location.

Removing a Range of Frames in the Timeline by Using the Lift and Extract Tools

In this section, you will remove a range of frames in the **Timeline** panel.

1. In the Program Monitor, set the Playhead at the beginning of the sequence.

2. Press the L key to play the sequence. Notice that the Playhead in the Program Monitor and CTI in the **Timeline** panel are moving.

3. Set the In and Out points at 00:00:42:16 and 00:00:54:22 frames, respectively, as discussed in Chapter 3. The In and Out points are displayed in the Program Monitor and on the time ruler in the **Timeline** panel. In this way, you can specify a range of frames that you need to remove from the sequence, refer to Figure 4-20.

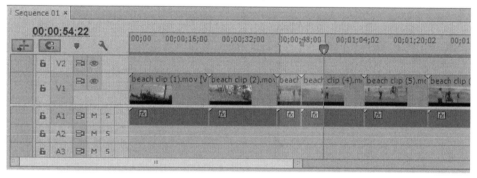

Figure 4-20 The In and Out points displayed in the time ruler

4. Invoke the **Lift** tool from the playback controls of the Program Monitor; the specified range of frames is removed, refer to Figure 4-21.

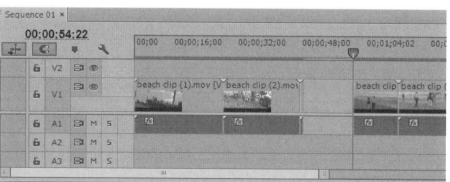

*Figure 4-21 The range of frames removed after using the **Lift** tool*

Note
*To add the **Lift** tool to the playback controls of the Program Monitor, choose the **Button Editor** button from the lower right corner of the Program Monitor; the **Button Editor** dialog box is displayed. Next, click-drag the **Lift** tool and other required buttons into the playback controls area. Now, choose the **OK** button to close this dialog box.*

5. Next, press the CTRL + Z keys to undo the **Lift** operation in the **Timeline** panel.

6. Invoke the **Extract** tool from the playback controls of the Program Monitor; the range of frames is removed. Note that on using this tool, the frames shift back simultaneously to fill the gap, refer to Figure 4-22.

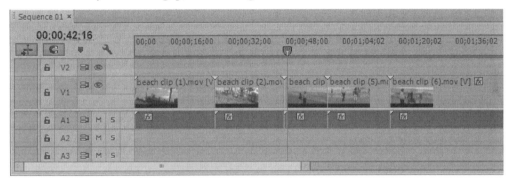

*Figure 4-22 The range of frames removed after using the **Extract** tool*

Trimming a Clip Using the Selection Tool

Making small adjustment in the In or Out points of a clip in the sequence is known as trimming. In Adobe Premiere Pro, you can trim a clip by using various options. In this section, you will trim a clip using the **Selection Tool**.

1. Choose the **Sequence 2** tab in the **Timeline** panel. Make sure the **Selection Tool** is invoked in the **Tools** panel.

    Next, you will trim the In point or the head of the **beach clip (4).mov**.

2. Move the cursor over the In point of the **beach clip (4).mov** clip in the **Timeline** panel; the cursor is displayed like an open bracket with an arrow, refer to Figure 4-23.

Figure 4-23 The cursor changed after moving it over the In point of the clip

3. Press and hold the left mouse button and drag the clip to the right of the frame +00:00:02:10. Note that while dragging the clip, a tooltip is displayed to show the status of the trimming, refer to Figure 4-24. You can also view the timecode displayed in the Program Monitor for reference. Release the mouse button; the In point of the clip is trimmed. Note that it leaves a gap between the **beach clip (3).mov** and **beach clip (4). mov**, as shown in Figure 4-25.

Figure 4-24 *The tooltip displayed in the* **Timeline** *Panel*

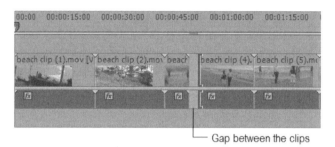

Figure 4-25 *The gap between the clips in the* **Timeline** *Panel*

4. To remove the gap between the clips, right-click on the gap; the **Ripple Delete** option is displayed, as shown in Figure 4-26. Choose the **Ripple Delete** option; the clips on the right of the gap shift to fill the gap between the clips.

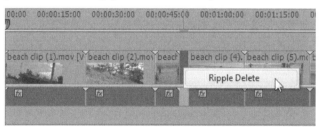

Figure 4-26 *The* **Ripple Delete** *option*

Trimming the In and Out Points Using the Ripple Edit Tool

The **Ripple Edit Tool** is used to trim the In or Out points of a clip in the **Timeline** panel. The **Ripple Edit Tool** is also used to close the gap caused by trimming. In this section, you will trim the In and Out points of the clips in the **Timeline** panel.

1. Choose the **Sequence 3** tab in the **Timeline** panel.

Note
*If the **Sequence 03** tab is not displayed in the **Timeline** panel then you need to create a new sequence with the name **Sequence 03** and then drag all the beach clips from the **Project** panel to the **Timeline** panel, as discussed in Tutorial 1 of this chapter.*

2. Invoke the **Ripple Edit Tool** from the **Tools** panel. Move the cursor over the Out point of the **beach clip (1).mov** in the **Timeline** panel; the cursor is displayed like a closed bracket, refer to Figure 4-27.

*Figure 4-27 The shape of the cursor changed to the **Ripple Edit Tool** icon*

3. Press and hold the left mouse button and drag the clip to the left to trim the Out point of the **beach clip (1).mov**. While dragging the cursor, a tooltip is displayed showing the duration of the clip that will be trimmed from the clip, refer to Figure 4-28. You can also view the new Out point in the Program Monitor, refer to Figure 4-29. Release the left mouse button; the Out point of the clip is trimmed. Note that the subsequent clips in the track shift simultaneously to fill the gap formed due to trimming.

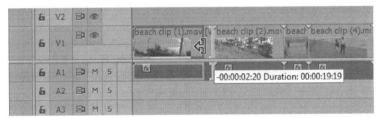

Figure 4-28 The tooltip displayed

Figure 4-29 The Program Monitor while trimming the Out point

Performing Rolling Edit On the Clips Using the Rolling Edit Tool

The **Rolling Edit Tool** is used to trim the frames adjacent to the In and Out points. This tool is used to move the edit point between the clips, preserve positions of other clips in the **Timeline** panel and maintain the total duration of the sequence.

1. Invoke the **Rolling Edit Tool** from the **Tools** panel and move the cursor on the edit point of the **beach clip (1).mov** and **beach clip (2).mov** clips in the **Timeline** panel; the shape of the cursor is changed to **Rolling Edit Tool** icon, as shown in Figure 4-30.

*Figure 4-30 The shape of the cursor changed to the **Rolling Edit Tool** icon*

2. Make sure the clip is trimmed. Next, press and hold the left mouse button and drag the clip to the right using the **Rolling Edit Tool** to +00:00:00:20, refer to Figure 4-31. Note that while dragging the clip, the Out point of **beach clip (1).mov** and the In point of **beach clip (2).mov** move simultaneously. Also, the output of the clips is displayed in the Program Monitor while dragging the clip, refer to Figure 4-32. Note that total duration of the sequence and total number of frames in the sequence is same.

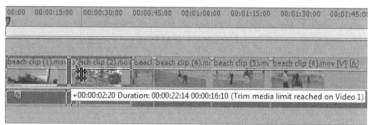

*Figure 4-31 Clips while dragging using the **Rolling Edit Tool***

Note
*You need to press the EQUAL (=) key to zoom in to the **Timeline** panel to view the edit point between the **beach clip (1).mov** and **beach clip (2).mov** clips clearly.*

3. Press the CTRL+S keys to save the file. Next, press the ENTER key to view the output of the sequence in the Program Monitor.

Figure 4-32 Output of the clips displayed while dragging the clip

Tutorial 3

In this tutorial, you will change the speed and duration of the clips using the **Rate Stretch Tool**. Also, you will split or cut a clip using the **Razor Tool**. The output of the sequence at frame 00:00:49:22 is shown in Figure 4-33.   **(Expected Time: 20 min)**

Figure 4-33 The output of the sequence at frame 00:00:49:22

The following steps are required to complete this tutorial:

a. Open the project.
b. Change the speed and duration of the clip.
c. Split or cut the clip.

Opening the Project

In this section, you will open the project.

1. Open the file *chapter04_rate_stretch.prproj* that you have downloaded from the CADCIM website.

2. Choose **File > Save As** from the menu bar; the **Save Project** dialog box is displayed. Browse to *\Documents\Adobe Premiere Tutorials\c04_premiere_cc_tut*. Type the name **chapter04_rate_stretch_01** in the **File name** text box and choose the **Save** button; the opened file is saved at the specified location.

Changing the Speed and Duration of the Clips Using Rate Stretch Tool

In this section, you will change the speed and duration of the clips by using the **Rate Stretch Tool**. This tool is used to shorten a clip by speeding up its playback or lengthen a clip by slowing down the playback speed. First, you will lengthen the clip by slowing down the playback speed.

1. Invoke the **Rate Stretch Tool** from the **Tools** panel and move the cursor to the end point of the **beach clip (10).mov** clip; the shape of the cursor is changed.

2. Press and hold the left mouse button and drag the endpoint of the **beach clip (10).mov** clip toward the right until the tooltip displays +00:00:04:12, as shown in Figure 4-34. Next, release the left mouse button.

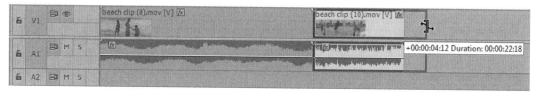

Figure 4-34 The tooltip displayed while dragging the clip toward the right

3. Move the CTI to the starting point of the **beach clip (10).mov** clip and press the L key to play it. Note that the duration of the clip is increased. Thus, the playback speed of the clip will be slowed down. Next, press the K key to stop it.

    Now, you will shorten the duration of the clip by increasing its playback speed.

4. Make sure the **Rate Stretch Tool** is invoked.

5. Move the cursor at the endpoint of the **beach clip (8).mov** clip; the shape of the cursor is changed.

6. Press and hold the left mouse button and drag the endpoint of the **beach clip (8).mov** clip toward left until the tooltip displays -00:00:07:09, as shown in Figure 4-35.

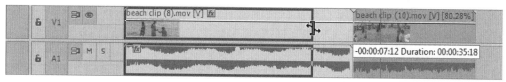

Figure 4-35 The tooltip displayed while dragging the clip toward left

7. Release the left mouse button; the selected clip is squeezed and its duration is shortened. Also, the speed of the clip is increased. Move the CTI to the starting point of the **beach clip(8).mov** clip and then press L to play the sequence. Next, press K to stop it.

8.   Right-click on the gap; a shortcut menu is displayed. Choose the **Ripple Delete** option; the clip on the right of the gap shifts to fill the gap between the clips.

Splitting or Cutting the Clip Using the Razor Tool

In this section, you will cut a clip into two clips and cut across clips in multiple tracks at once, using the **Razor Tool.** The resulting clips will have different In and Out points.

1.   Move the CTI to 00:00:15:00 frame.

2.   Choose the Razor Tool in the Tools panel. Next, move the cursor on the 00:00:15:00 frame; the shape of the cursor is changed to the **Razor Tool** icon, as shown in Figure 4-36.

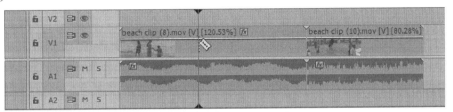

Figure 4-36 *The shape of the cursor changed to the* ***Razor Tool*** *icon*

3.   Click on the clip; it splits into two parts, as shown in Figure 4-37.

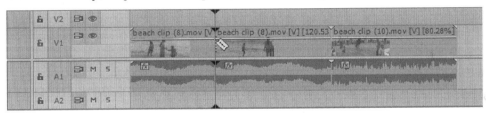

Figure 4-37 *The clip after splitting*

Next, you will split only the video portion of the **beach clip (10).mov.**

4.   Make sure the **Razor Tool** is invoked. Next, move the cursor to the 00:00:53:10 frame.

5.   Press and hold the ALT key and click on the **V1** track of the clip; it splits into two parts. Note that only the video portion of the clip splits, refer to Figure 4-38.

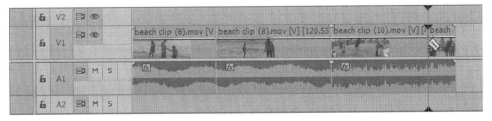

Figure 4-38 *The split video portion of the clip*

Next, you will cut across the clips in multiple tracks at once.

6. Choose the **Selection Tool** from the **Tools** panel. Next, drag the second part of the **beach clip (10).mov** clip from the **V1** track to the **V2** track in the **Timeline**, as shown in Figure 4-39.

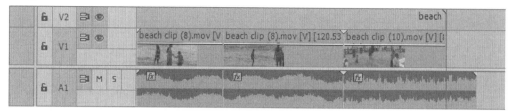

*Figure 4-39 The second part of **beach clip (10).mov** dragged to the V2 track*

7. Move the CTI to 00:00:49:22 frame in the **Timeline** panel. Also, move the cursor to 00:00:49:22 frame.

8. Invoke the **Razor Tool** from the **Tools** panel and then press the SHIFT key and click on the clip; all clips split into multiple tracks, as shown in Figure 4-40.

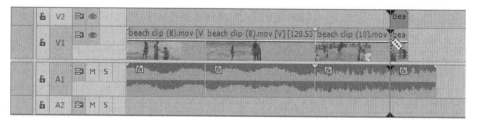

Figure 4-40 The clips split into multiple tracks

9. Press CTRL+S to save the file. Next, press the ENTER key to view the output of the sequence in the Program Monitor. The output of the sequence at frame 00:00:49:22 is shown in Figure 4-41.

Figure 4-41 The output of the sequence at frame 00:00:49:22

Tutorial 4

In this tutorial, you will perform Slip and Slide Edits in the trimmed clips. The output of the sequence at frame 00:00:28:00 is shown in Figure 4-42. **(Expected Time: 20 min)**

Figure 4-42 *The output of the sequence at frame 00:00:28:00*

The following steps are required to complete this tutorial:

a.   Open the project.
b.   Perform the Slip Edit.
c.   Perform the Slide Edit.

Opening the Project

In this section, you will open the project.

1.   Open the file *chapter04_slip and slide edit.prproj* that you have downloaded from the CADCIM website. Three clips are already placed in the sequence of this file.

2.   Choose **File > Save As** from the menubar; the **Save Project** dialog box is displayed. Browse to *Documents\Adobe Premiere Tutorials*. Type the name **chapter04_slip and slide edit_02** in the **File name** text box and then choose the **Save** button; the file is opened and saved at the specified location.

Performing the Slip Edit

The **Slip Tool** is used to change the In and Out points of a trimmed clip in the **Timeline** panel simultaneously. However, the time duration of the clip remains constant. For example, if you need to trim a 30-second clip to a 25-second clip, then you can use the **Slip Tool** to specify the 25-second of the clip that you want to display in the **Timeline** panel.

1.   In the **Timeline** panel, double-click on the **beach clip (2).mov** clip; the clip is opened in the Source Monitor. The total duration of the clip is 00:00:19:05 seconds.

Next, you need to trim the In and Out points of the selected clip.

2.   Make sure the **Selection Tool** from the **Tools** panel is invoked and move the cursor over the In point of the selected clip; the shape of the cursor changes to an open bracket, as shown in Figure 4-43.

Figure 4-43 The shape of the cursor changed to an open bracket

 Note
You need to press the EQUAL (=) key and the MINUS(-) key respectively to zoom in and zoom out the sequence in the **Timeline** *panel to locate the clip timings.*

3.   Press and hold the left mouse button and drag the In point of the clip toward the right until the tooltip displays +00:00:01:22. Then, release the left mouse button; the In point of the clip is trimmed. Also, a gap is formed before the In point of the clip.

4.   Right-click on the gap; a shortcut menu is displayed. Choose the **Ripple Delete** option; the clip shifts to the left to fill the gap.

5.   Trim the Out point of the **beach clip (2).mov** clip in the **Timeline** panel until the tooltip displays -00:00:01:16.

     Now, the total duration of the clip is 00:00:15:17 seconds.

6.   Right-click on the gap; a shortcut menu is displayed. Choose the **Ripple Delete** option; the **beach clip (3).mov** clip shifts to the left to fill the gap.

7.   Make sure the trimmed clip is selected. Next, invoke the **Slip Tool**.

8.   Move the cursor on the trimmed clip, press and hold the left mouse button and drag it to the left until the tooltip displays -00:00:01:16, as shown in Figure 4-44; the In and Out points adjust simultaneously in the clip. While dragging, the resultant In and Out points of the clip are displayed in the Program Monitor, as shown in Figure 4-45.

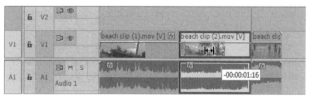

Figure 4-44 The tooltip after dragging the cursor

Figure 4-45 The In and Out points in the Program Monitor

Note that the In and Out points are updated in the Source Monitor as well. Also, the total duration of the clip and sequence is same in the **Timeline** panel.

Performing the Slide Edit

The **Slide Tool** is used to shift a clip in the **Timeline** panel and trim the adjacent clips to compensate for the move. In this edit process, the Out point of the preceding clip and the In point of the following clip get trimmed by the number of frames by which you shift the clip. However, the In and Out points of the clip remain constant. In this section, you will perform slide edit using the **Slide Tool**.

1. Make sure the file *chapter04_slip and slide edit_02.prproj* is opened.

2. Choose the **Selection Tool** from the **Tools** panel. Make sure the **beach clip(2).mov** clip is selected and invoke the **Slide Tool** from the **Tools** panel.

3. Move the cursor over the selected clip, press and hold the left mouse button, and drag the entire clip toward right until the tooltip displays +00:00:02:13, refer to Figure 4-46. Next, release the left mouse button; the clip shifts toward the right.

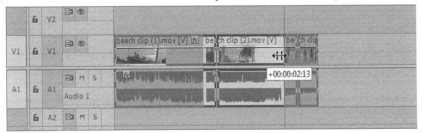

Figure 4-46 The tooltip after dragging the clip

While dragging the cursor, the Out point of the preceding clip and the In point of the following clip is displayed in the Program Monitor. In the slide edit, the duration of the selected clip and sequence remains constant in the **Timeline** panel. However, here the position of the selected clip gets changed.

Note

*While performing the **Slide Edit**, you need to drag the cursor toward the right to trim the Out point of the preceding clip. The In point of the following clip will be trimmed later in the **Timeline**.*

4. Press the CTRL+S keys to save the file. Next, press the ENTER key to view the output of the sequence in the Program Monitor. The output of the sequence at frame 00:00:28:00 is shown in Figure 4-47.

Figure 4-47 The output of the sequence at frame 00:00:28:00

Self-Evaluation Test

Answer the following questions and then compare them to those given at the end of this chapter:

1. Which of the following tools in the **Tools** panel is used to select all the clips on the right of the cursor in a sequence?

    (a) **Selection Tool**   (b) **Track Select Tool**
    (c) **Slip Tool**   (d) **Ripple Edit Tool**

2. Which of the following tools in the **Tools** panel is used to remove a range of frames in the **Timeline** panel?

    (a) **Lift**   (b) **Extract**
    (c) **Lift** and **Extract**   (d) **Slide Tool**

3. While trimming, which of the following tools in the **Tools** panel is used to fill the gap caused by editing a clip and shifts all edits to the left or right of the trimmed clip simultaneously?

    (a) **Ripple Edit Tool**   (b) **Razor Tool**
    (c) **Slide Tool**   (d) **Rate Stretch Tool**

4. To add the **Lift** tool in the playback controls of the Program Monitor, choose the _____ button from the lower right corner of the Program Monitor.

5. You need to press the _____ key to view all the clips properly in the **Timeline** panel.

6. The **Slide Tool** is used to simultaneously change the In and Out points of a trimmed clip in the **Timeline** panel. However, here the time duration of the clip remains constant. (T/F)

7. The **Slip Tool** is used to shift a clip in the **Timeline** and trim the adjacent clips to compensate the move. (T/F)

Review Questions

Answer the following questions:

1. Which of the following tools in the **Tools** panel is used to roll the edit point between two clips in the **Timeline** panel?

   (a) **Rolling Edit Tool**   (b) **Ripple Edit Tool**
   (c) **Track Select Tool**   (d) **Selection Tool**

2. Which of the following tools in the **Tools** panel is used to change the speed and duration of a clip?

   (a) **Track Select Tool**   (b) **Ripple Edit Tool**
   (c) **Rate Stretch Tool**   (d) All of the above

3. Which of the following tools in the **Tools** panel along with the SHIFT key is used to cut across clips in multiple tracks at one time?

   (a) **Rolling Edit Tool**   (b) **Ripple Edit Tool**
   (c) **Razor Tool**   (d) **Selection Tool**

4. You need to press the _____ key on the keyboard to zoom in the sequence, press the _____ key to zoom out the sequence, and press the _____ key to quickly view all the clips of the sequence.

5. The CTI indicates the current frame in the sequence which is also displayed in the Program Monitor. (T/F)

EXERCISE

Exercise 1

Create a new project in Premiere as per the settings of your video clip. Import your video clips in the **Project** panel. Add the clips in the sequence with the help of various tools in the **Tools** panel to edit the clips in the **Timeline** panel.

Answers to Self-Evaluation Test
1. b, **2.** c, **3.** a, **4.** Button Editor, **5.** BACKSLASH (\), **6.** F, **7.** F

Chapter 5

Creating Titles

Learning Objectives

After completing this chapter, you will be able to:

- *Create a new still title*
- *Create a title along the path*
- *Add images to the title*
- *Create Photoshop title*
- *Superimpose titles in the sequence*
- *Create rolling titles*
- *Create crawling titles*

INTRODUCTION

In this chapter, you will learn to create still, rolling, and crawling titles as well as credits and animated composites for your project by using the Titler window. This window contains all the panels related to a title. You will also learn to use Adobe Photoshop for creating titles in Premiere.

TUTORIALS

Before you start the tutorials, you need to download the *c05_premiere_cc_tut.zip* file from *www.cadcim.com*. The path of the file is as follows: *Textbooks > Animation and Visual Effects > Premiere Pro > Adobe Premiere Pro CC: A Tutorial Approach*

Next, extract the contents of the zip file to *\Documents\Adobe Premiere Tutorials*.

Tutorial 1

In this tutorial, you will create a still title. The output of the sequence at frame 00:00:03:18 is shown in Figure 5-1.   **(Expected Time: 15 min)**

Figure 5-1 The output of the sequence at frame 00:00:03:18

The following steps are required to complete this tutorial:

a.   Open the project file.
b.   Create a new bin for titles.
c.   Create a new still title.

Opening the Project File

In this tutorial, you will open the project file.

1.   Open the *chapter05_01.prproj* file that you have downloaded from the CADCIM website.

2.   Choose **File > Save As** from the menu bar; the **Save Project** dialog box is displayed. In this dialog box, browse to *\Documents\Adobe Premiere Tutorials\c05_premiere_cc_tut*. Enter the name **chapter05_01_still_title** in the **File name** text box and then choose the **Save** button; the opened file is saved with the specified name, refer to Figure 5-2.

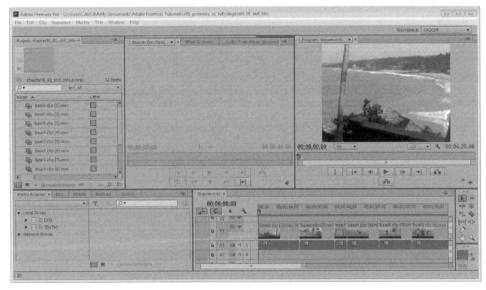

Figure 5-2 *The chapter05_01_still_title file displayed*

Creating a New Bin for Titles

To keep your media files organized, it is recommended that you create a separate bin for the titles of the project. In this section, you will create a bin for the titles.

1. Click on the triangle at the top right corner of the **Project** panel; a flyout is displayed, as shown in Figure 5-3.

2. Choose the **New Bin** option from the flyout; a new bin is created in the **Project** panel. Modify its name to **Titles**, refer to Figure 5-4.

3. Press and hold the CTRL key and double-click on the **Titles** bin; the bin is opened, as shown in Figure 5-5. Now, when you create new titles, they will be added to the **Titles** bin.

   In the **Project** panel, the **Project: chapter05_01_still_title** label is replaced with the **Bin:Titles** label, refer to Figure 5-5. To go back to the previous level, you need to choose the **chapter05_01_still_title.prproj\Titles** button.

   Note
   You can also open a bin in a floating window. To do so, double-click on the bin.

Figure 5-3 *The flyout displayed*   **Figure 5-4** *Modifying the name to* **Titles**

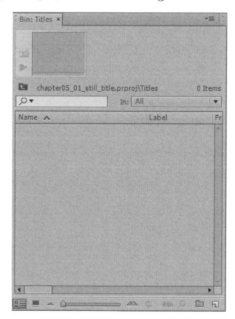

Figure 5-5 *The opened bin*

Creating a New Still Title

In this section, you will create a new still title.

1. Choose the **New Item** button located at the bottom of the **Project** panel; a flyout is displayed. Choose the **Title** option from the flyout; the **New Title** dialog box is displayed, as shown in Figure 5-6.

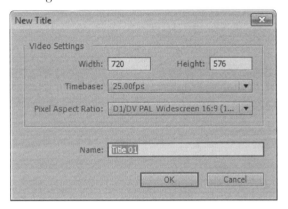

Figure 5-6 *The* **New Title** *dialog box*

Alternatively, you can choose **Title > New Title > Default Still** option from the menu bar to invoke the **New Title** dialog box. In the **New Title** dialog box, the parameters in the **Video Settings** area are set according to the settings of your current sequence.

2. In the **Name** text box, enter the name **title01** and choose the **OK** button; all panels are displayed in a floating window known as the Titler window, as shown in Figure 5-7. Also, the **title01** is displayed in the **Titles** bin of the **Project** panel, refer to Figure 5-8.

If the video background is not displayed in the Titler window, choose the **Show** **Background Video** button; the video background is displayed.

When the **Show Background Video** button is chosen, the background video of the frame on which CTI is placed is displayed in the Program Monitor and the Titler screen, refer to Figure 5-9. You can change the current frame by entering the new time in the **Background Video Timecode** edit box, refer to Figure 5-10. This edit box is located below the **Show Background Video** button in the Titler window.

The screen of the Titler window also displays the title safe frame, refer to Figure 5-7. It is recommended that the title is placed inside the title safe frame so that it is not cropped while being broadcast.

The Titler window has a number of panels such as **Tools**, **Actions**, **Title Properties**, and **Title Styles**. These panels are used to create and modify the titles.

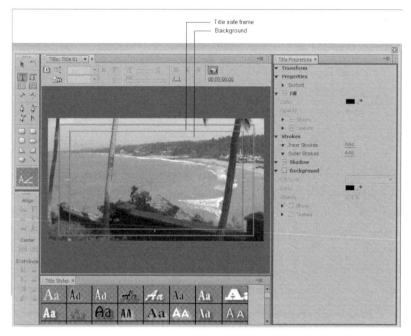

Figure 5-7 *The Titler window*

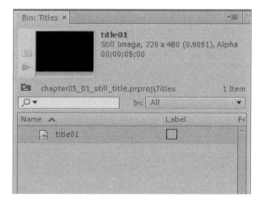

Figure 5-8 *The **title01** in the **Project** panel*

3. Choose the **Type Tool** from the **Title Tools** panel in the Titler window, if not already
    chosen.

4. Move the cursor over the Titler screen; the shape of the cursor is changed, as shown
    in Figure 5-11. Next, click on the screen to make the insertion point; a small text
    box is created in the Titler screen. Next, select **Caslon Pro 68** in the **Title Styles**
    panel. Again, click in the text box and enter **Sea Beach** in it, refer to Figure 5-12.

Figure 5-9 *The video background displayed*

Figure 5-10 *The **Background Video Timecode** edit box*

Figure 5-11 *The changed cursor*

Figure 5-12 *The text box on the screen*

Next, you will apply styles and effects to the title text. Also, you will align the title text with the background screen.

5. In the **Title Styles** panel, select the **Hobo Black 75** style; the text style is changed, as shown in Figure 5-13.

Next, you will change the font type and font size of the text.

6. In the **Title Properties** panel, expand the **Font Family** drop-down list in the **Properties** area and then select the **Bell Gothic Std** font from it; the text is modified as per the new font style, as shown in Figure 5-14.

Figure 5-13 *The changed text style*   *Figure 5-14* *The changed font type*

7. In the **Properties** area, click on the numeric value on the right of **Font Size**; it changes to an edit box. Enter **75** in the edit box, refer to Figure 5-15, and press ENTER; the font size is changed, as shown in Figure 5-16.

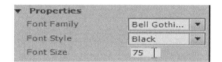

Figure 5-15 *The **Properties** area*   *Figure 5-16* *The changed font size*

Note
*You can also change the font size and font type using the options given in the **Title: title#** panel located above the Titler screen, refer to Figure 5-17.*

*You can also modify the other text properties of the title as per your requirement using the **Title: title#** panel.*

Figure 5-17 *Partial view of the **Title: title#** panel*

8. Invoke the **Selection** tool from the **Title Tools** panel. Next, press and hold the left mouse button over the title and move it to the bottom left corner of the screen. Release the left mouse button; the title is placed at the bottom of the screen, as shown in Figure 5-18.

Next, you will create a background for the title to make it properly visible.

9. Click in the empty area of the Titler screen to deselect the **Selection** tool and then invoke the **Rectangle Tool** from the **Title Tools** panel and create a rectangle around the title on the screen, refer to Figure 5-19. You will notice that after adding the rectangle, the title is hidden. Also, the rectangle takes the same title style properties as that of the newly created title text.

Figure 5-18 *The title at the bottom left corner*   *Figure 5-19* *The rectangle created*

Next, you will modify the properties of the rectangle to make the title visible on the screen.

10. Make sure the rectangle is selected and then right-click on it; a shortcut menu is displayed. Now, choose the **Arrange > Send to Back** option from the cascading menu, as shown in Figure 5-20. The title becomes visible on the screen, as shown in Figure 5-21.

Figure 5-20 *The shortcut menu*   *Figure 5-21* *The hidden title becoming visible on the screen*

11. Make sure the rectangle is selected. In the **Title Properties** panel, clear the **Shadow** check box in the **Shadow** area. Also, clear the **Outer Stroke** check box in the **Strokes** area.

12. In the **Fill** area, choose the color swatch corresponding to the **Color** parameter; the **Color Picker** dialog box is displayed.

13. In the **Color Picker** dialog box, enter **DAE7F4** in the text box at the bottom of the dialog box, refer to Figure 5-22. Choose the **OK** button; the modified rectangle is shown in Figure 5-23.

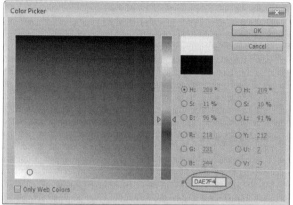

Figure 5-22 The **Color Picker** dialog box

Figure 5-23 The rectangle after modifying its properties

14. In the **Transform** area of the **Title Properties** panel, set the following parameters for the rectangle:

Opacity: **70.0**   Width: **467**   Height: **70**

Figure 5-24 displays the modified rectangle. Next, you will align the title text and rectangle.

15. Invoke the **Selection Tool** from the **Title Tools** panel. Press and hold the SHIFT key and select the title text and rectangle simultaneously.

16. In the **Align** area of the **Title Actions** panel, choose the **Vertical Center** and **Horizontal Center** buttons one by one; the title text and the rectangle are aligned, refer to Figure 5-25.

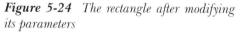

Figure 5-24 The rectangle after modifying its parameters

Figure 5-25 The aligned text and rectangle

17. Choose the Close button at the top right corner of the Titler window; the Titler window is closed.

18. Click-drag **title01** from the **Project** panel to the **Timeline** panel at the starting of the **V2** track.

19. Press CTRL+S to save the file. The output of the sequence at frame 00:00:03:18 is shown in Figure 5-26.

Figure 5-26 *The output of the sequence at frame 00:00:03:18*

Tutorial 2

In this tutorial, you will create a title along the path. Also, you will add images to the titles. The output of the sequence at frame 00:00:00:00 is shown in Figure 5-27.

(Expected Time: 20 min)

Figure 5-27 *The output of the sequence at frame 00:00:00:00*

The following steps are required to complete this tutorial:

a.   Open the project file.
b.   Create a title along a path.
c.   Add images to the title.

Opening the Project File

In this tutorial, you will open the project file.

1. Open the *chapter05_02.prproj* file that you have downloaded from the CADCIM website.

2. Choose **File > Save As** from the menu bar; the **Save Project** dialog box is displayed. In this dialog box, browse to *\Documents\Adobe Premiere Tutorials\c05_premiere_cc_tut*. Enter the name **chapter05_02_path_title** in the **File name** text box and choose the **Save** button; the opened file is saved with the specified name.

Creating a Title Along the Path

In this section, you will create a title along a path.

1. Choose **Title > New Title > Default Still** option from the menu bar; the **New Title** dialog box is displayed.

2. In the **Name** text box, enter the name **Title along the path** and choose the **OK** button; the Titler window is displayed along with various title panels.

3. Choose **Path Type Tool** from the **Title Tools** panel of the Titler window.

4. Move the cursor over the screen in the Titler window; the shape of the cursor is changed into a pen, refer to Figure 5-28.

5. Click on the screen to make an insertion point for the text.

6. Click and drag to create the second point of the path and continue clicking until you get the desired shape of the path on which the title will be created, refer to Figure 5-29.

Figure 5-28 The changed cursor   *Figure 5-29* The path created

7. Select **Caslon Pro 68** in the **Title Styles** panel. Again, choose the **Path Type** tool and click on the screen(at the start of the path). Next, enter the text **Title on a path**; the text is displayed.

8. If your title is not visible properly, you can adjust its path by rearranging the anchor points of the path, refer to Figure 5-30.

9. Select the title text and select the **Caslon Italic Bluesky 64** style from the **Title** **Styles** panel in the Titler window. Also, adjust the anchor points to display the title properly; the title is displayed, as shown in Figure 5-31.

Figure 5-30 *The text displayed along the path*

Figure 5-31 *The title after adjusting anchor points*

10. Choose the Close button at the top right corner of the Titler window; the Titler window is closed and the **Title along the path** text is displayed in the **Project** panel.

Note
In Tutorial 3, you will superimpose the titles created in the sequence.

Adding Images to the Titles

You can add an image, such as logo and graphic to the title in the Titler window. In this section, you will add an image to the title.

1. In the **Project** panel, double-click on **title01** title; the **title01** is opened in the Titler window.

2. Choose the **Title > Graphic > Insert Graphic** option from the menu bar; the **Import Graphic** dialog box is displayed.

3. Browse to the **Documents > Adobe Premiere Tutorials > c05_premiere_cc_tut > Media Files** folder that you have downloaded from the CADCIM website.

4. Select the **Logo.gif** image and choose the **Open** button; the logo is displayed on the Titler screen, as shown in Figure 5-32.

   Next, you need to modify the properties of the logo.

5. In the **Title Properties** panel, set the values of the properties as given below:

   Transform area
   Width: **69.2**   Height: **57.9**

   Also, make sure the **Outer Stroke** check box in the **Strokes** area and the **Shadows** check box is clear.

After modifying the properties, the logo is displayed, as shown in Figure 5-33.

Figure 5-32 *The logo displayed on the screen*   **Figure 5-33** *The logo after modifying its properties*

Next, you will align the logo with the title.

6. Make sure the **Selection Tool** is chosen and then select the logo.

7. Adjust the position and alignment of the logo, as shown in Figure 5-34.

8. Next, select the rectangle on the screen. In the **Transform** area of the **Title Properties** panel, modify the values of the **Width** and **Height** parameters such that logo fits in it. After modifying the rectangle, the title is displayed, as shown in Figure 5-35.

Figure 5-34 *The text, logo, and rectangle aligned*   **Figure 5-35** *The title after modifying the rectangle*

9. Choose the Close button at the top right corner of the Titler window; the Titler window is closed and the **title01** is modified with the logo in it.

10. Click and drag the **title01** from the **Project** panel to the beginning of the **V2** track in the **Timeline** panel.

11. Press CTRL+S to save the file. The output of the sequence at frame 00:00:00:00 is shown in Figure 5-36.

Figure 5-36 *The output of the sequence at frame 00:00:00:00*

Tutorial 3

In this tutorial, you will use Photoshop to create a title. Also, you will superimpose titles in the sequence. The output of the sequence at frame 00:00:05:00 is shown in Figure 5-37.

(Expected Time: 20 min)

Figure 5-37 *The output of the sequence at frame 00:00:05:00*

The following steps are required to complete this tutorial:

a. Open the project file.
b. Create photoshop title.
c. Superimpose titles in the sequence.

Opening the Project File
In this section, you will open the project file.

1. Open the *chapter05_03.prproj* file that you have downloaded from the CADCIM website.

2. Choose **File > Save As** from the menu bar; the **Save Project** dialog box is displayed. In this dialog box, browse to *\Documents\Adobe Premiere Tutorials\c05_premiere_cc_tut*. Enter the name **chapter05_03_superimpose_title** in the **File name** text box and choose the **Save** button; the opened file is saved with the specified name.

Creating Photoshop Title

In this section, you will create Photoshop title.

1. Choose **File > New > Photoshop File** from the menu bar; the **New Photoshop File** dialog box is displayed. In this dialog box, set the parameters as shown in Figure 5-38.

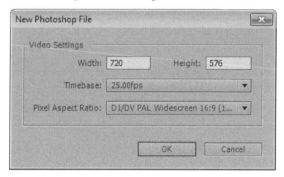

Figure 5-38 *The* **New Photoshop File** *dialog box*

2. Choose the **OK** button in the **New Photoshop File** dialog box; the **Save Photoshop File As** dialog box is displayed.

3. Browse to the location *\Documents\Adobe Premiere Tutorials\c05_premiere_cc_tut\Media Files\ Stills*. Enter the name **Photoshop title** in the **File name** text box and choose the **Save** button, refer to Figure 5-39; the Photoshop application opens with a new file, as shown in Figure 5-40. The dimension of this file is similar to the video frame size.

Note
If the **Adobe Photoshop CS6** *message box is displayed while opening the new photoshop file, choose the* **OK** *button to close it.*

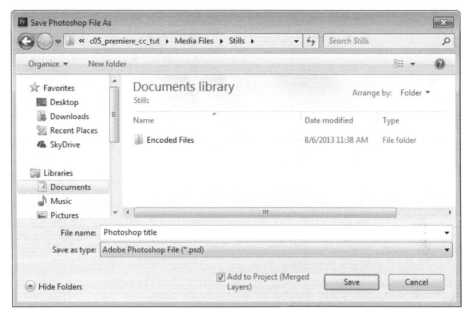

Figure 5-39 *The* **Save Photoshop File As** *dialog box*

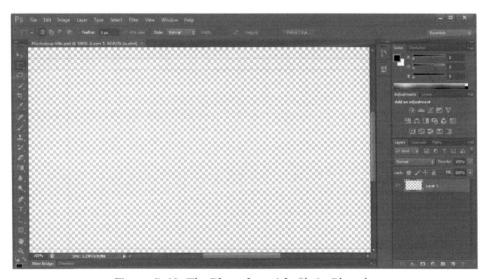

Figure 5-40 *The* **Photoshop title** *file in Photoshop*

4. Choose the **Horizontal Type Tool**. Next, click on the screen and enter **Photoshop Title** in the drawing area, refer to Figure 5-41.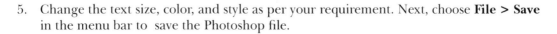

5. Change the text size, color, and style as per your requirement. Next, choose **File > Save** in the menu bar to save the Photoshop file.

6. Now, switch back to Premiere; the new **Photoshop title.psd** file is displayed in the **Project** panel, as shown in Figure 5-42.

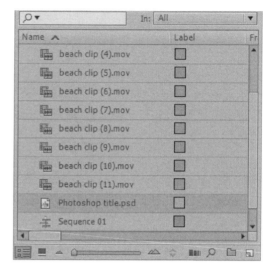

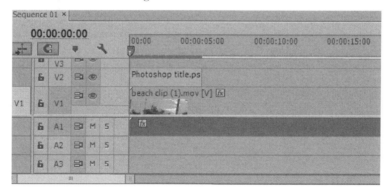

Figure 5-41 *The title text in the drawing area*

Figure 5-42 *The **Photoshop title.psd** in the **Project** panel*

Superimposing Titles in the Sequence

In this section, you will superimpose the "Photoshop title" on the sequence.

1. Make sure the CTI is positioned at the beginning of the sequence where you will add the title.

2. In the **Project** panel, press and hold the left mouse button over the **Photoshop title**, and drag it to the **V2** track in the sequence, refer to Figure 5-43. The title is displayed in the Program Monitor, as shown in Figure 5-44.

Figure 5-43 *The **Photoshop title** in the V2 track*

Using the above steps, you can also add other titles to the sequence. By default, the duration of the title is 5 seconds. Sometimes, you may need to change the duration of the title according to your project. In the following steps, you will change the default duration of the title.

Figure 5-44 *The **Photoshop Title** in the Program Monitor*

3. Press the EQUAL (=) key to zoom in the **Photoshop title** in the **V2** track to view it properly.

4. Place the cursor at the end of **Photoshop title** in the **Timeline**; the shape of the cursor changes into a closed bracket, as shown in Figure 5-45.

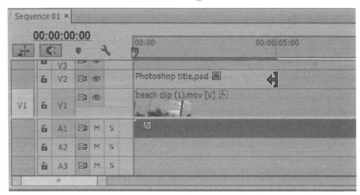

Figure 5-45 *The changed cursor shape*

5. Press and hold the left mouse button and drag the cursor to the left to shorten the duration of the appearance of the title on the screen. Alternatively, drag the cursor to the right to lengthen the duration of the display of the title. While dragging the cursor, a tooltip is displayed showing the added duration of the display of title, as shown in Figure 5-46.

6. Press CTRL+S to save the file. Next, press the ENTER key to view the output of the sequence in the Program Monitor. The output of the sequence at frame 00:00:05:00 is shown in Figure 5-47.

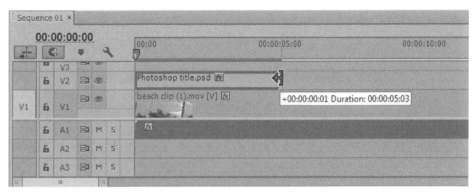

Figure 5-46 *The tooltip displayed*

Figure 5-47 *The output of the sequence at frame 00:00:05:00*

Tutorial 4

In this tutorial, you will create rolling and crawling titles. The output of the sequence at frame 00:00:03:02 is shown in Figure 5-48.   **(Expected Time: 25 min)**

Figure 5-48 *The output of the sequence at frame 00:00:03:02*

The following steps are required to complete this tutorial:

a.   Create a new project.
b.   Create rolling titles.
c.   Create crawling titles.

Creating a New Project

In this section, you will create a new project.

1.   Choose **File > New > Project** from the menu bar; the **New Project** dialog box is displayed.

2.   Type **chapter05_04** in the **Name** text box.

3.   In the **Location** area, make sure the location is \Documents\Adobe Premiere Tutorials\ c05_premiere_cc_tut.

4.   Choose the **Scratch Disks** tab and make sure the **Same as Project** is selected in the **Captured Video**, **Captured Audio**, **Video Previews**, and **Audio Previews** drop-down lists.

5.   Choose the **OK** button in the **New Project** dialog box; the project screen with various panels is displayed.

Creating Rolling Titles

The title that moves vertically over the screen is known as the rolling title whereas the title that moves horizontally over the screen is known as the crawling title. In this section, you will create rolling titles.

1.   Choose **Title > New Title > Default Roll** from the menu bar; the **New Title** dialog box is displayed. In this dialog box, set the parameters as shown in Figure 5-49.

2.   Enter the name **Rolling Title** in the **Name** text box and choose the **OK** button; the Titler window is opened. Also, the **Rolling Title** is displayed in the **Title** panel.

Note
You will use this rolling title at the end of the clips in the sequence.

3.   Choose the **Area Type Tool** from the **Title Tools** panel in the Titler window. Next, click-drag the cursor to create a text box from the top left corner to the bottom right corner, refer to Figure 5-50.

4.   Select the **Caslon Pro 68** style in the **Title Styles** panel. Next, click in the upper left corner of the text box and enter the text **CADCIM Technologies** in it; the text is displayed in the text box, refer to Figure 5-51.

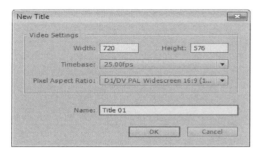

Figure 5-49 *The New Title dialog box*

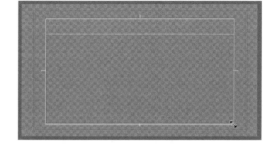

Figure 5-50 *The text box on the screen*

5. In the **Properties** area of the **Title Properties** panel, enter the following properties of the text:

Font Size: **50**   Font Family: **Book Antiqua**

Choose the **Center** button from the **Title: Rolling Title** properties panel to align the text at the center of the screen; the modified text is displayed, as shown in Figure 5-52.

Figure 5-51 *The text in the text box*

Figure 5-52 *The modified text in the text box*

6. Make sure the cursor is placed after the text CADCIM Technologies in the text box. Now, enter the following text: **525 St. Andrews Drive, Schererville, IN 46375, USA www.cadcim.com www.cadcimtech.com; Tel: (219) 614-7235 Fax: (270) 717-0185**, refer to Figure 5-53.

Figure 5-53 *The text entered in the text box*

Note
When you add the title to the sequence, the invisible offscreen text area rolls over the screen in the Program Monitor while the sequence is played.

7. Press the CTRL+A keys to select entire text on the Titler screen. In the **Title: Rolling Title** properties panel, modify the value in the **Leading** edit box to **20**. Now, choose the **Type Tool** from the **Title Tools** panel and align the entire text in the text box of the Titler screen, as shown in Figure 5-54.

If the text is not completely accommodated on the screen, a plus (+) sign may appear at the bottom right corner of the text box. This sign indicates that there is more text in that text box but it is not visible on the screen. To make the text visible, expand the text box.

Figure 5-54 *The text after aligning in the text box of the Titler screen*

8. Choose the **Selection Tool** from the **Title Tools** panel.

Next, you need to specify some parameters for the rolling title.

9. Choose the **Roll/Crawl Options** button from the **Title: Rolling Title** properties panel; the **Roll/Crawl Options** dialog box is displayed, as shown in Figure 5-55.

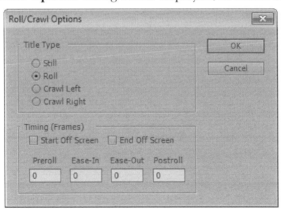

Figure 5-55 *The **Roll/Crawl Options** dialog box*

10. In the **Timing (Frames)** area of the **Roll/Crawl Options** dialog box, set the parameters as follows:

    Select the **Start Off Screen** check box.

    Ease-Out: **60**   Postroll: **90**

    The **Start Off Screen** check box is used to roll out the title or the text from the screen. The **Ease-Out** option is used to specify the number of frames through which the title scrolls at a gradually decreasing speed, until the roll is completed. The **Postroll** option is used to specify the number of frames that are played after the roll is completed.

11. Choose the **OK** button in the **Roll/Crawl Options** dialog box. Also, close the Titer window.

12. Create a sequence in the **Project** panel, as discussed in the previous chapters. Next, you need to add the Rolling Title to the sequence.

13. In the **Project** panel, press and hold the left mouse button over the **Rolling Title** title and drag it to the **V1** track, refer to Figure 5-56.

*Figure 5-56 The **Rolling Title** in the sequence*

 Note
*While dragging the clip from the **Project** panel to the **Timeline** panel if the **Clip Mismatch** message box is displayed, you need to choose the **Change Sequence Settings** button from this message box.*

14. Make sure the CTI is placed at the beginning of the **Rolling Title** in the sequence and press the SPACEBAR key to play it; the title rolls from bottom to top in the Program Monitor, refer to Figure 5-57.

15. To increase the total duration of the title, move the cursor over the end point of the title; the shape of the cursor changes to a closed bracket. Now, drag it as per your requirement; the duration of the title is increased.

 Note
The length of the title in the sequence determines the speed of the roll. More is the length of the title, slower will be the movement.

Figure 5-57 The rolling title at a frame in the Program Monitor

Creating Crawling Titles

In this section, you will create crawling titles.

1. Choose **Title > New Title > Default Crawl** from the menu bar; the **New Title** dialog box is displayed.

2. Enter the name **Crawling Title** in the **Name** text box and choose the **OK** button; the Titler window is opened. Also, **Crawling Title** is displayed in the **Project** panel.

3. In the Titler window, click on the **Show Background Video** button to deactivate it and then invoke the **Area Type Tool** from the **Title Tools** panel. Next, drag the cursor from left to right of the bottom of the screen; a text box is created, refer to Figure 5-58.

4. Select the **Caslon Pro 68** style in the **Title Styles** panel. Also, make sure 68 is displayed in the **Font Size** edit box of the **Properties** area in the **Title Properties** panel and then click in the upper left corner of the text box. Next, enter **CADCIM Technologies** in the text box; the text is displayed.

5. In the **Properties** area of the **Title: Properties** panel, enter the following properties of the text:

Font Size: **50**   Font Family: **Agency FB**

The text in the text box after modifying the values is shown in Figure 5-59.

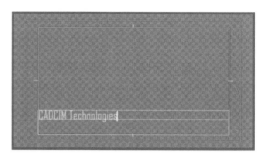

Figure 5-58 *The text in the text box*   *Figure 5-59* *The text after modifying the values*

Next, you need to set some crawl options.

6. Choose the **Roll/Crawl Options** button from the **Title: Crawling Title** properties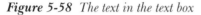
    panel; the **Roll/Crawl Options** dialog box is displayed.

7. In this dialog box, make sure the **Crawl Left** option and the **Start Off Screen** check box
    is selected and then choose the **OK** button.

8. Close the Titer window; the **Crawling Title** is displayed in the **Project** panel.

9. Delete **Rolling Title** from the **Timeline** panel. Now, add the **Crawling Title** to the sequence
    and then play the sequence; the **Crawling Title** moves horizontally in the Program Monitor,
    refer to Figure 5-60.

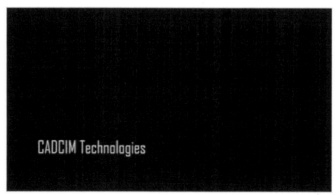

Figure 5-60 *The output of the sequence at frame 00:00:03:02*

Note
*When you modify a title, the modifications reflect both in the sequence and the **Project** panel.*

Self-Evaluation Test

Answer the following questions and then compare them to those given at the end of this chapter:

1. Which of the following options in the menu bar is used to create a new title?

   (a) **File**   (b) **Marker**
   (c) **Title**   (d) **Window**

2. Which of the following panels in the Titler window is used to set the alignment of the title?

   (a) **Title Tools**   (b) **Title Properties**
   (c) **Title Styles**   (d) **Actions**

3. Which of the following panels in the Titler window is used to apply styles to a title?

   (a) **Title Styles**   (b) **Title Properties**
   (c) **Title Tools**   (d) **Active**

4. Which of the following symbols is used to zoom in the clip in the Video track of the **Timeline** panel?

   (a) +   (b) =
   (c) ~   (d) -

5. The title that moves vertically over the screen is known as _____ title.

6. The length of the title in the sequence determines the _____ of the toll.

7. The **Title Properties** panel is used to quickly modify the font style, font size, and other properties of the title. (T/F)

8. You cannot use Photoshop to create a title in Premiere. (T/F)

Review Questions

Answer the following questions:

1. Which of the following buttons in the **Title Properties** panel is used to set the rolling and crawling options for the title?

   (a) **Show Background Video**   (b) **Templates**
   (c) **Roll/Crawl Options**   (d) None of these

2. The _____ check box in the **Roll/Crawl Options** dialog box is used to roll out the title or the text from the screen.

3. The _____ option in the **Roll/Crawl Options** dialog box is used to specify the number of frames that will play after the roll is completed.

4. The **Ease-Out** option in the **Roll/Crawl Options** dialog box is used to specify the number of frames through which the title will scroll at a gradually decreasing speed until the roll is completed. (T/F)

5. When you add a title to a sequence, the invisible offscreen text area disappears from the screen. (T/F)

6. The title that moves horizontally over the screen is known as the rolling title. (T/F)

EXERCISE

Exercise 1

Create a new project in Premiere as per the settings of your video clip. Create a new bin for the titles. Try to create still, rolling, and crawling titles. Also, try to create a title in Premiere using Photoshop.

Answers to Self-Evaluation Test
1. c, **2.** d, **3.** a, **4.** b, **5.** rolling, **6.** speed, **7.** T, **8.** F

Chapter 6

Adding Transitions to Clips

Learning Objectives

After completing this chapter, you will be able to:

- *Add video and audio transition effects*
- *Modify the transition*
- *Apply transitions to multiple clips*

INTRODUCTION

When you create a sequence by adding a number of clips together, a cut is formed between the clips. A cut or edit point is an instantaneous change from one shot to another. By adding transitions to the clips, the movement from one shot to another becomes smoother. There are two types of transition effects in Premiere: Audio Transition and Video Transition. You can add the Video Transition effects to the video clips and the Audio Transition effects to the audio clips. In this chapter, you will learn how to add transition effects to the clips in a sequence.

TUTORIALS

Before you start the tutorials, you need to download the *c06_premiere_cc_tut.zip* file from *www.cadcim.com*. The path of the file is as follows: *Textbooks > Animation and Visual Effects > Premiere Pro > Adobe Premiere Pro CC: A Tutorial Approach*

Next, extract the contents of the zip file at *\Documents\Adobe Premiere Tutorials*.

Tutorial 1

In this tutorial, you will add video transition effects to a sequence. The output of the sequence at frame 00:03:11:01 is shown in Figure 6-1.   **(Expected Time: 25 min)**

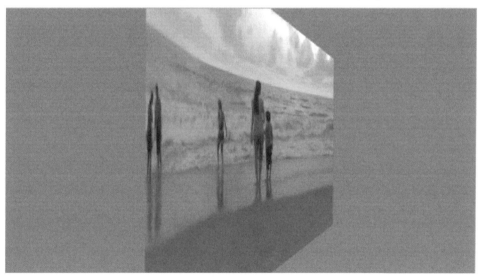

Figure 6-1 *The output of the sequence at frame 00:03:11:01*

The following steps are required to complete this tutorial:

a.   Open the project file.
b.   Add video transition.
c.   Modify the transition.

Opening the Project File

In this section, you will open the project file.

1.   Open the *chapter06.prproj* file that you have downloaded from the CADCIM website.

2.   Save the *chapter06.prproj* file with the name *chapter06_02.prproj* at *Documents**Adobe Premiere Tutorials**c06_premiere_cc_tut*. The *chapter06_02.prproj* file is displayed in the Premiere interface, refer to Figure 6-2.

Figure 6-2 The chapter06_02 file displayed

Adding a Video Transition Effect

In Premiere, video transitions are available in the **Effects** panel located on the lower left corner of its interface. You can add a transition effect to the clips using the drag and drop method. In this section, you will fade in and fade out the **Title 01** title of the *chapter06_02.prproj* file using video transitions.

1.   In the **Timeline** panel, press the EQUAL (=) key twice to zoom in the sequence so that you can view the **Title 01** properly, refer to Figure 6-3.

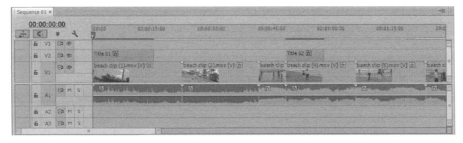

*Figure 6-3 The **Title 01** in the **Timeline** panel*

2. Choose the **Effects** tab located at the lower left corner of the interface; the **Effects** panel is displayed. In the **Effects** panel, click on the arrow on the left of the **Video Transitions** folder to expand it; different categories of video transition effects are displayed in folders, as shown in Figure 6-4.

*Figure 6-4 Video transitions in the **Effects** panel*

3. Click on the arrow on the left of the **Dissolve** folder; various types of transition effects under this category are displayed, as shown in Figure 6-5.

*Figure 6-5 Various types of transitions in the **Dissolve** category*

4. Select the **Additive Dissolve** transition by clicking on it. Press and hold the left mouse button on it and then drag it from the **Effects** panel to the **Timeline** panel at the beginning of the **Title 01**; the shape of the cursor changes, refer to Figure 6-6. This cursor indicates that the transition will start on the edit point at the beginning of the **Title 01**. Next, release the left mouse button; the **Additive Dissolve** transition is placed at the start point of the **Title 01**.

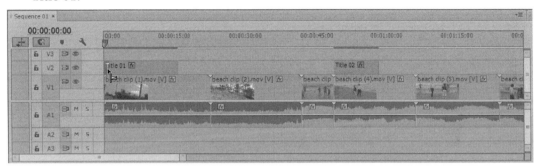

Figure 6-6 *The changed cursor while dropping the transition in the* **Timeline** *panel*

5. Press the EQUAL key twice to zoom in the sequence to view the transition effect properly, as shown in Figure 6-7.

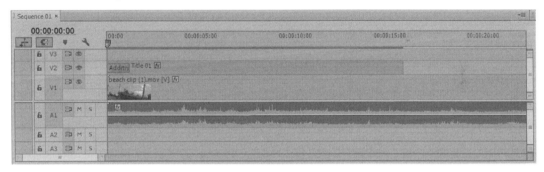

Figure 6-7 *The* **Additive Dissolve** *transition in the zoomed sequence*

6. Move the mouse over the **Additive Dissolve** transition; a tooltip is displayed showing the default duration, as shown in Figure 6-8. The default duration of the **Additive Dissolve** effect is about 1 second.

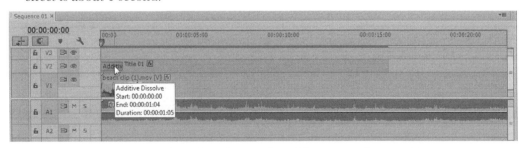

Figure 6-8 *The tooltip showing the* **Additive Dissolve** *transition*

You can increase or decrease the duration of the effect based on your requirement.

7. Move the cursor over the last edge of the **Additive Dissolve** transition; the shape of the cursor changes into a closed bracket, refer to Figure 6-9. Now, press and hold the left mouse button and drag it toward right to increase the duration of the transition or drag it toward left to decrease the duration of the transition. Next, press CTRL + Z to undo the changes.

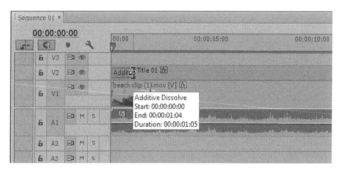

Figure 6-9 *The shape of the cursor changed at the end of the transition*

8. Make sure the CTI is at the beginning of the **Additive Dissolve** transition.

9. Press the SPACEBAR key to play the sequence and view the result of the **Additive Dissolve** transition effect. The transition effect is displayed in the Program Monitor, refer to Figures 6-10 and 6-11.

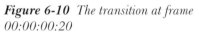

Figure 6-10 *The transition at frame*
00:00:00:20

Figure 6-11 *The transition at frame*
00:00:01:03

Next, you will use the **Additive Dissolve** transition to fade out the title.

10. Make sure the **Additive Dissolve** transition is selected in the **Effects** panel. Press and hold the left mouse button on it and drag it from the **Effects** panel to the **Timeline** panel at the end of the **Title 01**. On doing so, the shape of the cursor changes, refer to Figure 6-12. The cursor indicates that the transition will be at the end of the cut of **Title 01**. Next, release the left mouse button; the **Additive Dissolve** transition is placed at the end of **Title 01**, as shown in Figure 6-13.

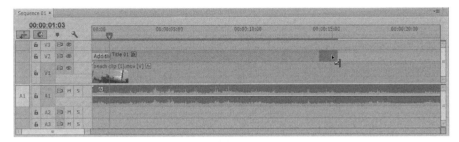

Figure 6-12 *The cursor at the end of the* **Title 01** *clip*

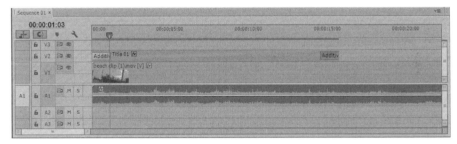

Figure 6-13 *The* **Additive Dissolve** *transition applied at the end of the clip*

Note
You may need to zoom in or zoom out the sequence to place the **Additive Dissolve** *at the end of the* **Title 01**.

11. Play the sequence to view the result of the **Additive Dissolve** transition at the end of the **Title 01**; the **Title 01** fades out.

    Next, you will add a transition between two clips in the **V1** track to move from one clip to another.

12. Press the BACKSLASH (\) key to view all clips in the **Timeline** panel.

    Next, you will add a transition between the **beach clip (6).mov** and **beach clip (7).mov**.

13. Move the CTI at the cut point of the **beach clip (6).mov** and **beach clip (7).mov**. Press the EQUAL (=) key twice to view these clips clearly in the **Timeline** panel, as shown in Figure 6-14.

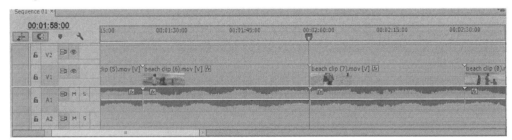

Figure 6-14 *The* **beach clip (6).mov** *and* **beach clip (7).mov** *in the* **Timeline** *panel*

14. Select the **Cross Dissolve** transition in the **Effects** panel. Press and hold the left mouse button on it and drag it from the **Effects** panel to the **Timeline** panel in between the **beach clip (6).mov** and **beach clip (7).mov**. Release the mouse button; the **Transition** message box is displayed with the message "**Insufficient media. This transition will contain repeated frames**", as shown in Figure 6-15.

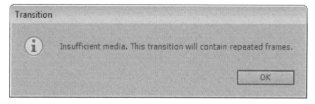

Figure 6-15 *The* ***Transition*** *message box*

15. Choose the **OK** button in the **Transition** message box.

16. Make sure the CTI is placed at the cut point of the **beach clip (6).mov** and **beach clip (7).mov**. Press the EQUAL (=) key five times to zoom in the sequence. The transition is displayed as diagonal lines on the video clip, as shown in Figure 6-16. These diagonal lines indicate that the clips lack the head and tail frames.

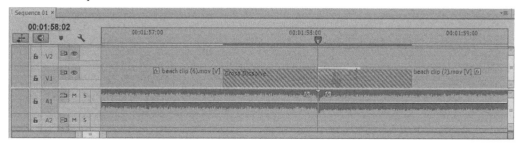

Figure 6-16 *The transition displayed as diagonal lines on the video clip*

Note that there are little triangles at the upper right and upper left corners of the **beach clip (6).mov** and **beach clip (7).mov** before adding transition in between them, refer to Figure 6-14. These triangles indicate that the clips are at their full length and there are no additional frames at the beginning or at the end of the clips. To add the transitions smoothly between the clips, you need to trim both the clips. By doing so, you will get some unused head and tail frames or clip handles to overlap between the clips.

17. Invoke the **Ripple Edit Tool** and then move the cursor to the end of the **beach** **clip(6).mov**; the cursor gets changed to a yellow colored closed bracket. Press and hold the left mouse button and move the cursor toward left till the tooltip displays about -00:00:00:15, refer to Figure 6-17. Release the left mouse button.

18. Move the cursor to the beginning of the **beach clip (7).mov**; the cursor gets changed to a yellow colored open bracket. Press and hold the left mouse button and move the cursor toward right till the tooltip displays about +00:00:00:15. Next, release the left mouse button; the diagonal lines on the transition disappear, refer to Figure 6-18.

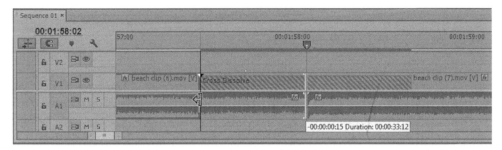

Figure 6-17 *The tooltip displayed while using the **Ripple Edit Tool***

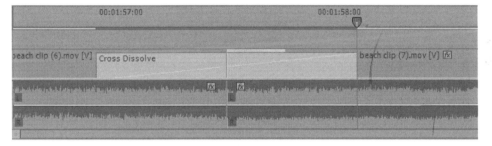

Figure 6-18 *The transition without diagonal lines*

19. Next, play the sequence to view the **Cross Dissolve** transition in the Program Monitor.

    Now, you will add the **Wipe** transition to the **beach clip (8).mov** and **beach clip (9).mov** using different methods.

20. Press the BACKSLASH (\) key to view all the clips in the **Timeline** panel.

21. Move the CTI to the cut point between the **beach clip (8).mov** and **beach clip (9).mov** clips. Press the EQUAL (=) key thrice to view the cut between the clips properly.

    Note that there are triangles at the upper corners of the clips. So, you need to trim the endpoint of **beach clip (8).mov** and the starting point of **beach clip (9).mov**.

22. Make sure the **Ripple Edit Tool** is chosen. Move the cursor at the end of the **beach** **clip (8).mov**; the cursor gets changed to a closed bracket. Press and hold the left mouse button and move the cursor toward left till the tooltip displays about -00:00:15:00.

23. Move the cursor to the beginning of the **beach clip (9).mov**; the shape of the cursor gets changed to an open bracket. Press and hold the left mouse button and move the cursor toward right till the tooltip displays about +00:00:01:00.

    Note that after trimming the clips, there are no triangles at the upper right corner of the **beach clip (8).mov** and at the upper left corner of the **beach clip (9).mov**.

24. In the **Effects** panel, click on the arrow on the left of the **Wipe** folder; a list of wipe transition effects is displayed in it. Select the **Checker Wipe** transition, press and hold the left mouse button on it, and drag it from the **Effects** panel to the **Timeline** panel and then to the cut between the **beach clip (8).mov** and **beach clip (9).mov.** Now release the left mouse button; the **Wipe** transition is placed between the clips. While holding down the left mouse button, you can also move the cursor to the left or to the right of the cut.

You will notice that cursor and the highlighted rectangle on the clips get changed, refer to Figure 6-19. If you apply the transition effect on the left of the cut, as shown in Figure 6-19; the transition will end at the cut point. If you place the transition on the right of the cut, as shown in Figure 6-20, the transition will start at the cut point. If you apply the transition between the two clips, the transition will be positioned on both the clips.

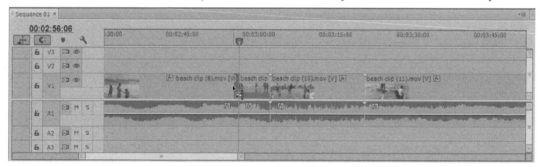

Figure 6-19 *The transition on the left of the cut*

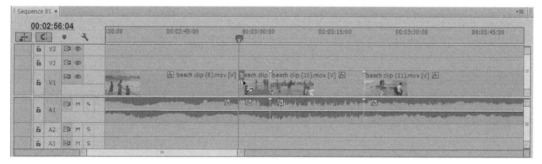

Figure 6-20 *The transition on the right of the cut*

25. Move the CTI to the left of the transition and press SPACEBAR to view the transition in the Program Monitor.

Modifying the Transition

In this section, you will modify the transition effect. You will replace the **Checker Wipe** transition which you applied in the earlier section, with the **Flip Over** transition.

1. In the **Effects** panel, click on the arrow on the left of the **3D Motion** folder; a list of 3D transitions is displayed in it. Select the **Flip Over** transition, press and hold the left mouse

button on it, and drag it from the **Effects** panel to the **Timeline** panel over the **Checker Wipe** transition; the **Checker Wipe** transition is replaced with the **Flip Over** transition, refer to Figures 6-21 and 6-22.

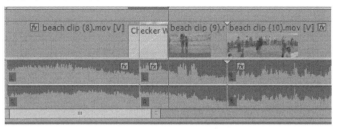

Figure 6-21 *The* ***Checker Wipe*** *transition*

Figure 6-22 *The* ***Flip Over*** *transition*

2. Move the CTI to the beginning of the transition and press the SPACEBAR key to play the sequence; the **Flip Over** transition is displayed in the Program Monitor, as shown in Figure 6-23.

Figure 6-23 *The* ***Flip Over*** *transition in the Program Monitor*

The transition can be adjusted or customized in the **Timeline** panel. To control them more precisely, you need to use the **Effect Controls** panel. The **Effect Controls** panel is located as a tab in the Source Monitor. You can modify almost all properties of the transition using this panel. In this section, you will modify the **Flip Over** transition that you applied between the **beach clip (8).mov** and **beach clip (9).mov** clips using the **Effect Controls** panel.

Make sure the *Chapter06_02.prproj* file is opened with the **Flip Over** transition applied between **beach clip (8).mov** and **beach clip (9).mov**.

3. Invoke the **Selection** tool from the **Tools** panel and then select the **Flip Over** transition in the **Timeline** panel. Next, choose the **Effect Controls** tab; its settings are displayed in the **Effect Controls** panel, refer to Figure 6-24.

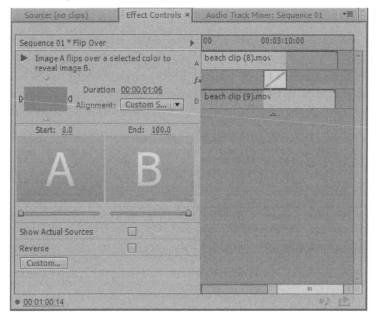

*Figure 6-24 The **Flip Over** transition settings in the **Effect Controls** panel*

4. Choose the **Play the transition** button at the top left corner of the **Effect Controls** panel; the sample transition starts playing in the preview window, as shown in Figure 6-25.

    The default duration of the **Flip Over** transition is displayed in the **Duration** edit box on the right of the preview window. The default duration is 00:00:01:05. Next, you will change the default duration of the transition.

5. Move the cursor over the text **Duration**; the shape of the cursor gets changed, as shown in Figure 6-26. Next, press and hold the left mouse button on it and drag the mouse till the point where edit box displays 00:00:02:05.

    Note that after increasing the duration, the length of the **Flip Over** transition is also increased in the **Timeline** panel.

    In the **Effect Controls** panel, the **A** and **B** windows represent the **beach clip (8).mov** and **beach clip (9).mov**, respectively.

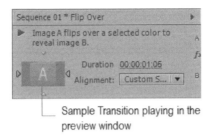

Figure 6-25 *The **Flip Over** transition*   **Figure 6-26** *The shape of the cursor changes*

6. Select the **Show Actual Sources** check box at the bottom of these windows; the **A** and **B** windows are replaced with the **beach clip (8).mov** and **beach clip (9).mov**, as shown in Figure 6-27.

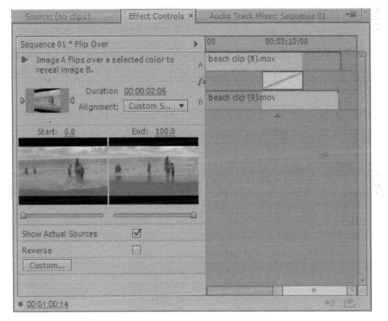

Figure 6-27 *The **beach clip (8).mov** and **(9).mov** in the **Effect Controls** panel*

7. Select the **Reverse** check box; the direction of the **Flip Over** transition is reversed.

8. Choose the **Custom** button on the bottom of the **Effect Controls** panel; the **Flip Over Settings** dialog box is displayed, as shown in Figure 6-28.

Figure 6-28 *The **Flip Over Settings** dialog box*

9. Set the value **2** in the **Bands** edit box and choose the **OK** button. Move the CTI to the beginning of the transition. Now, press the SPACEBAR key; the CTI starts moving in the **Timeline** panel and you will notice that **Flip Over** transition is displayed with 2 bands, refer to Figure 6-29.

*Figure 6-29 The **Flip Over** transition with 2 bands*

10. Choose the **Custom** button in the **Effects Control** panel; the **Flip Over Settings** dialog box is displayed. Next, choose the **Fill Color** color swatch in this dialog box, refer to Figure 6-28; the **Color Picker** dialog box is displayed. Now, select the color of your choice and choose the **OK** button. Now, choose the **OK** button from the **Flip Over Settings** dialog box; the selected color is displayed in the **Flip Over** transition, as shown in Figure 6-30.

*Figure 6-30 The changed color in the **Flip Over** transition effect*

11. Select the **Center at Cut**, **Start at Cut**, or **End at Cut** option from the **Alignment** drop-down list in the **Effects Control** panel; the transition is aligned with the clips as per the option selected. You can also view the changes as per the option selected in the Program Monitor.

The **Effect Controls** panel displays the timeline view on its right. The beach clips and the transition is displayed in the timeline view of the **Effect Controls** panel. Also, a triangle is displayed in this panel, indicating the original cut point, refer to Figure 6-31.

Note
*1. If you change the alignment of the transition from the **Alignment** drop-down list or change the duration of the transition, then the result will also be displayed in the timeline view of the **Effect Controls** panel.*

*2. The settings in the **Effect Controls** panel may vary for different transition effects.*

Next, you will manually change the duration of the transition in the **Effect Controls** panel.

12. Move the cursor to the starting point of the transition in the **Effect Controls** panel; the shape of the cursor is changed into an open bracket, as shown in Figure 6-32.

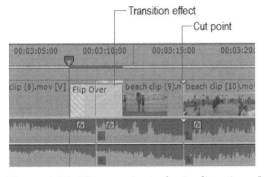

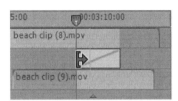

*Figure 6-31 The cut point in the timeline view of the **Effect Controls** panel*

Figure 6-32 The changed cursor at the starting point of the transition

13. Press and hold the left mouse button and drag the cursor toward left as much as you need; the duration of the transition is changed. Also, the changed duration is displayed in the **Duration** edit box.

Next, you will manually change the alignment of the transition in the **Effect Controls** panel.

14. Move the cursor over the transition in the **Effect Controls** panel; the shape of the cursor is changed, as shown in Figure 6-33.

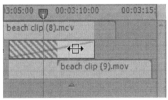

Figure 6-33 The changed cursor over the transition

15. Press and hold the left mouse button and place the transition at the desired place; the **Alignment** drop-down list will display the **Custom Start** option.

16. Choose the **Custom** button; the **Flip Over Settings** dialog box is displayed. Set the value **1** in the **Bands** edit box, refer to steps 8 and 9.

17. Press CTRL+S to save the file. Next, press the ENTER key to view the output of the sequence in the Program Monitor. The output of the sequence at frame 00:03:11:01 is shown in Figure 6-34.

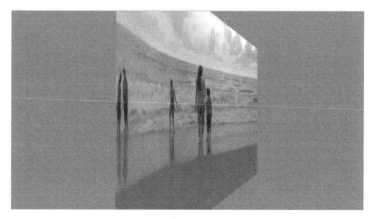

Figure 6-34 *The output of the sequence at frame 00:03:11:01*

Tutorial 2

In this tutorial, you will apply transition effects to multiple clips. Also, you will add audio transition to the clips. The output of the sequence at frame 00:00:56:24 is shown in Figure 6-35.

(Expected Time: 20 min)

Figure 6-35 *The output of the sequence at frame 00:00:56:24*

The following steps are required to complete this tutorial:

a. Open the project file.
b. Apply transitions to multiple clips at once.
c. Add audio transitions.

Opening the Project File

In this section, you will open the composition.

1. Make sure *Chapter06_02.prproj* is opened. Next, press the BACKSLASH (\) key to view all the clips properly.

Applying Transitions to Multiple Clips at Once

In this section, you will apply transitions to multiple clips automatically at the same time.

1. Drag a selection box around all the clips using the **Selection Tool** to select them simultaneously in the **Timeline** panel, refer to Figure 6-36.

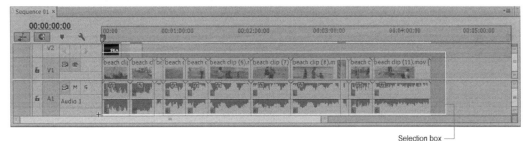

Selection box

*Figure 6-36 All clips selected in the **Timeline** panel*

2. Press the DELETE key; all clips are deleted from the sequence in the **Timeline** panel.

3. In the **Project** panel, select **beach clip (1).mov**, **beach clip (2).mov**, **beach clip (3).mov**, **beach clip (4).mov**, and **beach clip (5).mov** using the CTRL key.

4. Move the CTI to the beginning of the sequence. Choose the **Automate To Sequence** button in the **Project** panel; the **Automate To Sequence** dialog box is displayed, as shown in Figure 6-37.

    The **Automate To Sequence** dialog box is used to place multiple clips in sequential order in the **Timeline** panel. Various options in the **Automate to Sequence** dialog box are discussed next.

    The **Ordering** drop-down list is used to specify the method that will be used to determine the order of the clips when they are added to the sequence. By default, the **Selection Order** option is selected in the **Ordering** drop-down list. As a result, the clips will be placed in the order in which you selected them in the **Project** panel. If you select the **Sort Order** option, then clips will be placed in the same order in which they are placed in the **Project** panel.

    The **Placement** drop-down list is used to specify how clips will be placed in the sequence. By default, the **Sequentially** option is selected in this drop-down list. As a result, clips are placed one after another in the **Timeline** panel. If you select the **At Unnumbered Markers** option from the **Placement** drop-down list, then the clips will be placed at unnumbered sequence markers.

Figure 6-37 The **Automate To Sequence** *dialog box*

The **Method** drop-down list is used to choose the edit type to be performed.

When you apply default transitions to the clips, then the **Clip Overlap** option is used to specify the duration of the transition.

5. Accept the default settings in the **Automate To Sequence** dialog box by choosing the **OK** button; all selected clips are added to the sequence with the default **Cross Dissolve** transition applied between them, refer to Figure 6-38.

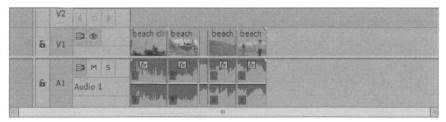

Figure 6-38 The **Cross Dissolve** *transition effect applied between the clips*

6. Make sure the CTI is placed at the beginning of the clips. Next, press the SPACEBAR key to play the sequence. You can view the result in the Program Monitor. All clips in the sequence are connected with the **Cross Dissolve** transition.

The **Cross Dissolve** transition is set by default. If you want to set some other transition effect as the default effect, then follow the steps given below:

7. In the **Effects** panel, make sure the **Video Transitions** folder is expanded. Various categories for video transition are displayed in this folder.

8. Next, expand the **Iris** category folder; various transitions are displayed in it, as shown in Figure 6-39.

9. Select the **Iris Cross** transition and right-click on it; a shortcut menu is displayed, as shown in Figure 6-40.

*Figure 6-39   Various **Iris** transition effects*

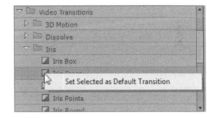

Figure 6-40   The shortcut menu

10. Choose the **Set Selected as Default Transition** option to make it the default video transition.

    There are other methods to apply the default transition to multiple clips simultaneously.

11. Delete all clips in the **Timeline** panel. Next, select all clips in the **Project** panel and drag them to the **V1** track in the **Timeline** panel. Invoke the **Ripple Edit Tool** and trim the In and Out points of all clips to get the clip handles. Next, select all clips in the **V1** track of the sequence using the **Selection Tool**. Choose **Sequence > Apply Default Transitions to Selection** from the menu bar; the **Iris Cross** transition is added to the sequence between all clips, refer to Figure 6-41.

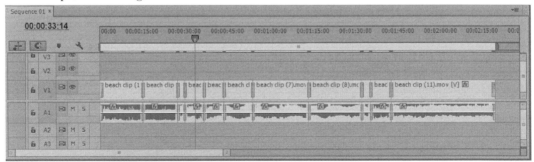

*Figure 6-41   The **Iris Cross** transition between the clips*

Note
If the **Clip Mismatch Warning** *message box is displayed, choose the* **Keep Existing Settings** *button from it.*

Play the sequence to view the effect in the Program Monitor. To add the transition only between few clips, press the CTRL + Z keys to undo the last step which was to apply default transition to the selection. Now, you will have beach clips with trimmed In and Out points in the sequence. Move the CTI to the beginning of the clips in the sequence. Choose the **Go to Next Edit Point** button in the Program Monitor; the CTI is moved to the cut ➜| point between the two clips where transition is to be applied. Also, click in the **Timeline** panel to deselect the clips. Next, press the CTRL + D keys; the **Iris Cross** transition is added to the cut between the two clips.

Adding Audio Transitions
In this section, you will add audio transitions to the audio clips in the sequence.

1. Press the BACKSLASH (\) key to view the clips properly in the **Timeline** panel.

2. In the **Effects** panel, click on the arrow on the left of the **Audio Transitions** folder to expand it; the **Crossfade** folder is displayed.

3. Next, click on the arrow on the left of the **Crossfade** folder to expand it; various audio transitions are displayed, as shown in Figure 6-42.

Figure 6-42 The audio transitions in the **Effects** *panel*

4. Select the **Constant Power** audio transition in the **Effects** panel. Next, drag it from the **Effects** panel to the end of the **beach clip (5).mov** in the **A1** track, refer to Figure 6-43.

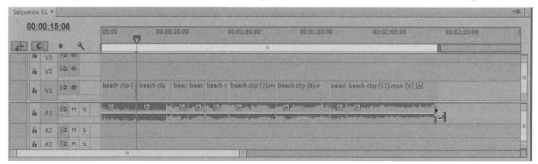

Figure 6-43 The transition at the end of the **beach clip (5).mov**

5. Press the EQUAL key four times to view the added transition properly.

6. Move the CTI to the beginning of the **beach clip (5).mov** and play the sequence.

    Note that after adding the **Constant Power** audio transition, the fade out effect is created for the music track.

 Tip. *Press the SHIFT+CTRL+D keys to add the default audio transition to the cut point near the current-time indicator on the selected audio track.*

7. Press CTRL+S to save the file. Next, press the ENTER key to view the output of the sequence in the Program Monitor. The output of the sequence at frame 00:00:56:24 is shown in Figure 6-44.

Figure 6-44 The output of the sequence at frame 00:00:56:24

Self-Evaluation Test

Answer the following questions and then compare them to those given at the end of this chapter:

1. Which of the following panels have different transition effects?

    (a) **Effect Controls**   (b) **Effects**
    (c) **Info**   (d) **Project**

2. Which of the following panels in Premiere is used to control the settings of the transition?

    (a) **Media Browser**   (b) **Info**
    (c) **Effect Controls**   (d) **Effects**

3. Which of the following buttons in the **Effect Controls** panel is used to preview the transition?

    (a) **Show/Hide Timeline View**   (b) **Stop the Transition**
    (c) **Play the transition**   (d) None of these

4. Which of the following buttons in the **Project** panel is used to add multiple clips at once?

    (a) **Find**   (b) **New Item**
    (c) **New Bin**   (d) **Automate to Sequence**

5. Which of the following options is available in the **Alignment** drop-down list in the **Effect Controls** panel?

    (a) **Center at Cut**   (b) **End at Cut**
    (c) **Start at Cut**   (d) All of these

6. Select the _____ check box to replace the A and B windows with the actual clips in the **Effect Controls** panel.

7. The _____ folder in the **Effects** panel is used to add video transitions to the clips.

8. You can increase or decrease the duration of the transition based on your requirement. (T/F)

9. The transition cannot be adjusted or customized in the **Timeline** panel. (T/F)

10. The **Automate To Sequence** dialog box is used to place multiple clips in sequential order in the **Timeline** panel. (T/F)

Review Questions

Answer the following questions:

1. Which of the following options is used to view the default duration of the transition in the **Effect Controls** panel?

    (a) **Alignment**   (b) **Show Actual Sources**
    (c) **Duration**   (d) None of these

2. Which of the following options is used to align the transition in the **Effect Controls** panel?

    (a) **Duration**   (b) **Alignment**
    (c) **Show Actual Sources**   (d) None of these

3. Which of the following buttons in the **Effect Controls** panel is used to hide the timeline view?

   (a) **Show/Hide Timeline View**   (b) **Stop the Transition**
   (c) **Play the Transition**   (d) None of these

4. Which of the following combinations of shortcut keys is used to add the default audio transition to the cut point near the CTI on the selected audio track?

   (a) SHIFT+CTRL+D   (b) CTRL+D
   (c) SHIFT+D   (d) None of the above

5. Press the _____ keys to add the default video transition to the cut between two clips.

6. The options in the _____ drop-down list in the **Automate To Sequence** dialog box are used to specify how clips will be placed in the sequence.

7. If you change the alignment of the transition by selecting an option from the **Alignment** drop-down list or change the duration of the transition, then the result will also be displayed in the timeline view of the **Effect Controls** panel. (T/F)

8. The settings in the **Effect Controls** panel are the same for different transition effects. (T/F)

9. You cannot apply the transition to multiple clips at once. (T/F)

EXERCISE

Exercise 1

Create a new project in Premiere as per the settings of your video clip. Add some of your clips to the sequence. Also, add various audio and video transitions from the **Effect** panel to the clips to view their results. Next, use various settings of different transition in the **Effect Controls** panel.

Answers to Self-Evaluation Test
1. b, **2.** c, **3.** c, **4.** d, **5.** d, **6. Show Actual Sources**, **7. Video Transitions**, **8.** T, **9.** F, **10.** T

Chapter 7

Previewing a Sequence

Learning Objectives

After completing this chapter, you will be able to:

- *Render and preview a sequence*
- *Render the audio and video tracks together*
- *Locate missing media files*
- *Convert an online clip to an offline clip*

INTRODUCTION

In this chapter, you will learn to create the preview of the sequence so that you can view the sequence in real time and at full frame rate. Also, you will learn how to locate a missing media file. In addition to this, you will learn to make an offline file.

TUTORIALS

Before you start the tutorials, you need to download the *c07_premiere_cc_tut.zip* file from *www.cadcim.com*. The path of the file is as follows: *Textbooks > Animation and Visual Effects > Premiere Pro > Adobe Premiere Pro CC: A Tutorial Approach*

Next, extract the contents of the zip file at *\Documents\Adobe Premiere Tutorials*.

Tutorial 1

In this tutorial, you will render and preview a sequence. Also, you will render audio and video tracks together. The output of the sequence at frame 00:00:07:00 is shown in Figure 7-1.

(Expected Time: 25 min)

Figure 7-1 *The output of the sequence at frame 00:00:07:00*

The following steps are required to complete this tutorial:

a. Open the project file.
b. Render and preview a sequence.
c. Render audio and video tracks together.

Opening the Project File

In this section, you will open the project file.

1. Open the *chapter07.prproj* file that you have downloaded from the CADCIM website; the project is displayed in the Premiere interface, as shown in Figure 7-2.

Figure 7-2 The chapter07_preview file displayed

2. Choose **File > Save As** from the menu bar; the **Save Project** dialog box is displayed. Browse to the location *\Documents\Adobe Premiere Tutorials\c07_premiere_cc_tut*. Enter **chapter07_preview** in the **File name** text box and choose the **Save** button; the opened file is saved with the specified name with the titles and transitions displayed in a sequence.

Rendering and Previewing a Sequence

In Premiere, the unrendered and rendered sections of a sequence are marked in different colored render bars. Note that there is a red colored render bar in the time ruler of the sequence, refer to Figure 7-2. This red colored render bar specifies an unrendered section that must be rendered in order to play the sequence in real-time and at full frame rate. However, the yellow colored render bar specifies an unrendered section that does not need to be rendered in order to play in real-time and at full frame rate. Similarly, the green colored render bar specifies a section that already has rendered preview files associated with it.

In this section, you will define work area for rendering.

Note
*You can display the work area bar in the **Timeline** panel if is not so. To display it, click on the arrow at the top right corner of the **Timeline** panel; a flyout is displayed. Choose the Work Area Bar option from this flyout to make this bar available in the **Timeline** panel.*

1. Make sure the CTI is at the beginning of the **Timeline** panel and press the ALT+[keys to set the starting point of the work area bar.

2. Move the CTI to 00:03:43:08 frame and press the ALT+] keys to set the endpoint of the Work Area Bar; the Work area bar is set, as shown in Figure 7-3.

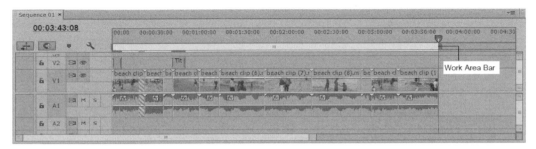

Figure 7-3 *Setting the Work Area Bar*

 Note
*If you move the cursor over the Work area bar, then a tooltip will be displayed showing the **Start**
timecode, **End** timecode, and **Duration** timecode of the Work area bar, refer to Figure 7-4.*

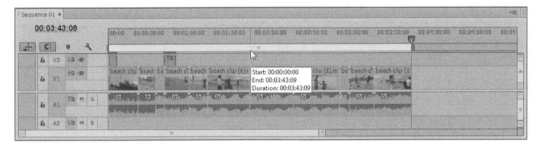

Figure 7-4 *The tooltip for the Work area bar*

Next, you will render the section of the sequence specified by the Work area bar.

3. Choose **Sequence > Render Effects in Work Area** from the menu bar; the **Rendering**
   dialog box is displayed, showing the status of the rendering process, as shown in Figure 7-5.
   After the completion of rendering process, the **Rendering** dialog box closes and the
   rendered video is played in the Program Monitor.

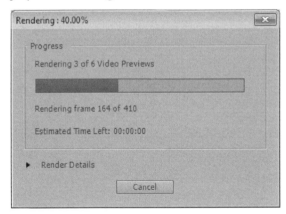

Figure 7-5 *The **Rendering** dialog box*

Tip. *After defining the work area for rendering, you can also press the ENTER key to start the rendering process.*

Note that after the rendering process is completed, the red colored render bar turns into a green colored bar.

 Note
The rendering time of a sequence depends on its complexity as well as on the system resources on which the rendering process is performed.

4. Select all clips and titles in the sequence by dragging a selection box around them, as shown in Figure 7-6.

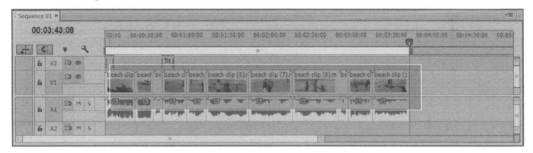

Figure 7-6 All clips and titles selected in the sequence

5. Drag the selected clips and titles toward right; the colored bars also move simultaneously, refer to Figure 7-7. Next, deselect the clips by clicking on an empty area in the sequence.

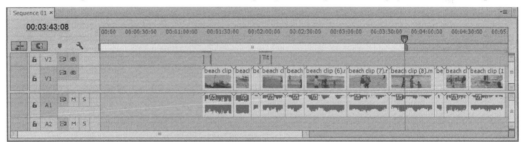

Figure 7-7 The selected clips and titles moved to right in the sequence

6. Press the CTRL+Z keys to undo the last command.

Now, you need to use the **Ripple Edit Tool** to trim the clips.

7. Make sure the CTI is placed at the beginning of the sequence. Press the EQUAL (=) key thrice; the **beach clip (1).mov** and **beach clip (2).mov** are zoomed, as shown in Figure 7-8.

8. Choose the **Ripple Edit Tool**. Next, move the cursor over the endpoint of the **beach clip (1).mov** and move the endpoint toward left until the tooltip displays -00:00:17:01, refer to Figure 7-9; the **beach clip (1).mov** is trimmed. Also, some portion in the green colored bar turns red, refer to Figure 7-10, indicating that you need to render that portion again.

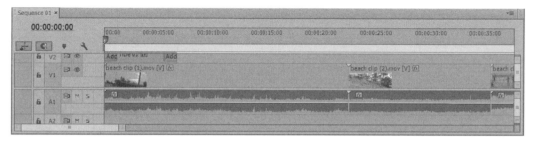

Figure 7-8 The beach clip (1).mov and beach clip (2).mov zoomed

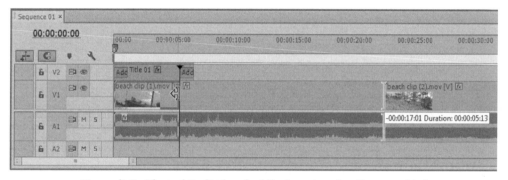

Figure 7-9 The tooltip displayed while dragging the clip toward left

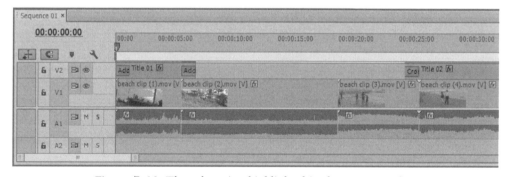

Figure 7-10 The red portion highlighted in the green area bar

9. Press the CTRL+Z keys to undo the last trimming action.

Rendering the Audio and Video Tracks Together

By default, the audio tracks are not rendered on rendering a sequence. You need to follow the steps given below to render the audio tracks while rendering a video sequence.

1. Choose **Edit > Preferences > General** from the menu bar; the **Preferences** dialog box is displayed.

2. Next, select the **Render audio when rendering video** check box, as shown in Figure 7-11.

3. Choose the **OK** button in the **Preferences** dialog box. Now, the audio track will also be rendered while rendering the video sequence.

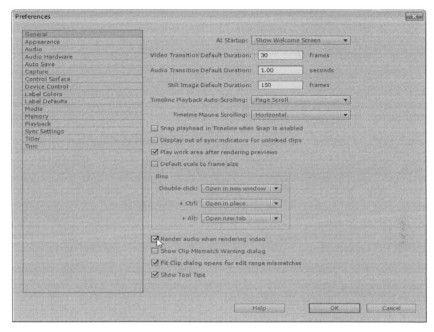

*Figure 7-11 The **Preferences** dialog box*

Note

*After rendering the sequence, the preview files automatically get stored in the hard disk at a location specified by you in the scratch disk. In the **Scratch Disks** tab of the **Project Settings** dialog box, the preview files contain the results of the effects that Premiere processed during the preview process. If you preview the same work area more than once, without making any change, then Premiere will instantly play the preview files instead of processing the sequence again. The preview files move along with their associated segment of sequence as you edit the project. When a segment of a sequence is changed, Premiere automatically changes the corresponding files, and saves the remaining unchanged segment.*

Tip. *After completing a project, it is recommended that you delete the preview files to save the disk space.*

To delete the rendered preview files, make sure the **Timeline** panel is active. Next, you will delete the rendered preview files for the selected range of clips.

4. Choose **Sequence > Delete Work Area Render Files** from the menu bar; the **Confirm Delete** message box is displayed, as shown in Figure 7-12. Choose the **OK** button in the **Confirm Delete** message box; all rendered preview files for the selected range are deleted. Also, the green colored bar of that range in the time ruler turns red.

5. Press CTRL+S to save the file. Next, press the ENTER key to view the output of the sequence at frame 00:00:07:00 in the Program Monitor, as shown in Figure 7-13.

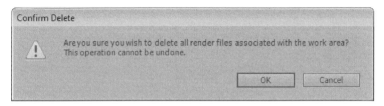

*Figure 7-12 The **Confirm Delete** message box*

Figure 7-13 The output of the sequence at frame 00:00:07:00

Tutorial 2

In this tutorial, you will locate and link missing media files.   **(Expected Time: 25 min)**

The following steps are required to complete this tutorial:

a.   Move files to different location.
b.   Locate the missing media file.
c.   Convert an online clip to an offline clip.

Moving Files to Different Location
In this section, you will move files to another location for the illustration purpose.

1.   Open the Windows Explorer and then browse to the location *\Documents\Adobe Premiere Tutorials\c07_premiere_cc\Media Files*. Next, move the **beach clip (1).mov** and **beach clip (2).mov** files from this location to another location.

Locating the Missing Media File
In this section, you will locate the missing media file.

1.   Open the *chapter07_02.prproj* file that you have downloaded from the CADCIM website; the **Link Media** dialog box is displayed, as shown in Figure 7-14.

Note
When you open the chapter07_02.prproj file, the dialog box will display the name of the missing media file on its title bar.

If you know the location of the missing media file that the dialog box is referring to, browse to the location of the missing media file in the dialog box. Next, select the missing media file and then choose the **Select** button; the **chapter07_02.prproj** file is opened.

If you do not know the location of the missing media file, then you need to either skip the file or make it offline. If you skip the file, then Premiere Pro assumes that you do not have the file right now. If you open the same project file again and the media file is still missing, then Adobe Premiere Pro will prompt you to locate the missing media file again.

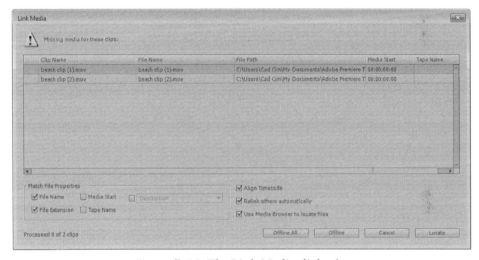

*Figure 7-14 The **Link Media** dialog box*

2. Choose the **Offline** button in the **Link Media** dialog box; you are prompted to specify the location of another missing media file. Choose the **Offline All** button; the **chapter07_02. prproj** file is opened with the missing media files highlighted by different icons in the **Project** panel, as shown in Figure 7-15. Additionally, the Program Monitor displays a red colored screen with **Media offline** written on it in various languages, refer to Figure 7-15.

The offline clip indicates that the clip information is present in the project but the media associated with the clip is not available, which means the clip will be present in the sequence but the content of the clip will not be available. When you choose the **Offline** button in the **Link Media** dialog box, then Premiere Pro allows you to actively locate the missing media file in the Premiere Pro project. In the next section, you will learn how to actively locate the missing media file.

Figure 7-15 *The missing media files highlighted by different icons in the* **Project** *panel*

3. In the **Project** panel, right-click on the **beach clip (1).mov** file; a shortcut menu is displayed, as shown in Figure 7-16.

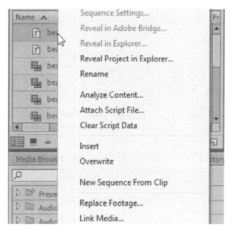

Figure 7-16 *Partial view of the shortcut menu*

4. Choose the **Link Media** option from the shortcut menu; the **Link Media** dialog box is displayed, as shown in Figure 7-17.

5. Browse to the missing media file in the **Link Media** dialog box by choosing the **Locate** button. Next, select the missing media file and then choose the **OK** button; the icon for the missing media file is changed to the original one in the **Project** panel. Also, the media is displayed in the Program Monitor.

6. Repeat steps 3, 4, and 5 for the **beach clip (2).mov** file to locate the missing media file.

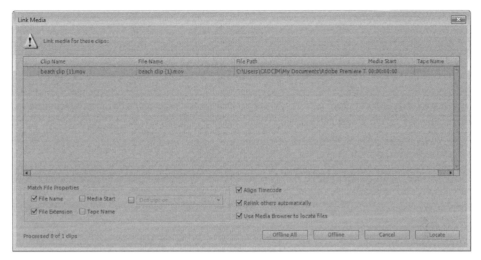

*Figure 7-17 The **Link Media** dialog box*

Converting an Online Clip to an Offline Clip

If you do not need a media file in the current project from the **Project** panel, then you can either delete it or make it offline for the current project. To make the clip offline, follow the steps given below:

1. Select the media file in the **Project** panel that you need to make offline and right-click on it; a shortcut menu is displayed.

2. Choose the **Make Offline** option from the shortcut menu; the **Make Offline** dialog box is displayed, as shown in Figure 7-18.

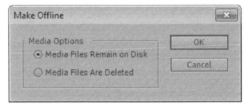

*Figure 7-18 The **Make Offline** dialog box*

3. Make sure the **Media Files Remain on Disk** radio button is selected to make the selected file offline for the project so that the source file of the selected file does not get erased from the hard disk. Next, choose the **OK** button to close the dialog box.

    If you select the **Media Files Are Deleted** radio button in the **Make Offline** dialog box, then the selected file will become offline for the project. Also, the source file will be deleted from the hard disk.

4. Press CTRL+S to save the file.

Self-Evaluation Test

Answer the following questions and then compare them to those given at the end of this chapter:

1. Which of the following keys are used to set the starting point of the Work area bar?

    (a) ALT + [(b) CTRL + [
    (c) ALT + CTRL + [(d) All of these

2. Which of the following options is used link the missing media file by right-clicking on that file in the **Project** panel?

    (a) **Link Media**   (b) **Make Offline**
    (c) **Edit Offline**   (d) None of these

3. Which of the following bars in the **Timeline** panel indicates an unrendered section that must be rendered in order to play in real-time and at full frame rate?

    (a) Green colored render bar   (b) Yellow colored render bar
    (c) Red colored render bar   (d) None of these

4. You need to press the _____ keys to set the endpoint of the Work area bar in the **Timeline** panel.

5. Select the _____ radio button in the **Make Offline** dialog box to make the selected file offline for the current project only.

6. The _____ render bar shows a section in the **Timeline** panel that already has rendered preview files associated with it.

7. The rendering time depends on the complexity of the portion being rendered and the system resources on which the rendering process will be performed. (T/F)

Review Questions

Answer the following questions:

1. Which of the following keys is used to start the rendering process for the sequence?

    (a) BACKSPACE   (b) K
    (c) ENTER   (d) SPACEBAR

2. Which of the following options is used to convert an online clip to an offline clip in the **Project** panel?

    (a) **Link Media**   (b) **Edit Offline**
    (c) **Make Offline**   (d) None of these

3. Which of the following bars in the **Timeline** panel indicates an unrendered section that does not need to be rendered in order to play the sequence in real-time and at full frame rate?

       (a) Red colored render bar   (b) Yellow colored render bar
       (c) Green colored render bar   (d) None of these

4. The _____ dialog box is used to check the location of the scratch disk settings.

5. Select the _____ radio button in the **Make Offline** dialog box to make the selected file offline for the current project and also to delete the source files from the hard disk.

6. To view the start timecode, end timecode, and duration of the work area bar, you need to move the cursor over the work area bar in the **Timeline** panel. (T/F)

7. By default, Adobe Premiere Pro automatically renders the audio tracks on rendering the sequence. (T/F)

EXERCISE

Exercise 1

Create a new project in Premiere as per the settings of your video clip. Add some of your clips to the sequence. Also, add various audio and video effects to the clips and then preview the sequence. In the **Project** panel, convert an online clip to an offline clip.

Chapter 8

Editing Audio

Learning Objectives

After completing this chapter, you will be able to:

- *Understand audio levels*
- *Control the gain and volume*
- *Map the source audio channels*
- *Adjust the track volume level with keyframes*
- *Modify the track volume level using transitions*
- *Analyze speech*

INTRODUCTION

In Premiere, you can edit audio clips, add effects to them, and mix as many tracks as you want in your sequence. Tracks may have mono, stereo, or 5.1 surround channels. Generally, an audio clip is linked with a video clip. But you can import separate audio clips to the audio tracks in your sequence. You can also view the waveform of an audio clip in the Source Monitor, trim it based on your requirement, and then add it to the sequence. In the sequence, you can edit audio clips just like video clips. You can adjust the volume settings of audio tracks in the **Timeline** as well as in the **Effect Controls** panel. You can also add effects to audio tracks in the sequence. In this chapter, you will adjust and edit audio clips in a sequence.

UNDERSTANDING AUDIO LEVELS

Audio levels are used to specify the sound settings of a sequence. Before adjusting the audio level, first import the audio and make sure the **Timeline** panel is active. Next, press the SPACEBAR key to play the sequence; the music starts playing. Note that as the music starts playing, the audiometer in the **Audio Meters** panel also starts moving up and down based on the audio level of the music track, refer to Figure 8-1. The **Audio Meters** panel is located on the right of the **Timeline** panel and shows the audio output graphically.

In the **Audio Meters** panel, numbers are written vertically, such as -12, -24, -36, and so on. These numbers show the level of the audio track. When the peak level of the audio rises higher than 0, then the audiometer shows a red mark at its top, as shown in Figure 8-2. The red mark indicates that the audio will distort if you do not make any adjustment. Therefore, it is recommended that you keep an eye on the audiometers while working with audio clips.

Figure 8-1 The **Audio Meters** panel

Figure 8-2 The red mark highlighted at the top

TUTORIALS

Before you start the tutorials, you need to download the *c08_premiere_cc_tut.zip* file from *www.cadcim.com*. The path of the file is as follows: *Textbooks > Animation and Visual Effects > Premiere Pro > Adobe Premiere Pro CC: A Tutorial Approach*

Next, extract the contents of the zip file at *\Documents\Adobe Premiere Tutorials*.

Tutorial 1

In this tutorial, you will add and edit audio clips in a sequence.

(Expected Time: 20 min)

The following steps are required to complete this tutorial:

a.   Create a new project.
b.   Import audio clips.
c.   Add audio clips to the sequence.
d.   Control the gain and volume.
e.   Map the source audio channels.

Creating a New Project

In this section, you will create a new project.

1.   Start Adobe Premiere Pro CC; the **Welcome to Adobe Premiere Pro** dialog box is displayed.

2.   In this dialog box, choose the **New Project** button; the **New Project** dialog box is displayed.

3.   In the **General** tab of the **New Project** dialog box, type **chapter08** in the **Name** text box.

4.   Choose the **Browse** button on the right of the **Location** area; the **Please select the destination path for your new project** dialog box is displayed. Next, browse to *\Documents\ Adobe Premiere Tutorials\c08_premiere_cc_tut*.

5.   Choose the **Scratch Disks** tab. In the **Captured Video**, **Captured Audio**, **Video Previews**, and **Audio Previews** areas, select the **Same as Project** option from the drop-down list corresponding to these areas.

6.   Choose the **OK** button in the **New Project** dialog box; the interface is displayed with various panels and the file is saved with the name *chapter08.prproj*.

7.   In the **Project** panel, right-click in the empty area; a shortcut menu is displayed. Choose **New Item > Sequence**; the **New Sequence** dialog box is displayed.

8.   Make sure **Sequence 01** is displayed in the **Sequence Name** text box, and **Standard 48KHz** is selected in the **DV-PAL** preset in the **Available Presets** area. Next, choose the **OK** button in the **New Sequence** dialog box; the **Sequence 01** is displayed in the **Project** panel, as shown in Figure 8-3.

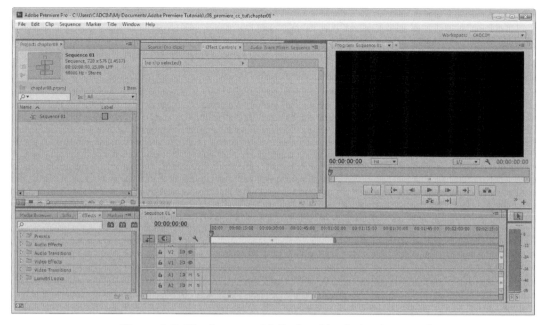

Figure 8-3 *The **Sequence01** displayed in the **Project** panel*

Importing Audio Clips

In this section, you will import audio clips.

1. Double-click on the empty area in the **Project** panel; the **Import** dialog box is displayed.

2. Browse to *\Documents\Adobe Premiere Tutorials\c08_premiere_cc_tut\Media Files\Audio* folder and then select **audio_1.mp3**. Next, choose the **Open** button; the selected audio clip is imported and displayed in the **Project** panel, as shown in Figure 8-4.

Figure 8-4 *The audio clip in the **Project** panel*

Adding Audio Clip to the Sequence

In this section, you will add an audio clip to the sequence.

1. Select the **audio_1.mp3** clip in the **Project** panel, if not already selected. Press and hold the left mouse button on it and drag it from the **Project** panel to the **A1** track of the **Timeline** panel. The audio clip is displayed in the **Timeline** panel, as shown in Figure 8-5.

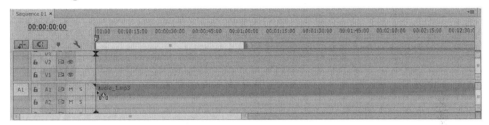

*Figure 8-5 The **audio_1.mp3** clip in the **A1** track*

2. Move the cursor at the bottom of the **A1** track; the shape of the cursor is changed, as shown in Figure 8-6. Press and hold the left mouse button and drag it down to expand the track and view it properly, refer to Figure 8-7.

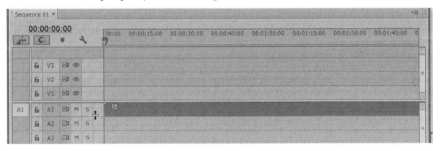

Figure 8-6 The changed cursor

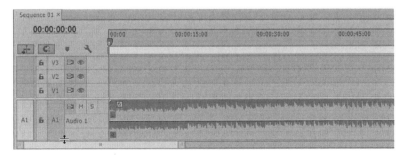

*Figure 8-7 Viewing the **A1** track*

Controlling the Gain and Volume

In the previous section, you learned that if the peak level goes higher than 0 dB, the audiometer shows red mark at some points in the audio track. To change the audio peak level to -12, you need to adjust the gain and volume.

1. Press the BACKSLASH (\) key to view the entire audio clip properly, as shown in Figure 8-8.

Figure 8-8 *The audio clip waveform*

2. Right-click on the audio clip; a shortcut menu is displayed, as shown in Figure 8-9. Next, choose the **Audio Gain** option from the shortcut menu; the **Audio Gain** dialog box is displayed, as shown in Figure 8-10. Alternatively, choose **Clip > Audio Options > Audio Gain** from the menu bar to display the **Audio Gain** dialog box.

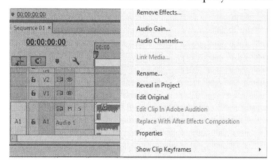

Figure 8-9 *Partial view of the shortcut menu*   *Figure 8-10* *The **Audio Gain** dialog box*

3. In this dialog box, select the **Normalize Max Peak to** radio button and click on the text box on the right of this radio button. Next, type **-12** in the edit box and choose the **OK** button; the audio waveform in the sequence becomes shorter, as shown in Figure 8-11.

Figure 8-11 *The waveform after setting the peak level to -12*

Note
You can compare Figure 8-8 with Figure 8-11 to view the difference in the waveform after setting the peak level to -12. The taller waveform indicates louder volume and shorter waveform indicates lower volume.

4. Play the audio clip again and view the audiometer. Now, the volume level is not higher than -6. Also, there is no red mark in the audiometer while playing the clip. On changing the peak level value, the quality of the audio also changes.

Mapping the Source Audio Channels

An audio clip can have one audio channel (mono), two audio channels (stereo), or 5.1 audio surround channels. When you add an audio to a sequence, it gets adjusted to the corresponding audio track.

The stereo clips have two audio channels, left and right. When you add a stereo clip to the sequence, both the left and right audio channels are placed in one track, refer to Figure 8-12. At times, you may need to manipulate or apply audio effect separately to individual channels in a stereo clip. To do so, you need to change the track format in stereo clips so that the two audio channels are placed on separate mono tracks while adding them to the sequence. The process of specifying the type and number of audio tracks in which they will appear in a sequence is known as mapping the audio channels. In this section, you will map audio channels.

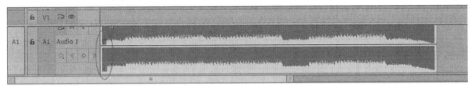

Figure 8-12 The stereo audio clip with the left and right channels

 Note
You can change the track format of an audio clip only before adding it to the sequence.

1. Select the **audio_1.mp3** audio clip in the **A1** track in the **Timeline** panel. Next, press the DELETE key; the **audio_1.mp3** audio clip is deleted from the **Timeline** panel.

2. Make sure the **audio_1.mp3** audio clip is selected in the **Project** panel.

3. Choose **Clip > Modify > Audio Channels** from the menu bar; the **Modify Clip** dialog box is displayed, as shown in Figure 8-13.

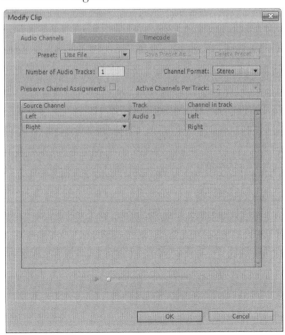

*Figure 8-13 The **Modify Clip** dialog box*

By default, the **Audio Channels** tab is chosen in the **Modify Clip** dialog box. The **Use File** option is selected in the **Preset** drop-down list. Also, the number **1** is displayed in the **Number of Audio Tracks** attribute. These options indicate that the selected audio clip has the stereo audio channel. Next, you will modify the options in the **Modify Clip** dialog box.

4. Select the **Mono** option in the **Preset** drop-down list, refer to Figure 8-14. Notice that the number in the **Number of Audio Tracks** edit box is changed. Now, **Audio 1** is displayed in the **Left Source Channel** and **Audio 2** is displayed in the **Right Source Channel**. This indicates that on adding the audio clip to the sequence, the left channel will appear on track 1 and the right channel will appear on track 2.

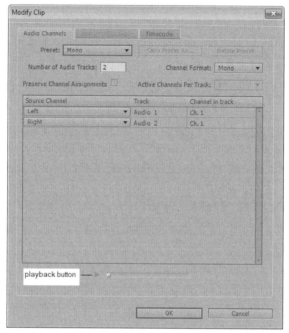

*Figure 8-14 The **Mono** track format selected*

Note
*To examine the audio of a particular channel, select **Audio 1** in the **Track** column and then choose the playback button at the bottom of the **Modify Clip** dialog box. Alternatively, you can drag the slider on the right of the playback button.*

5. Choose the **OK** button in the **Modify Clip** dialog box to close it.

6. Make sure the **audio_1.mp3** clip in the **Project** panel is selected. Press and hold the left mouse button and drag it from the **Project** panel to the **A1** track in the current sequence.

Note
*Note that the selected audio clip does not move to the stereo audio track, refer to Figure 8-15. Since you changed the track format of the **audio_1.mp3** clip from stereo to mono, the clip will now go to the mono audio track.*

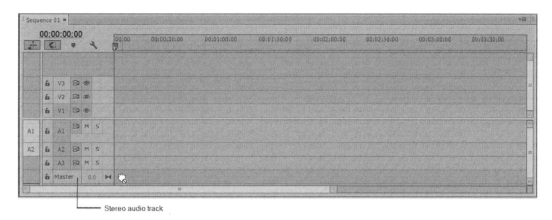

Figure 8-15 *The* **audio_1.mp3** *clip in the sequence*

7. Release the left mouse button; the left and right channels of the **audio_1.mp3** clip are placed separately in the mono audio tracks, **A1** and **A2**, as shown in Figure 8-16.

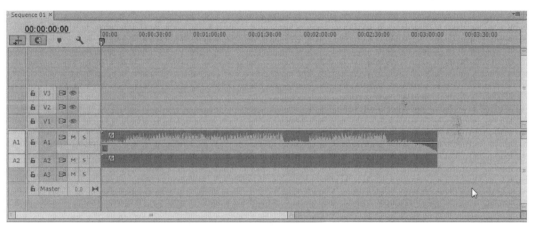

Figure 8-16 *The* **audio_1.mp3** *clip in the mono audio tracks*

8. Right-click on one of the audio track labels; a shortcut menu is displayed, refer to Figure 8-17.

Figure 8-17 *The shortcut menu*

9. Choose the **Delete Tracks** option from the shortcut menu; the **Delete Tracks** dialog box is displayed, as shown in Figure 8-18.

Figure 8-18 The **Delete Tracks** dialog box

10. In the **Audio Tracks** area, select the **Delete Audio Tracks** check box and make sure the **All Empty Tracks** option is selected in the drop-down list.

11. Choose the **OK** button in the **Delete Tracks** dialog box; all empty audio tracks are deleted from the sequence, as shown in Figure 8-19.

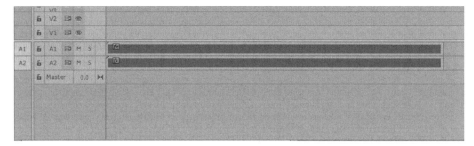

Figure 8-19 The empty tracks deleted from the sequence

12. Press CTRL+S to save the file. Next, press the ENTER key to render the output of the sequence.

Note
*You can also specify the track format for the audio clip before importing the clip into the **Project** panel.*

*1. To do so, choose **Edit** > **Preferences** > **Audio** from the menu bar; the **Preferences** dialog box is displayed with the audio settings.*

2. In the **Default Audio Tracks** area, select the desired option from the drop-down lists available in this area. Next, choose the **OK** button in the **Preferences** dialog box to save the changes made. Now, import a clip in the **Project** panel and then add it to the sequence.

Tutorial 2

In this tutorial, you will adjust the volume level of an audio track at different points using keyframes. Also, you will modify the volume level using transitions.

(Expected Time: 20 min)

The following steps are required to complete this tutorial:

a.   Create a new project.
b.   Keyframe track volume level using transitions.
c.   Modify the track volume level using transitions.

Creating a New Project

In this section, you will create a new project.

1.   Choose **File > New > Project** from the menu bar; the **New Project** dialog box is displayed, as shown in Figure 8-20.

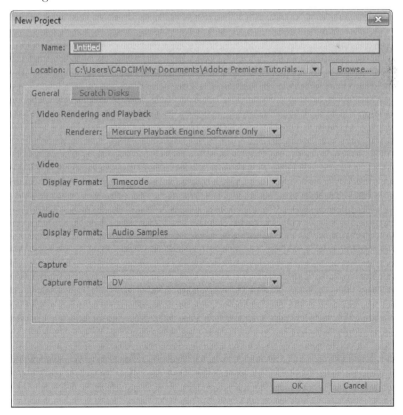

*Figure 8-20 The **New Project** dialog box*

2. Choose the **Browse** button on the right of the **Location** area in the **New Project** dialog box and browse to the location *\Documents\Adobe Premiere Tutorials\c08_premiere_cc_tut* and then choose the **Select Folder** button.

3. Choose the **Scratch Disks** tab in the **New Project** dialog box. In the **Captured Video**, **Captured Audio**, **Video Previews**, and **Audio Previews** areas, make sure the **Same as Project** option is selected from the drop-down lists corresponding to these areas.

4. Type **chapter08_volumelevel** in the **Name** text box.

5. Choose the **OK** button in the **New Project** dialog box; the interface is displayed with various panels. Also, the file is saved with the name *chapter08_volumelevel.prproj*.

6. Right-click in the empty area of the **Project** panel; a shortcut menu is displayed. Choose **New Item > Sequence**; the **New Sequence** dialog box is displayed.

7. In the **Available Presets** area of the **Sequence Presets** tab, expand the **DV-NTSC** option, if not already expanded. Now, select the **Widescreen 48KHz** preset; the settings of this preset are displayed on the right in the **Preset Description** area.

8. In the **Sequence Name** text box, make sure the **Sequence 01** is displayed. Next, choose the **OK** button in the **New Sequence** dialog box; the **Sequence 01** is displayed in the **Project** panel.

9. Choose **Edit > Preferences > Audio** from the menu bar; the **Preferences** dialog box is displayed. In the **Default Audio Tracks** area, make sure the **Use File** option is selected in all the drop-down lists in this area, as shown in Figure 8-21. Choose the **OK** button in the **Preferences** dialog box.

Keyframing the Track Volume Level
In this section, you will keyframe the track volume level.

1. Double-click on the empty area in the **Project** panel; the **Import** dialog box is displayed.

2. Choose *\Documents\Adobe Premiere Tutorials\c08_premiere_cc_tut\Media Files\Video* folder and then select the **biking.mp4** clip. Next, choose the **Open** button; the selected video clip is imported and displayed in the **Project** panel.

3. Again, double-click on the empty area in the **Project** panel; the **Import** dialog box is displayed.

4. Browse to the location *\Documents\Adobe Premiere Tutorials\c08_premiere_cc_tut\Media Files\Audio* and then select the **audio_1.mp3** clip. Choose the **Open** button; the selected audio clip is imported and displayed in the **Project** panel. Now, both the audio and video clips are displayed in the **Project** panel.

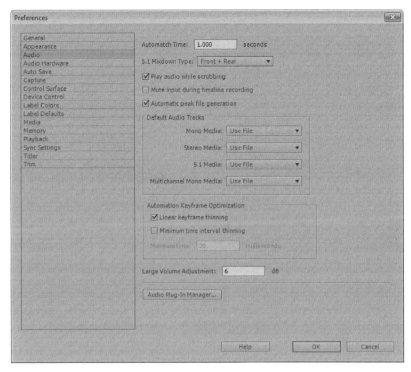

Figure 8-21 The **Preferences** dialog box

5. Select the **biking.mp4** clip in the **Project** panel and drag it to the **V1** track sequence in the **Timeline** panel; the **Clip Mismatch Warning** message box is displayed.

6. Choose the **Keep Existing Settings** option in this message box; the **biking.mp4** clip is placed in the **Timeline** panel with existing settings.

7. Choose the **Play-Stop Toggle** button in the Program Monitor; the **biking.mp4** starts playing, refer to Figure 8-22. Choose this button again to stop the playback.

   Note that the size of the **biking.mp4** clip is different from the screen size of the Program Monitor. Next, you will manually modify the size of the **biking.mp4** clip.

8. Make sure the **biking.mp4** clip is selected in the sequence. The properties of the **biking. mp4** clip are displayed in the **Effect Controls** panel, as shown in Figure 8-23.

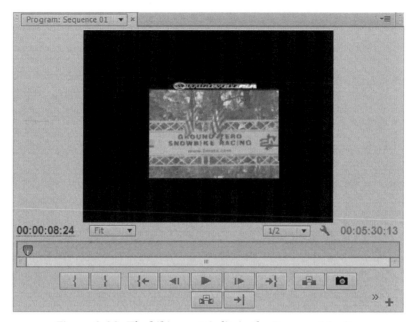

Figure 8-22 *The **biking.mp4** clip in the Program Monitor*

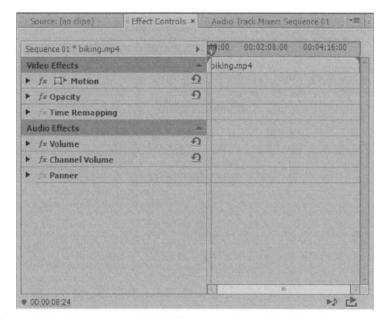

Figure 8-23 *The properties of the **biking.mp4** clip in the **Effect Controls** panel*

9. Expand the **Motion** node by clicking on the arrow on the left of the **Motion** label; various parameters such as **Scale**, **Rotation**, and so on are displayed.

10. Click on the numeric value on the right of the **Scale** parameter; it is converted into an edit box, refer to Figure 8-24.

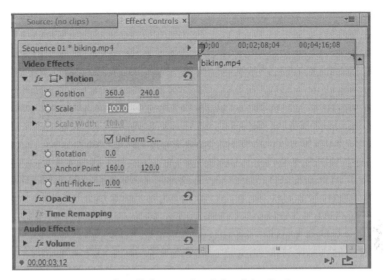

Figure 8-24 *The edit box on the right of the* **Scale** *parameter*

11. Enter **199** in the edit box; the size of the **biking.mp4** clip is increased in the Program Monitor, as shown in Figure 8-25.

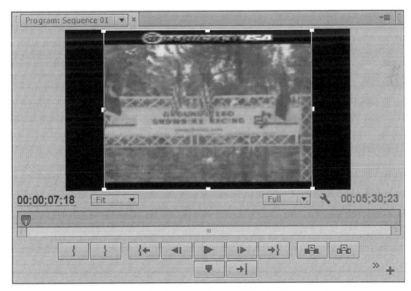

Figure 8-25 *The increased size of the* **biking.mp4** *clip*

12. Add the **audio_1.mp3** clip to the sequence in the **A2** audio track; the **audio_1.mp3** clip in the **Timeline** panel is displayed, as shown in Figure 8-26.

13. Adjust the peak level of the **audio_1.mp3** and **biking.mp4** clips to **-12**, as discussed in the Tutorial 1 of this chapter.

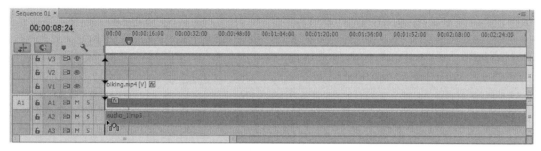

*Figure 8-26 The **audio_1.mp3** clip displayed in the **Timeline** panel*

14. Drag the bottom border of the **A2** track to make it wider and visible, as shown in Figure 8-27.

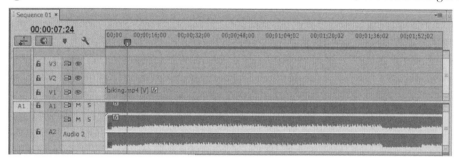

*Figure 8-27 The expanded **A2** audio track*

Next, you will adjust the volume level at different points in the **audio_1.mp3** audio clip to match it with the audio track of the **biking.mp4** clip.

Most of the time you would like to hear the volume of **audio_1.mp3** at normal level. But, at some point in the **biking.mp4** clip, you need to lower the volume of the **audio_1.mp3** clip, so that you can hear the important audio properly.

Next, you will lower the **audio_1.mp3** clip volume from 00:00:02:06 to 00:00:05:00 frames to hear the sound of the **biking.mp4** clip properly through those frames.

15. Click on **Playhead Position** below the **Sequence 01** label; it is converted into an edit box. Enter **2:06** in the edit box and press ENTER; the CTI is moved to 00:00:02:06 frame.

16. Next, zoom in the sequence based on your requirement.

17. Press the SHIFT+left arrow keys twice to go back about 10 frames. Now, the CTI is at 00:00:01:26 frame.

Next, you will set a keyframe at this point on the volume graph of the **A2** track.

18. Move the cursor in between the left and right channels of the volume graph in the **A2** track where the CTI is placed at 00:00:01:26 frame. Press and hold the CTRL key; the shape of the cursor is changed to arrow with a plus (+) sign. Also, a tooltip is displayed showing the frame and volume level, as shown in Figure 8-28.

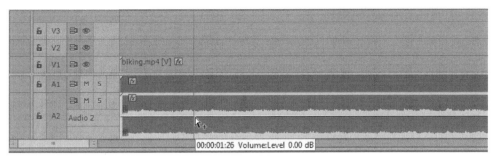

Figure 8-28 *The tooltip at 00:00:01:26 frame*

19. Click on the specified frame; a keyframe is created on the volume graph, as shown in Figure 8-29.

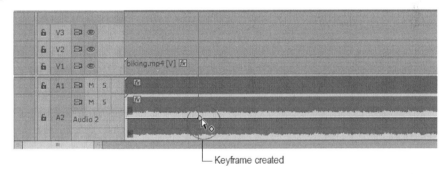

Figure 8-29 *A keyframe created on the volume graph*

20. Similarly, create a keyframe at 00:00:02:11 frame.

Now, you will keep the first keyframe at its place and move the second keyframe to bring the volume down.

21. Move the cursor on the volume graph next to the second keyframe. Press and hold the left mouse button and move the cursor down until the tooltip displays approximately -7.82 dB; the graph is modified, as shown in Figure 8-30. Now, you will notice a slight audio fade effect.

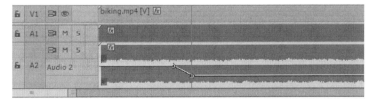

Figure 8-30 *The modified graph*

Next, you need to add the fade effect to **audio_1.mp3** after the biking logo audio is finished.

22. Move the CTI to 00:00:05:00 frame and create a keyframe on the volume graph, as discussed earlier.

23. Again, create a keyframe at 00:00:05:10 frame.

24. Move the cursor on the volume graph next to the second keyframe at 00:00:05:10 frame. Press and hold the left mouse button and move the cursor up until the tooltip displays 0.00dB; the graph is modified, as shown in Figure 8-31.

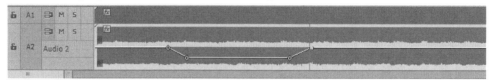

Figure 8-31 *The modified graph*

25. Move the CTI to the beginning of the sequence and play it.

In the above steps, you added keyframes using the keyboard shortcuts in the **Timeline** panel. Next, you will add keyframes to **audio_1.mp3** using the **Effect Controls** panel.

26. Make sure the **audio_1.mp3** clip in the **Timeline** panel is selected. The properties of the **audio_1.mp3** clip are displayed in the **Effect Controls** panel, refer to Figure 8-32.

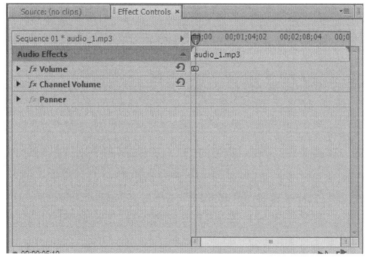

Figure 8-32 *The properties of the **audio_1.mp3** clip in the*
***Effect Controls** panel*

27. Next, move the CTI to 00:00:08:29 frame; the CTI on the right of the **Effect Controls** panel is also moved to 00:00:08:29 frame.

28. Expand the **Volume** area and then expand the **Level** parameter. Next, click on the numeric value on the right of the **Level** parameter; it is converted into an edit box, as shown in Figure 8-33. Enter **-5** in it and press the ENTER key; a new keyframe is created on the volume graph, as shown in Figures 8-34 and 8-35.

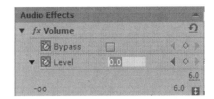

Figure 8-33 *The edit box on the right in the **Level** parameter*

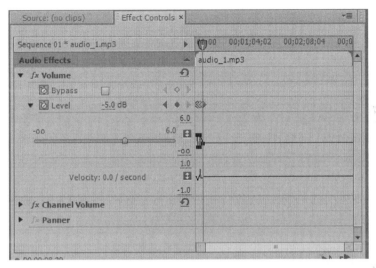

Figure 8-34 *A new keyframe on the volume graph in the **Effect Controls** panel*

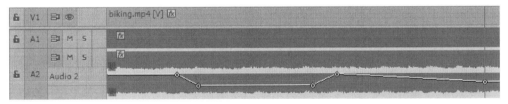

Figure 8-35 *The new keyframe created in the volume graph of the **Timeline** panel*

Similarly, you can add new keyframes to the volume graph of the **audio_1.mp3** clip using the keyboard shortcuts or using the **Effect Controls** panel to match it with the volume of the **biking.mp4** clip.

Modifying the Track Volume Level Using Transitions

In this section, you will modify the track volume level in the **Timeline** panel using audio transitions.

1. Make sure the **audio_1.mp3** clip is selected in the **Timeline** panel. Next, in the **Effect Controls** panel, choose the **Toggle animation** button on the left of the **Level** parameter; the **Warning** message box is displayed, as shown in Figure 8-36.

*Figure 8-36 The **Warning** message box*

2. Choose the **OK** button in the **Warning** message box; all the existing keyframes are deleted from the **audio_1.mp3** track.

3. Choose the **Reset** button on the right of the **Volume** area in the **Effect Controls**  panel to reset the volume level.

    Next, you need to cut the **audio_1.mp3** audio clip at a location where you need to change the volume of this clip across time.

4. Move the CTI to 00:00:09:03 frame.

5. Invoke the **Razor Tool** from the **Tools** panel and move the cursor over the **audio_1.mp3** clip on the CTI, as shown in Figure 8-37 and then click on it; the **audio_1.mp3** clip is divided into two parts, as shown in Figure 8-38.

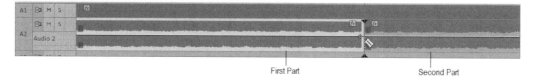

Figure 8-37 The cursor on the clip

*Figure 8-38 The **audio_1.mp3** clip divided into two parts*

6. Choose the **Selection Tool** from the **Tools** panel. In the **Timeline** panel, move the cursor to the start of the second part of the **audio_1.mp3** clip in between the left and right channels of the volume graph of the same clip.

7. Press and hold the left mouse button and drag the volume graph downward until the tooltip displays approximately -8.68 dB, refer to Figure 8-39. Release the left mouse button; the volume of the second **audio_1.mp3** clip is now lowered.

*Figure 8-39 The volume graph of the second **audio_1.mp3** clip lowered*

Next, you will add transition effect between the two separate audio clips on the **Audio 2** track.

8. Choose the **Effects** panel if not already chosen; various categories of effects and transitions are displayed.

9. Expand **Audio Transitions > Crossfade** category in the **Effects** panel; various audio transitions are displayed in it.

10. Select the **Constant Power** audio transition and drag it from the **Effects** panel to the **Timeline** panel between the two audio clips in the **Audio 2** track, as shown in Figure 8-40.

Figure 8-40 *The transition added between the clips*

You may need to zoom in the sequence to view the transition properly. You can also drag the In and Out points of the **Constant Power** transition effect to increase its duration.

11. Next, play the sequence and notice the difference after lowering the volume level of the second **audio_1.mp3** clip and adding the transition between the clips.

12. Press CTRL+S to save the file. Next, press the ENTER key to render the output of the sequence.

Tutorial 3

In this tutorial, you will analyze speech using the **Metadata** panel in Adobe Premiere.

(Expected Time: 20 min)

The following steps are required to complete this tutorial:

a. Create a new project file.
b. Analyze the speech.

Creating a New Project File

In this section, you will create a new project file.

1. Choose **File > New > Project** from the menu bar; the **New Project** dialog box is displayed.

2. Choose the **Browse** button on the right of the **Location** area in the **New Project** dialog box and browse to the location *Documents\\Adobe Premiere Tutorials* and then choose the **Select Folder** button.

3. Choose the **Scratch Disks** tab in the **New Project** dialog box. In the **Captured Video**, **Captured Audio**, **Video Previews**, and **Audio Previews** areas, make sure the **Same as Project** option is selected from the drop-down lists corresponding to these areas.

4. Type the name **chapter08_speech analysis** in the **Name** text box.

5. Choose the **OK** button in the **New Project** dialog box; the interface is displayed with various panels. Also, the file is saved with the name *chapter08_speech analysis*.

6. Choose the **New Item** button located at the bottom of the **Project** panel; a flyout is displayed. Next, choose the **Sequence** option from the flyout; the **New Sequence** dialog box is displayed.

7. In the **Available Presets** area of the **Sequence Presets** tab, expand the **DV-NTSC** option. Now, select the **Widescreen 48KHz** preset; the settings of this preset are displayed on the right in the **Preset Description** area.

8. In the **Sequence Name** text box, make sure the **Sequence 01** is displayed. Next, choose the **OK** button in the **New Sequence** dialog box; the **Sequence 01** is displayed in the **Project** panel.

Analyzing Speech

In this section, you will analyze speech.

1. Double-click on the empty area in the **Project** panel; the **Import** dialog box is displayed. Choose *\Documents\Adobe Premiere Tutorials\c08_premiere_cc_tut\Media Files\Audio* folder and then select the **audio_speech.wav** clip.

2. Choose the **Open** button; the selected file is imported to the **Project** panel.

3. Add the **audio_speech.wav** clip to the **A1** track in the **Timeline** panel.

4. Make sure the **audio_speech.wav** clip is selected in the **Timeline** panel. Choose **Window > Metadata** from the menu bar; the **Metadata** panel is displayed as a tab on the right of the Source Monitor, as shown in Figure 8-41.

5. Select the **audio_speech.wav** clip in the **Timeline** panel. Expand the **Metadata** panel to view the **Analyze** button and then choose this button; the **Analyze Content** dialog box is displayed, as shown in Figure 8-42.

    The **Analyze Content** dialog box is used to select the language, quality options, and reference script.

6. Make sure the **English - U.S.** option is selected in the **Language** drop-down list and the **High (slower)** option is selected in the **Quality** drop-down list.

7. In the **Script** area, select the **Add** option from the **Reference Script** drop-down list; the **Open** dialog box is displayed.

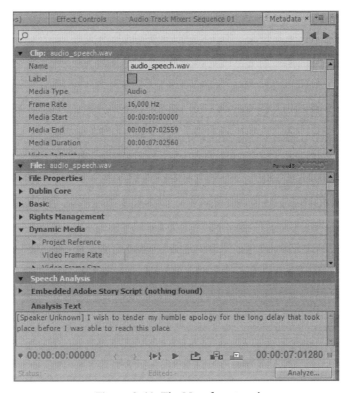

Figure 8-41 The **Metadata** *panel*

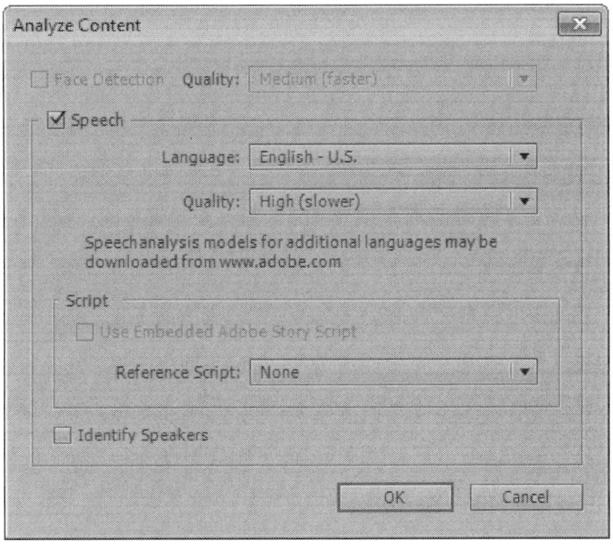

Figure 8-42 The **Analyze Content** *dialog box*

8. Navigate to the location *Documents\Adobe Premiere Tutorials\c08_premiere_cc_tut\Media Files*
Script and then select the *speech.txt* file. Next, choose the **Open** button; the **Import Script**
dialog box is displayed, as shown in Figure 8-43. Choose the **OK** button in this dialog
box.

*Figure 8-43 The **Import Script** dialog box*

9. Choose the **OK** button in the **Analyze Content** dialog box; the **Adobe Media Encoder**
screen is displayed and the encoding process is started, as shown in Figure 8-44.

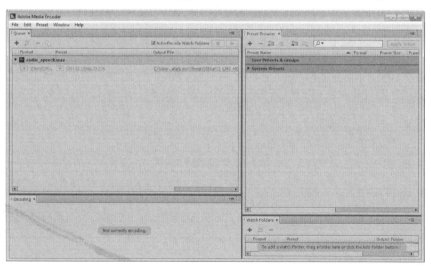

*Figure 8-44 The **Adobe Media Encoder** dialog box*

Note
*If Adobe Media Encoder does not open automatically, run it from the **Start** menu.*

10. On completion of the encoding process, close or minimize the **Adobe Media Encoder** dialog box; the speech analysis of the clip is displayed in the **Speech Analysis** area of the **Metadata** panel.

11. Choose the **Play** button at the bottom of the **Metadata** panel; the clip starts playing in the Source Monitor. Also, the text gets highlighted simultaneously with the speech in the **Speech Analysis** area of the **Metadata** panel, as shown in Figure 8-45.

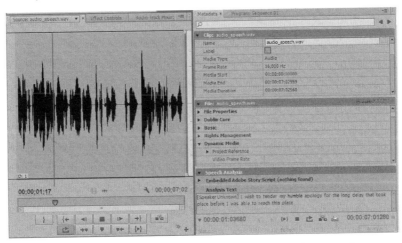

*Figure 8-45 The highlighted text in the **Metadata** panel*

12. Press CTRL+S to save the file. Next, press the ENTER key to render the output of the sequence in the Program Monitor.

Self-Evaluation Test

Answer the following questions and then compare them to those given at the end of this chapter:

1. In which of the following panels the audio tracks can be adjusted?

    (a) **Timeline**   (b) **Effect Controls**
    (c) **Project**   (d) Both **Timeline** and **Effect Controls**

2. Which of the following audio peak levels is appropriate for an audio in a sequence?

    (a) -6   (b) more than -6
    (c) -12   (d) between -12 and -24

3. Which of the following keys is used to add a keyframe to an audio track in the sequence?

    (a) CTRL   (b) ALT
    (c) SHIFT   (d) None of these

4. The stereo clips have two audio channels, _____ and _____ .

5. The taller waveform indicates the _____ volume whereas the shorter waveform specifies the _____ volume.

6. The **Audio Meters** panel shows the audio output graphically. (T/F)

7. While playing the audio, the red mark on **Audio Meters** panel indicates that your audio is perfect. (T/F)

Review Questions

Answer the following questions:

1. Which of the following buttons in the **Effect Controls** panel is used to delete the keyframe on the volume graph of an audio track?

    (a) **Reset**   (b) **Go to Next Keyframe**
    (c) **Add/Remove Keyframe**   (d) None of these

2. Which of the following panels in Adobe Premiere Pro is used to analyze speech?

    (a) **Project**   (b) **Metadata**
    (c) **Effects**   (d) **Effect Controls**

3. In the audio track of a sequence, you can adjust the volume level at some points by using the _____ so that it can be mixed with the other audio in the sequence.

4. You can add keyframes to an audio track by using the _____ and _____ panels.

5. An audio clip can have one audio channel (mono), two audio channels (stereo), or 5 audio surround channels. (T/F)

EXERCISE

Exercise 1

Create a new project in Premiere based on the settings of your video clip. Add some of your audio clips to the sequence. Play the sequence and try to maintain the gain and volume of the audio track, and then notice the difference in **Audio Meter** panel. Try to change the track format of the audio clip. Adjust the track volume at different points using keyframes.

Answers to Self-Evaluation Test
1. d, **2.** d, **3.** a, **4.** left, right, **5.** louder, lower, **6.** T, **7.** F

Chapter 9

Adding Effects to a Sequence-I

Learning Objectives

After completing this chapter, you will be able to:

- *Understand Waveform Monitors and Vectorscope*
- *Modify Fixed and apply Standard effects*
- *Remove effects from a clip*
- *Apply the Color Correction effect to a video clip*
- *Apply lighting effect to a clip*

INTRODUCTION

In Premiere, there are various audio and video effects that can be applied to the clips in a sequence. An effect can give a special visual or audio characteristic to a clip and make it attractive. By adding an effect to a clip, you can perform color correction, manipulate sound, add artistic effects, and so on. In this chapter, you will learn about video effects and also about the methods to apply these effects to clips.

UNDERSTANDING WAVEFORM MONITORS AND VECTORSCOPE

In NTSC standard, some colors cannot be legally broadcast on television. If you are creating a video for the web or for your own use on the computer, then you do not need to worry about the legality of the colors. However, if you are creating a video to be broadcast on television, then you need to be careful about the legality of the colors. The colors should follow the broadcast standard of NTSC. It is very important to make sure that the colors being used are legally allowed to be used for broadcast when you work with the **Color Correction** effects in NTSC. In this section, you will learn how to analyze the legality of colors.

Open the new project in Premiere and import any video clip in the **Project** panel. Next, choose **Window > Workspace > Color Correction** from the menu bar; the **Color Correction** workspace is displayed, as shown in Figure 9-1.

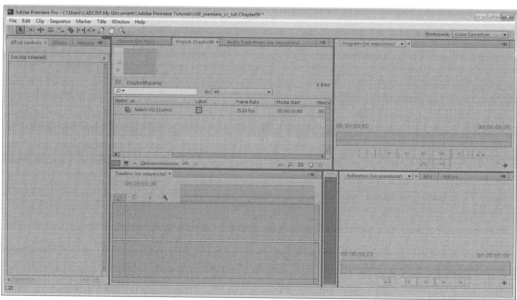

Figure 9-1 *The* ***Color Correction*** *workspace*

Note that the Reference Monitor is displayed on the bottom right of the screen in the **Color Correction** workspace. Double-click on the video clip to display in the Source Monitor. Choose the **Settings** button at the top right of the Reference Monitor; a flyout is displayed. Choose the **Vectorscope** option from the flyout, if not already chosen; the Reference Monitor displays the Vectorscope. The Vectorscope displays a circular chart that shows the chrominance of a video signal including hue and saturation. The chrominance is the color component of a video signal.

In Vectorscope, the small target boxes show the location of fully saturated magenta, blue, cyan, green, yellow, and red colors, refer to Figure 9-2.

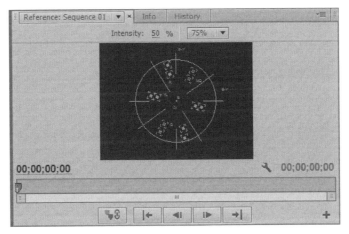

Figure 9-2 The Vectorscope in the Reference Monitor with target boxes highlighted

In NTSC videos, if the color pixels appear till these target boxes, the colors are legal. But, if they appear beyond these target boxes, then the colors are illegal. So, while working with the final output of a video, it is recommended that you view the Vectorscope to check whether the colors are legal.

The Waveform Monitors include **YC Waveform**, **YCbCr Parade**, and **RGB Parade**. Choose the **Settings** button at the top right of the Reference Monitor; a flyout is displayed. Choose the **YC Waveform** option from the flyout; the Reference Monitor now displays the **YC Waveform**, as shown in Figure 9-3.

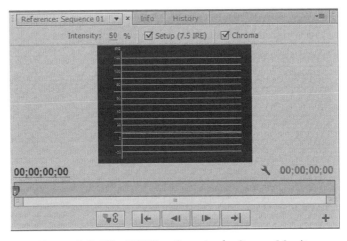

*Figure 9-3 The **YC Waveform** in the Source Monitor*

The **YC Waveform** represents a graph showing the brightness intensity or luminance over colors. The horizontal axis of the graph corresponds to the video image and the vertical axis corresponds to the signal intensity in IRE units. IRE refers to the Institute for Radio Engineers.

For NTSC video in United States, luminance level should be between 7.5 and 100 IRE. However, for NTSC video in Japan, luminance level should be between 0 and 100 IRE.

TUTORIALS

Before you start the tutorials, make sure you reset the workspace to CADCIM. Next, you need to download the *c09_premiere_cc_tut.zip* file from *www.cadcim.com*. The path of the file is as follows: *Textbooks > Animation and Visual Effects > Premiere Pro > Adobe Premiere Pro CC: A Tutorial Approach*

Next, extract the contents of the zip file at *\Documents\Adobe Premiere Tutorials*.

Tutorial 1

In this tutorial, you will edit the fixed effects (built-in) and apply the standard effects to the clip. The output of the sequence is displayed at frame 00:00:07:08, as shown in Figure 9-4. You will also remove the effects from the clip.   **(Expected Time: 30 min)**

Figure 9-4 *The output of the sequence at frame 00:00:07:08*

The following steps are required to complete this tutorial:

a.   Create a new project.
b.   Import clips.
c.   Modify fixed effects.
d.   Apply standard effects.
e.   Remove effects from a clip.

Creating a New Project

In this section, you will create a new project.

1.   Start Premiere as discussed earlier; the **Welcome to Adobe Premiere Pro** dialog box is displayed.

2.   Choose the **New Project** button; the **New Project** dialog box is displayed.

3.   In the **General** tab of the **New Project** dialog box, enter **chapter09** in the **Name** text box.

4. In the **Location** area, choose the **Browse** button; the **Please select the destination path for your new project** dialog box is displayed. Next, navigate to *\Documents\Adobe Premiere Tutorials\c09_premiere_cc_tut* and then choose the **Select Folder** button from the dialog box.

5. Choose the **Scratch Disks** tab in the **New Project** dialog box. In the **Captured Video**, **Captured Audio**, **Video Previews**, and **Audio Previews** drop-down lists, make sure the **Same as Project** option is selected.

6. Choose the **OK** button in the **New Project** dialog box; the interface is displayed with various panels. Also, the file is saved with the name *chapter09.prproj*.

7. Make sure the **CADCIM** workspace is active. In the **Project** panel, right-click in the empty area; a shortcut menu is displayed. Choose **New Item > Sequence**; the **New Sequence** dialog box is displayed.

8. In the **Available Presets** area of the **Sequence Presets** tab, expand the **DV-PAL** option. Now, select the **Widescreen 48kHz** preset; the settings of this preset are displayed on the right in the **Preset Description** area.

9. In the **Sequence Name** text box, make sure the **Sequence 01** is displayed. Next, choose the **OK** button in the **New Sequence** dialog box; the **Sequence 01** is displayed in the **Project** panel.

Importing Clips
In this section, you will import clips in the project panel.

1. Choose the **Media Browser** panel, if it is not already chosen; the drives of your computer are displayed in it.

2. Browse to the location *\Documents\Adobe Premiere Tutorials\Media Files\Video\beach clips*; all the video clips are displayed on the right in the **Media Browser** panel, refer to Figure 9-5.

3. Double-click on the **beach clip (11).mov**; it is displayed in the Source Monitor.

4. Press and hold the left mouse button on the clip in the Source Monitor and drag the clip to the **V1** video track sequence in the **Timeline** panel and release the left mouse button; the **Clip Mismatch Warning** message box is displayed. Choose the **Keep existing settings** button in this message box; the **beach clip (11).mov** clip is added to the sequence. It is automatically added to the **Project** panel as well, refer to Figure 9-6.

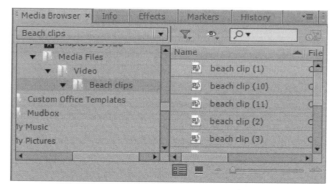

Figure 9-5 *The video clips displayed in the **Media Browser** panel*

Figure 9-6 *The **beach clip (11).mov** in the **Timeline** and **Project** panels*

Modifying Fixed Effects

In Premiere, there are two types of effects, Fixed and Standard. When you add a clip to the sequence in the **Timeline** panel, some effects are automatically added to it, such as **Motion**, **Opacity**, **Volume**, and **Time Remapping**. These pre-applied effects are known as Fixed effects. However, when you add additional effects to the video or audio clip from the **Effects** panel to get the desired result, they are known as Standard effects. You can add a number of effects to any of the clips in the sequence. The Fixed and Standard effects are displayed in the **Effect Controls** panel and their parameters are also modified using this panel.

In this section, you will modify the parameters of the Fixed effects using the **Effect Controls** panel.

1.   Select the **beach clip (11).mov** clip in the **Timeline** panel. Next, choose the **Effect Controls** panel, which is displayed as a tab on the right of the Source Monitor; all the Fixed effects are displayed, as shown in Figure 9-7.

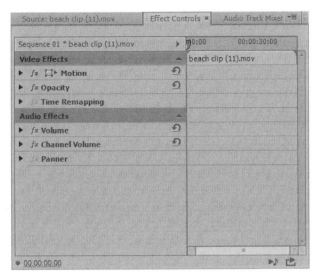

Figure 9-7 The Fixed effects displayed

2. Expand the **Motion** node by clicking on the arrow on its left; the parameters such as **Position**, **Scale**, **Rotation**, **Anchor point**, and **Anti-flicker** are displayed, as shown in Figure 9-8.

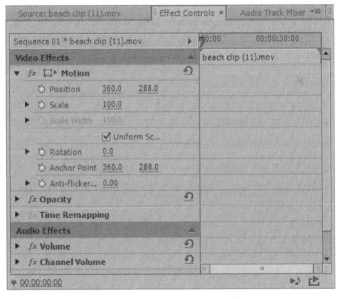

*Figure 9-8 The parameters in the **Motion** area*

Next, you will position, scale, and rotate the clip using the parameters in the **Motion** area.

3. To change the position of the clip, click on the **Motion** label; the control points and handles are displayed on the clip in the Program Monitor, as shown in Figure 9-9. Alternatively, you can directly double-click on the clip in the Program Monitor to display the control points and handles.

Figure 9-9 *The control points on the clip*

4. In the **Effect Controls** panel, move the cursor over the value 360.0 on the right of the **Position** parameter; the shape of the cursor is changed into a hand cursor, as shown in Figure 9-10. Next, press and hold the left mouse button and drag the cursor based on your requirement; the position of the clip is changed, refer to Figure 9-11.

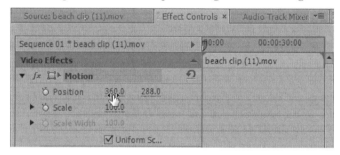

Figure 9-10 *The shape of the cursor changed in the*
Effect Controls panel

Figure 9-11 *The changed position of the clip*

You can also drag the clip in the Program Monitor to change the position of the clip. On doing so, the values on the right of the **Position** parameter in the **Motion** area will change automatically.

Next, you will scale the selected clip.

5. Choose the **Reset** button on the right of the **Motion** label; all the parameters in the **Motion** node are reset to their original values.

6. Make sure the **Uniform Scale** check box is selected. Next, move the cursor over one of the control points of the clip in the Program Monitor; a double-headed arrow is displayed in place of the cursor. Next, press and hold the left mouse button and drag it to scale the clip based on your requirement. The clip is scaled, refer to Figure 9-12. Also, the value on the right of the **Scale** parameter is modified accordingly.

Figure 9-12 The scaled clip in the Program Monitor

 Note
*If you clear the **Uniform Scale** check box, the **Scale Height** and **Scale Width** parameters will be activated. You can enter new values for these parameters to scale the clip according to your requirement.*

Next, you will rotate the selected clip.

7. Move the cursor slightly away from the control point of the clip in the Program Monitor; the cursor changes into a rotate icon, as shown in Figure 9-13.

Figure 9-13 The rotate icon

8. Press and hold the left mouse button and drag the mouse up or down; the clip is rotated, refer to Figure 9-14. Also, the value on the right of the **Rotation** parameter is modified in the **Effect Controls** panel.

Figure 9-14 The rotated clip

When you select a clip in the Program Monitor, you will notice a small circular point in the middle of the clip. This circular point is known as the anchor point, refer to Figure 9-15.

Figure 9-15 The anchor point in the middle of the clip

The position of the clip refers to the location where this anchor point will be placed with respect to the entire viewable area. The anchor point is the point of origin for the parameters or transformations in the **Motion** area.

9. Press the CTRL+Z to undo the rotate command.

10. In the **Motion** node, move the cursor on the first value located on the right of the **Anchor Point** parameter; the shape of the cursor is changed, as shown in Figure 9-16. Next, click on this value; it is converted into an edit box, as shown in Figure 9-17.

Figure 9-16 *The changed cursor*   **Figure 9-17** *The edit box*

11. Enter the value **0** and press the ENTER key. Again, enter the value **0** in the second edit box on the right of the **Anchor Point** parameter; the anchor point is moved, as shown in Figure 9-18.

Figure 9-18 *The changed position of anchor point*

12. Next, rotate the clip, as discussed in the previous section. The clip rotates with respect to the new origin or new position of the anchor point, refer to Figure 9-19.

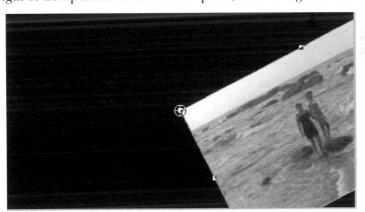

Figure 9-19 *The clip rotated according to the new position of the anchor point*

13. Choose the **Reset** button on the right of the **Motion** node; the clip comes back to its original place with the original size.

14. Expand the **Opacity** node by clicking on the arrow on its left. Enter the value **70** in the edit box given on the right of the **Opacity** parameter; the clip becomes transparent, as shown in Figure 9-20.

Figure 9-20 *The clip after modifying the* **Opacity** *parameter*

The value 100 for the **Opacity** parameter specifies that the clip is opaque and the value 0 for the **Opacity** parameter specifies that the clip is transparent.

15. Press the ENTER key to view the output of the sequence in the Program Monitor.

Applying Standard Effects

In Premiere, all the standard effects are located in the **Effects** panel. These Standard effects are categorized into two parts, Audio effects and Video effects, refer to Figure 9-21. On the top of the **Effects** panel, there is a search text box, which is used to search the required effect from the **Effects** panel. For example, enter **color** in the search text box; all the effects with the word "color" will be displayed, as shown in Figure 9-22. Choose the close icon on the right of the search text box to close the search results.

Figure 9-21 *The* **Effects** *panel*

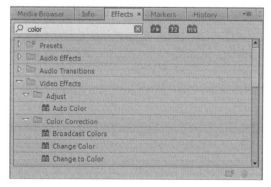

Figure 9-22 *All effects with the word "color"*

There are three buttons: **Accelerated Effects**, **32-bit Color**, and **YUV Effects** just next to the search text box. Choose the **Accelerated Effects** button; all the accelerated effects will be displayed in the **Effects** panel, as shown in Figure 9-23. Now, deactivate the **Accelerated Effects** button and choose the **32-bit Color** button; the 32-bit color effects will be displayed in the **Effects** panel, as shown in Figure 9-24. Next, deactivate the **32-bit Color** button and choose the **YUV Effects** button; the YUV effects will be displayed in the **Effects** panel, as shown in Figure 9-25. Next, deactivate the **YUV Effects** button.

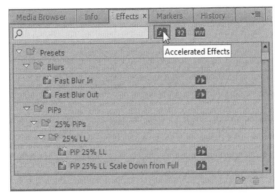

Figure 9-23 *The accelerated effects in the **Effects** panel*

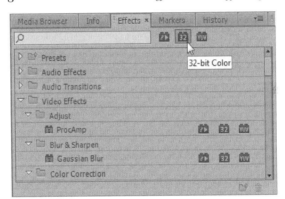

Figure 9-24 *The 32-bit color effects in the **Effects** panel*

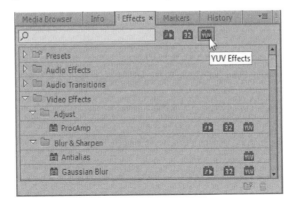

Figure 9-25 *The YUV effects in the **Effects** panel*

You can apply a Standard effect to a clip in your sequence by simply dragging it from the **Effects** panel and dropping it over the clip in the **Timeline** panel. Next, you will apply the **Gaussian Blur** effect to the clip in the **Timeline** panel.

1. Make sure the **Timeline** panel is selected. Next, press the BACKSLASH (\) key to zoom in the sequence in the **Timeline** panel.

2. In the **Effects** panel, expand the **Video Effects** bin by clicking on the arrow on its left; various video effects such as **Adjust**, **Blur & Sharpen**, **Channel**, **Color Correction**, and so on are displayed.

3. Expand **Blur & Sharpen** by clicking on the arrow on its left; various blur effects are displayed.

4. Select the **Gaussian Blur** effect, press and hold the left mouse button on it, and drag it from the **Effects** panel to the **beach clip (11).mov** in the **Timeline** panel. Release the left mouse button; the **Gaussian Blur** effect is applied to the clip. Also, it is added to the **Effect Controls** panel.

5. In the **Effect Controls** panel, expand the **Gaussian Blur** node, if not already expanded, by clicking on the arrow on its left; the parameters for the effect are displayed, as shown in Figure 9-26.

Figure 9-26 *The parameters for the* **Gaussian Blur** *effect*

6. Specify the value **50** for the **Blurriness** parameter; the clip is blurred accordingly in the Program Monitor, refer to Figures 9-27 and 9-28.

Figure 9-27 *The video clip before applying the* **Gaussian Blur** *effect*

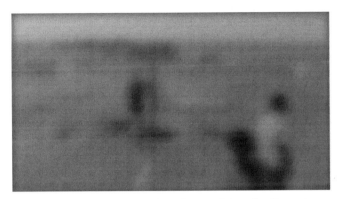

Figure 9-28 *The video clip after applying the **Gaussian Blur** effect*

When you apply an effect to a clip, it remains active for the entire duration of the clip. However, you can make an effect more or less intense at specific frames using the keyframes.

7. Make sure the CTI is placed at the beginning of the sequence in the **Timeline** panel.

8. In the **Effect Controls** panel, choose the **Toggle animation** button on the left of the **Blurriness** parameter; a keyframe is created at 00:00:00:00 frame, as shown in Figure 9-29. Make sure the value for the **Blurriness** parameter is set to **50**.

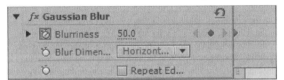

Figure 9-29 *A keyframe created*

9. In the **Timeline** panel, enter the value **5.15** in the **Playhead Position** edit box; the CTI is moved to that frame.

10. In the **Effect Controls** panel, choose the **Reset** button on the right of the **Gaussian Blur** parameter; another keyframe is created at 00:00:05:15 frame, as shown in Figure 9-30.

Figure 9-30 *Another keyframe created at 00:00:05:15 frame*

11. Next, play the sequence from frame 00:00:00:00 to 0000:05:15 and view the effect of adding keyframes. You will notice that the blur effect fades away over the time.

12. Press the ENTER key to view the output of the sequence in the Program Monitor.

Note
*You can copy an effect from one clip and paste it to the other clips easily. You can also copy all the effect values including keyframes. To do so, select the clip in the **Timeline** panel whose effects or attributes you need to copy and then choose **Edit > Copy** from the menu bar. Now, select the clips where you need to paste the effects or attributes and then choose **Edit > Paste Attributes** from the menu bar to paste the copied effects or attributes.*

Removing Effects from a Clip

You can remove a selected effect or all effects from the selected clip in the **Timeline** panel. In this section, you will remove effects from the clip.

1. Make sure the **beach clip (11).mov** clip is selected in the **Timeline** panel.

2. In the **Effect Controls** panel, right-click on the **Gaussian Blur** parameter; a flyout is displayed.

3. Choose the **Clear** option from the flyout; the effect is removed from the video clip. Alternatively, select the **Gaussian Blur** effect from the **Effect Controls** panel. Next, choose the button on the right of the **Effect Controls** panel; a flyout is displayed, as shown in Figure 9-31. Choose the **Remove Selected Effect** option from the flyout; the **Gaussian Blur** effect is removed from the clip and the **Effect Controls** panel. Also, you can press the BACKSPACE key to remove the selected effect from the clip.

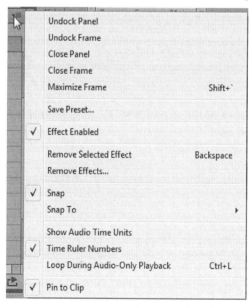

Figure 9-31 The flyout displayed

Next, you will remove all the effects from the clip.

4. Select the **beach clip (11).mov** clip in the **Timeline** panel.

5. Choose the button on the right of the **Effect Controls** panel; a flyout is displayed.

6. Choose the **Remove Effects** option from the flyout; the **Remove Effects** dialog box is displayed, as shown in Figure 9-32.

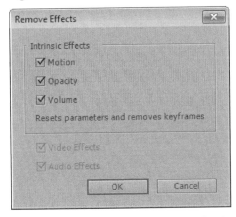

Figure 9-32 *The* ***Remove Effects*** *dialog box*

7. In the **Remove Effects** dialog box, select the check boxes corresponding to the effects that you need to remove from the clip. Then, choose the **OK** button; all the effects corresponding to the selected check boxes are removed from the clip and the **Effect Controls** panel. Next, press CTRL+Z to undo the changes.

    If you do not want to permanently remove the effects but need to disable them for a while, then use the following steps:

    In the **Effect Controls** panel, choose the **Toggle the effect on or off** button on the left of an effect; the effect is disabled. To enable the effect, choose the **Toggle the effect on or off** button again.

8. Press CTRL+S to save the file.

9. Press the ENTER key to view the output of the sequence in the Program Monitor.

    The output of the sequence is displayed at frame 00:00:07:08, as shown in Figure 9-33.

Figure 9-33 *The output of the sequence at frame 00:00:07:08*

Tutorial 2

In this tutorial, you will color correct the clip and then apply light effect to the clip. The output of the sequence at frame 00:00:00:00 is displayed, as shown in Figure 9-34.

(Expected Time: 30 min)

Figure 9-34 The output of the sequence at frame 00:00:00:00

The following steps are required to complete this tutorial:

a.   Open the project file.
b.   Apply color correction to the clip.
c.   Apply lighting effect to the clip.

Opening the Project File

In this section, you will open the project file.

1.   Open the *chapter09_color_correction.prproj* file that you have downloaded from the CADCIM website.

2.   Save the *chapter09_color_correction.prproj* file with the name *chapter09_color_correction_02.prproj* at the location *\Documents\Adobe Premiere Tutorials\c09_Premiere_cc_tut*. The *chapter09_color_correction_02.prproj* file is displayed. Now, switch to **Color Correction** workspace.

Applying Color Correction to the Clip

In this section, you will apply color correction to the clip.

1.   In the **Project** panel, double-click on the **beach clip_CC.avi** clip; the clip is displayed in the Source Monitor.

    Note that the clip has an extreme blue effect. You will correct this effect by using one of the color correction effects in the **Effects** panel.

2. Press and hold the left mouse button on the clip in the Source Monitor and drag it from the Source Monitor to the sequence in the **V1** video track. Release the left mouse button; the **beach clip_CC.avi** clip is added to the sequence. It is also displayed in the Program Monitor. Note that the clip does not have any audio.

3. Choose the **Settings** button at the top right of the Reference Monitor; a flyout is displayed. Choose the **Vectorscope** option from the flyout; the Reference Monitor now displays the **Vectorscope**, refer to Figure 9-35.

*Figure 9-35 The **beach clip_CC.avi** in the **Color Correction** workspace*

Next, you will apply the **Fast Color Correction** effect to the **beach clip_CC.avi** clip.

4. In the **Effects** panel, expand **Video Effects > Color Correction**; various color correction effects are displayed under the **Color Correction** category.

5. Select the **Fast Color Corrector** effect from the **Color Correction** category in the **Effects** panel. Press and hold the left mouse button on the effect and drag it from the **Effects** panel to the **Timeline** panel over the **beach clip_CC.avi** clip. Release the left mouse button; the **Fast Color Corrector** effect is applied to the **beach clip_CC.avi** clip.

6. Make sure the **beach clip_CC.avi** clip is selected in the **Timeline** panel. Next, choose the **Effect Controls** panel; the effects of the selected clip are displayed in it.

7. Next, expand the **Fast Color Corrector** node in the **Effect Controls** panel, if not already expanded; all the parameters of this effect are displayed, as shown in Figure 9-36.

    The **Fast Color Corrector** effect is used to perform the primary color correction. In primary color correction, you can adjust all the pixels of an image.

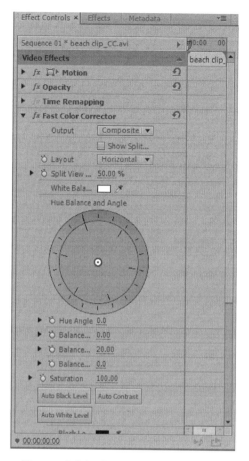

Figure 9-36 *Parameters of the **Fast***
Color Corrector *effect*

However, in the secondary color correction, you can adjust only some of the pixels of the image. While doing color correction, it is recommended that first the primary color corrections are performed and then the secondary corrections.

8. In the **Fast Color Corrector** properties, press and hold the left mouse button on the middle of the color wheel, refer to Figure 9-37. Next, drag the cursor away from the blue color, refer to Figure 9-37. On doing so, the **beach clip_CC.avi** is modified in the Program Monitor, refer to Figure 9-38.

You can view the original clip in the Source Monitor, modified clip in the Program Monitor, and the luminance in the Reference Monitor. You can also see the pixels in the Vectorscope, as discussed earlier.

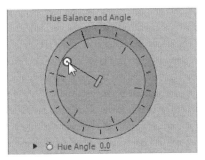
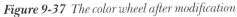

Figure 9-37 *The color wheel after modification*

Figure 9-38 *The color of the clip modified in the Program Monitor*

9. Next, modify the values for other parameters of the **Fast Color Corrector** effect as given next.

Hue Angle: **15.0**
Balance Magnitude: **67.60**
Balance Gain: **27.00**
Balance Angle: **-123.1**
Input Gray Level: **2.66**

The clip after modifying the values is shown in Figure 9-39.

Figure 9-39 *The modified clip*

Next, you will add secondary color correction and **RGB curves** to the **beach clip_CC.avi** clip.

10. Choose the **Effects** panel and expand **Video Effects > Color Correction**, if not already expanded.

11. Select the **RGB Curves** effect from the **Color Correction** category in the **Effects** panel. Press and hold the left mouse button on it and then drag it from the **Effects** panel to the **Timeline** panel over the **beach clip_CC.avi** clip. Release the left mouse button; the **RGB Curves** effect is applied to the **beach clip_CC.avi** clip.

12. Make sure the **beach clip_CC.avi** is selected in the **Timeline** panel. Choose the **Effect Controls** panel; the effects of the selected clip are displayed in it.

13. Expand the **RGB Curves** node, if not already expanded; all the parameters of this effect are displayed, as shown in Figure 9-40.

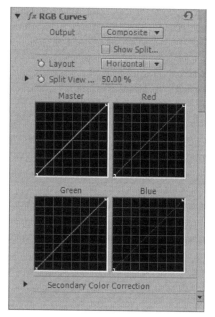

Figure 9-40 *Parameters of the* **RGB Curves** *effect*

Note

The effects in the **Effect Controls** *panels must be in the same order in which they are applied to the clip.*

The **RGB Curves** effect is used to adjust the color of a clip by adjusting the curve for each channel. The **Master** channel is used to adjust the brightness and contrast of all the channels by changing the shape of the curve. If you move the curve upward, the clip will be lightened. However, on moving the curve downward, the clip will become darker. To move the curve upward or downward, you need to add points on it.

You can alter the brightness and contrast of the red, green, and blue channels of the clip by changing the shape of their respective curves in the **Red**, **Green**, and **Blue** areas.

14. In the **Master** area, move the cursor over the curve; it is changed to a plus sign, as shown in Figure 9-41.

15. Click on the lower side of the curve; a point is added to the curve, as shown in Figure 9-42.

16. Press and hold the cursor on the point and move the curve downward; the curve moves downward, refer to Figure 9-43. It is recommended that you view the result of the effects on the clip in the Program Monitor.

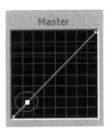
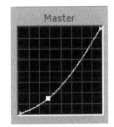

Figure 9-41 *The changed shape of the cursor*

Figure 9-42 *The point added to the curve*

Figure 9-43 *The curve moved downward*

Note that the shadows and the midtones of the clip are bit down. Now, you will bring the midtones up.

17. Add another point on the curve and move it upward, refer to Figure 9-44. Also, make adjustments in the curve by moving both the points as required. The clip is modified in the Program Monitor, refer to Figure 9-45.

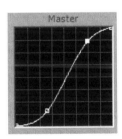

Figure 9-44 *The modified curve*

Figure 9-45 *The modified clip*

Note
To view the effect on the clip in the Program Monitor, you can choose the **Toggle the effect** *on or off button on the left of the* **RGB Curves** *effect.*

18. Make adjustment in the **Green** channel and view the difference in the clip in the Program Monitor, refer to Figures 9-46 and 9-47.

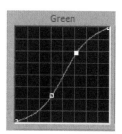

Figure 9-46 *The modified*   *Figure 9-47* *The clip after modifying the* **Green** *channel*
Green *channel*

19. Press the ENTER key to view the output of the sequence in the Program Monitor.

    Next, you will save the preset for the effect.

20. Choose **Window > Workspace > CADCIM** from the menu bar; the current workspace
    is changed to the **CADCIM** workspace, as shown in Figure 9-48.

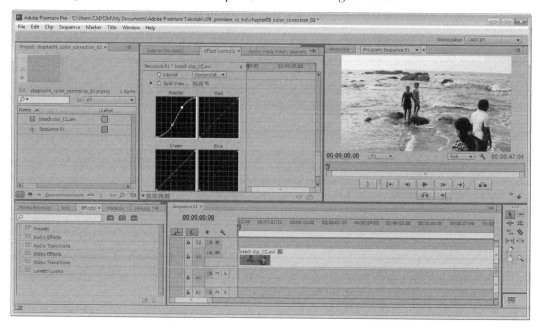

Figure 9-48 *The* **CADCIM** *workspace*

21. Select the **beach clip_CC.avi** clip in the **Timeline** panel, if it is not already selected.

22. In the **Effect Controls** panel, select the **Fast Color Corrector** node and right-click on it;
    a shortcut menu is displayed, as shown in Figure 9-49.

23. Choose the **Save Preset** option from the shortcut menu; the **Save Preset** dialog box is displayed, as shown in Figure 9-50.

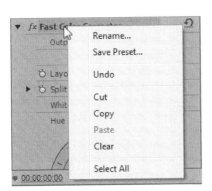

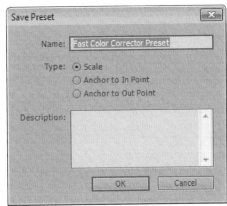

Figure 9-49 *The shortcut menu displayed*   *Figure 9-50* *The **Save Preset** dialog box*

24. Accept the default name and then choose the **OK** button; the preset for the selected effect is saved. It is also displayed in the **Presets** bin of the **Effects** panel, as shown in Figure 9-51.

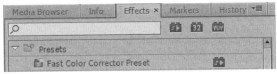

Figure 9-51 *The preset in the **Effects** panel*

Next, you will apply the saved preset to other clips in the sequence.

25. Import a clip of your choice and add it to the sequence.

26. In the **Effects** panel, expand the **Presets** bin. Next, select the preset effect that you saved in the previous section of this tutorial. Press and hold the left mouse button and drag the selected effect from the **Effects** panel to the **Timeline** panel over the clip on which you want to apply the preset. The clip now shows the same effects in the Program Monitor.

27. Press CTRL+S to save the file. Next, press the ENTER key to view the output of the sequence in the Program Monitor.

Applying the Lighting Effect to the Clip

In this section, you will apply the lighting effect to the clip.

1. Import the **beach clip (3).mov** clip to the **Project** panel and then drag it to the sequence in the **V2** track of the **Timeline** panel from the **Project** panel.

   Next, you will apply the **Lighting Effects** effect to the **beach clip (3).mov** clip.

2. In the **Effects** panel, expand **Video Effects**, if it is not already expanded. Next, expand **Adjust**; various effects are displayed, as shown in Figure 9-52.

*Figure 9-52 Various effects in the **Adjust** bin*

3. Select the **Lighting Effects** effect and drag it from the **Effects** panel to the **beach clip(3).mov** clip in the **Timeline** panel. The **Lighting Effect** is applied to the clip. Also, it is displayed in the Program Monitor, as shown in Figure 9-53.

Figure 9-53 The clip in the Program Monitor after applying the **Lighting Effects** *effect*

4. Make sure the **beach clip (3).mov** clip is selected in the sequence. Next, choose the **Effect Controls** panel; the **Lighting Effects** effect is displayed in it.

5. Expand the **Lighting Effects** effect, if not already expanded; various parameters of this effect are displayed, as shown in Figure 9-54.

6. Expand the **Light 1** option; the parameters are displayed, as shown in Figure 9-55.

The parameters of the **Light 1** node are used to set the light type, intensity, light color, and other properties of the light. The **Light Type** drop-down list is used to specify the type of light. By default, the **Spotlight** option is selected in the **Light Type** drop-down list. This type of light is used to create a spotlight that casts an elliptical beam of light. The **Directional** light type is used to cast a sunlight effect in which the light seems to be coming from a distant source, unaffecting the light angle. The **Omni** light type is used to spread light in all directions just like a light bulb.

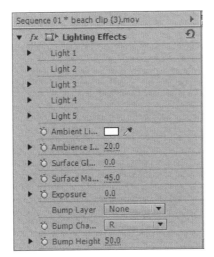

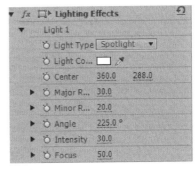

Figure 9-54 *The parameters of the* **Lighting Effects** *effect*

Figure 9-55 *The parameters of* **Light 1** *node*

7. Select the **Directional** option from the **Light Type** drop-down list; the clip now displays the directional light effect, as shown in Figure 9-56.

Figure 9-56 *The directional light effect on the clip*

8. Choose the color swatch on the right of the **Light Color** option; the **Color Picker** dialog box is displayed, as shown in Figure 9-57. Enter the following values in this dialog box:

R: **250**   G: **203**   B: **142**

After modifying the values, the clip displays the sunset light effect in the Program Monitor, as shown in Figure 9-58.

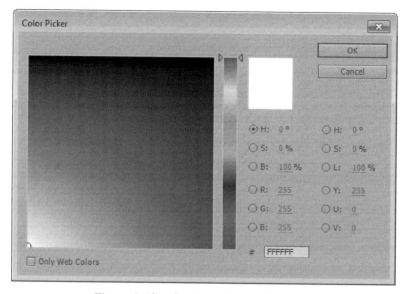

Figure 9-57 The **Color Picker** *dialog box*

Figure 9-58 The clip after changing the color of the light

9. Select the **Omni** option from the **Light Type** drop-down list; the clip now displays the omni light effect, as shown in Figure 9-59.

10. Choose the color swatch located on the right of the **Color** option; the **Color Picker** dialog box is displayed. Next, enter the following values to give sunset light effect to the clip:

Light Color
R: **244**   G: **168**   B: **68**

Figure 9-59 The omni light effect on the clip

11. Enter the following values in the **Light1** option of the **Effect Controls** panel:

Center:	**360.0**	**154.0**
Major Radius:	**10.0**	
Intensity:	**35.0**	

After modifying the values, the clip displays the sunset light effect in the Program Monitor, as shown in Figure 9-60.

Figure 9-60 The sunset light effect on the clip

12. Choose the color swatch located on the right of the **Color** option; the **Color Picker** dialog box is displayed. Next, select the **Spotlight** option from the **Light Type** drop-down list. Now, specify the values of parameters as follows:

Light Color
R: **249**   G: **219**   B: **177**

13. Enter the following values in the **Light1** option of the **Effect Controls** panel:

Center:	**276**		**372**
Major Radius:	**8.0**	Minor Radius:	**8.0**
Angle:	**225.0**	Intensity:	**40.0**
Focus:	**70.0**		

After modifying the values, the spotlight effect is applied on the clip in the Program Monitor, as shown in Figure 9-61.

Figure 9-61 The spotlight effect on the clip

Note

*1. If you select the **None** option from the **Light Type** drop-down list, there will be no light in the clip.*

2. To animate the light according to the motion of your clip, you need to use the keyframes. You will learn about animating light effects using keyframes in the later chapters.

14. Press CTRL+S to save the file. Next, press the ENTER key to view the output of the sequence in the Program Monitor.

Self-Evaluation Test

Answer the following questions and then compare them to those given at the end of this chapter:

1. Which of the following panels displays the properties of the Standard and Fixed effects applied to a clip?

    (a) **Effect Controls**   (b) **Info**
    (c) **Effects**   (d) All of these

2. Which of the following effects comes under the Fixed effects category?

    (a) **Motion**   (b) **Adjust**
    (c) **Color Correction**   (d) None of these

3. Which of the following options in the Reference Monitor is used to accurately evaluate the colors and brightness?

    (a) **Vectorscope**   (b) **YC Waveform**
    (c) Both (a) and (b)   (d) None of these

4. In Premiere, there are two types of effects, _____ and _____.

5. The _____ Monitor displays the original uncorrected image. The _____ Monitor displays the image after applying the effects and the _____ Monitor indicates the legality of the colors in NTSC videos.

6. The circular chart in the Vectorscope shows the _____ of a video signal including hue and saturation.

7. You cannot remove the effect that is applied to a clip. (T/F)

8. While working with the **Color Correction** effects in NTSC, it is very important to make sure that the colors being used in the clip are legally allowed to be broadcast on television. (T/F)

Review Questions

Answer the following questions:

1. Which of the following effects comes under the Fixed effects category?

    (a) **Motion**   (b) **Volume**
    (c) **Opacity**   (d) All of these

2. Which of the following effects in the **Effects** panel is used to blur the clip?

    (a) **Color Correction**   (b) **Lighting Effects**
    (c) **Gaussian Blur**   (d) All of these

3. Which of the following options is included in the Waveform Monitors?

    (a) **RGB Parade**   (b) **YC Waveform**
    (c) **YCbCr Parade**   (d) All of these

4. To view the effect on the clip in the Program Monitor, choose the _____ button on the left of that in the **Effect Controls** panel.

5. The term IRE refers to the _____ .

6. In United States, the luminance level for the NTSC video should be between 0 and 100 IRE. However, for NTSC video in Japan, luminance level should be between 7.5 and 100 IRE.(T/F)

7. The chrominance is the color component of a video signal. (T/F)

8. In primary color correction, you can adjust all the pixels of an image. (T/F)

EXERCISE

Exercise 1

Create a new project in Premiere as per the settings of your video clip. Add some of your video clips to the sequence. Try and apply various video effects to the clips in the sequence. Next, modify the properties in the **Effect Controls** panel and view the difference.

Answers to Self-Evaluation Test
1. a, **2.** a, **3.** c, **4.** Fixed, Standard, **5.** Source, Program, Reference, **6.** chrominance, **7.** F, **8.** T

Chapter *10*

Adding Effects to a Sequence-II

Learning Objectives

After completing this chapter, you will be able to:

• *Apply various audio effects to audio clips*
• *Edit Audio using the Audio Mixer*
• *Automate changes in audio tracks using Audio Track Mixer*
• *Apply the Time Remapping effect in video clips*
• *Apply the Ultra Key effect in video clips*

INTRODUCTION

In the previous chapter, you learned to add video effects to video clips. In this chapter, you will learn about audio effects in the **Effects** panel. You will also learn about **Audio Mixer**, the **Time Remapping** effects, and the **Ultra Key** effect.

TUTORIALS

Before you start the tutorials, you need to download the *c10_premiere_cc_tut.zip* file from *www.cadcim.com*. The path of the file is as follows: *Textbooks > Animation and Visual Effects > Premiere Pro > Adobe Premiere Pro CC: A Tutorial Approach*

Next, extract the contents of the zip file at *\Documents\Adobe Premiere Tutorials*.

Tutorial 1

In this tutorial, you will apply various audio effects to the audio clip.

(Expected Time: 20 min)

The following steps are required to complete this tutorial:

a.   Open the project file.
b.   Apply audio effects to the audio clip.

Opening the Project File

In this section, you will open the project file.

1.   Open the *chapter10.prproj* file that you have downloaded from the CADCIM website.

2.   Save the file at the location *\Documents\Adobe Premiere Tutorials\c10_premiere_cc_tut* with the name *chapter10_audio effects*. The *chapter10_audio effects.prproj* file is displayed, refer to Figure 10-1.

Applying Audio Effects to the Audio Clip

In Premiere, there are various audio effects that can be used to alter and modify the properties of audio clips by changing their pitch, creating echoes, removing extra noise, and so on. You can add a number of audio effects to an audio clip. In this section, you will apply some of the audio effects to the audio clip.

First, you will apply the **Bass** audio effect to the audio clip. The **Bass** audio effect is used to increase or decrease the frequencies that are below or equal to 200 Hz.

1.   Select the **audio_speech.wma** clip in the **Timeline** panel.

2.   In the **Effects** panel, expand the **Audio Effects** folder by clicking on the arrow on its left, refer to Figure 10-2; various audio effects are displayed, as shown in Figure 10-3.

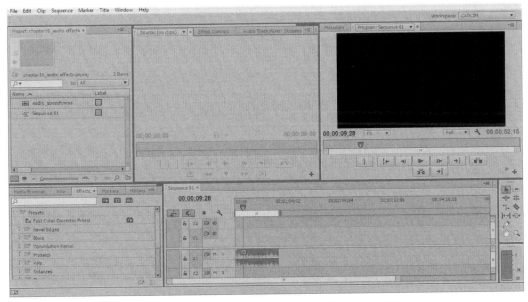

Figure 10-1 *The chapter10_audio effects.prproj file*

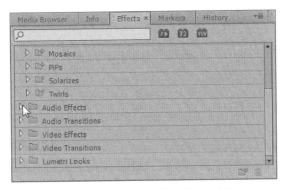

Figure 10-2 The **Audio Effects** *folder*

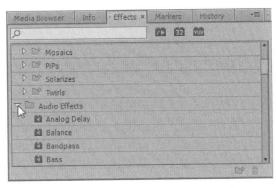

Figure 10-3 *Various audio effects in the*
Audio Effects *folder*

3. Select the **Bass** audio effect in the **Effects** panel. Press and hold the left mouse button on it and drag it to the **audio_speech.wma** clip in the **Timeline** panel. Release the left mouse button; the **Bass** effect is applied to the clip.

4. Make sure the **audio_speech.wma** clip is selected in the **Timeline** panel. In the **Effect Controls** panel, the **Bass** effect you just applied is displayed.

5. Expand the **Bass** effect, if not already expanded; the **Bypass** and **Boost** properties are displayed, refer to Figure 10-4.

6. Expand the **Boost** property; its parameters are displayed, as shown in Figure 10-4.

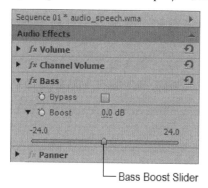

Figure 10-4 The **Boost** and **Bypass** *properties of the* **Bass** *audio effect*

7. Move the CTI to the beginning of the sequence in the **Timeline** panel. Press the SPACEBAR key to play the clip.

8. In the **Effect Controls** panel, move the Bass Boost Slider to left or right, refer to Figure 10-4. While moving the Bass Boost Slider, notice the difference in the frequency of the clip. It increases or decreases based on the movement of the slider. Set the frequency based on your requirement.

   Next, you will apply the **Delay** audio effect to the audio clip. The **Delay** effect is used to add an echo to the audio clip that will play after a specified period of time.

9. Select the **Bass** audio effect in the **Effect Controls** panel and press the DELETE key to delete the effect.

10. Select the **Delay** audio effect in the **Effects** panel. Press and hold the left mouse button on it and drag it to the **audio_speech.wma** clip in the **Timeline** panel. Release the left mouse button; the **Delay** effect is applied to the clip.

11. Make sure the **audio_speech.wma** clip is selected in the **Timeline** panel. In the **Effect Controls** panel, the **Delay** effect is displayed.

12. Expand the **Delay** effect by clicking on the arrow on its left, if not already expanded; various properties such as **Delay**, **Bypass**, **Feedback**, and **Mix** are displayed.

    The **Delay** property determines the time lapse occurred before the echo starts playing. It is between 0 to 2 seconds. The **Feedback** property is used to specify the percentage of echo added to the audio to create multiple decaying echoes. The **Mix** property is used to control the amount of echo. The **Bypass** property is used to specify whether to apply the **Delay** effect or not.

13. Expand the **Delay**, **Feedback**, and **Mix** properties; the corresponding sliders are displayed, as shown in Figure 10-5.

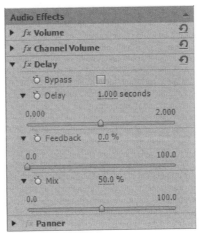

Figure 10-5 *The properties with their sliders*

14. Move the CTI to the beginning of the sequence in the **Timeline** panel. Press the SPACEBAR key to play the clip.

15. Next, drag the sliders corresponding to the **Delay**, **Feedback**, and **Mix** properties and notice the difference in the echoes of the **audio_speech.wma** clip. Also, set the properties of the audio based on your requirement.

    Next, you will apply the **PitchShifter** effect to the **audio_speech.wma** audio clip. The **PitchShifter** effect is used to adjust the pitch of the incoming signal.

16. Delete the **Delay** audio effect from the **Effect Controls** panel as discussed earlier.

17. Select the **PitchShifter** audio effect in the **Effects** panel. Press and hold the left mouse button on it and drag it to the **audio_speech.wma** clip in the **Timeline** panel. Release the left mouse button; the **PitchShifter** effect is applied to the clip.

18. Make sure the **audio_speech.wma** clip is selected in the **Timeline** panel. Select the **Effect Controls** panel; the applied **PitchShifter** effect is displayed in it.

19. Expand the **PitchShifter** effect by clicking on the arrow on its left, if not already expanded; the **Custom Setup** and **Individual Parameters** properties are displayed.

20. Expand the **Individual Parameters** property; the parameters corresponding to this property are displayed, as shown in Figure 10-6.

   You can adjust the pitch of an audio clip either by using the graphical controls in the **Custom Setup** property or by modifying parameters in the **Individual Parameters** property. Next, you will adjust the pitch of the **audio_speech.wma** clip by using the parameters in the **Individual Parameters** property.

21. Expand the **Pitch**, **FineTune**, and **FormantPreserve** parameters; the sliders corresponding to these parameters are displayed, as shown in Figure 10-7.

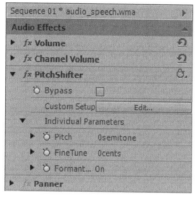

Figure 10-6 *The parameters of the PitchShifter effect*

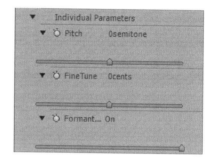

Figure 10-7 *The parameters and their corresponding sliders*

The **Pitch** parameter is used to specify the change in pitch in semitone steps. It ranges between -12 and +12 semitones. The **FineTune** parameter is used to specify the fine tuning between the semitone grid of the pitch property. The **FormantPreserve** parameter is used to prevent formants in the audio clip from being affected.

22. Move the CTI to the beginning of the sequence in the **Timeline** panel. Press the SPACEBAR key to play the clip.

23. Drag the sliders corresponding to the **Pitch**, **FineTune**, and **FormantPreserve** properties and notice the difference in the pitch of the **audio_speech.wma** clip. Also, set the pitch based on your requirement.

24. Choose the **Edit** button next to the **Custom Setup** property; the **Clip Fx Editor** dialog box is displayed, refer to Figure 10-8.

   You can also use some of the available presets for modifying the pitch of the audio clip.

25. Choose the **Reset** button available on the left in the **Clip Fx Editor** dialog box, refer to Figure 10-8; the parameters are set to their default values. Next, close this dialog box.

26. Choose the **Presets** button on the right of the **PitchShifter** effect in the **Effect** **Controls** panel; a flyout is displayed with a list of available presets, as shown in Figure 10-9.

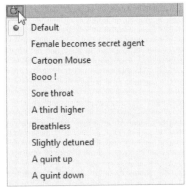

*Figure 10-8 The **Clip Fx Editor** dialog box*

*Figure 10-9 The flyout displayed on choosing the **Presets** button*

27. Choose one of the presets from the flyout. Note that the parameters in the **Custom Setup** and **Individual Parameters** change accordingly.

28. Next, play the clip and view the difference in the pitch after applying the preset.

    Now, you will apply the **Treble** audio effect to the **audio_speech.wma** clip. The **Treble** audio effect is used to increase or decrease the frequencies that are equal or above 4000 Hz.

29. Delete the **PitchShifter** audio effect from the **Effect Controls** panel.

30. Select the **Treble** audio effect in the **Effects** panel. Press and hold the left mouse button on it and drag it to the **audio_speech.wma** clip in the **Timeline** panel. Release the left mouse button; the **Treble** effect is applied to the clip.

31. Make sure the **audio_speech.wma** clip is selected in the **Timeline** panel. In the **Effect Controls** panel, the **Treble** effect that you have applied is displayed.

32. Expand the **Treble** effect by clicking on the arrow on its left, if not already expanded; the **Bypass** and **Boost** properties are displayed, refer to Figure 10-10.

33. Expand the **Boost** property; its parameters are displayed, refer to Figure 10-10.

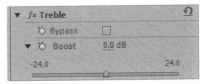

*Figure 10-10 The properties of the **Treble** effect*

34. Move the CTI to the beginning of the sequence in the **Timeline** panel. Press the SPACEBAR key to play the clip.

35. In the **Effect Controls** panel, move the **Boost** slider left or right. While moving the **Boost** slider, notice the difference in the frequency of the clip. It increases or decreases depending on the movement of the slider. Set the frequency based on your requirement.

    Next, you will apply the **Reverb** effect to the **audio_speech.wma** clip. This effect is used to add an effect similar to the sound of an audio playing in a room.

36. Delete the **Treble** audio effect from the **Effect Controls** panel.

37. Select the **Reverb** audio effect in the **Effects** panel. Press and hold the left mouse button on it and drag it to the **audio_speech.wma** clip in the **Timeline** panel. Release the left mouse button; the **Reverb** effect is applied to the clip.

38. Make sure the **audio_speech.wma** clip is selected in the **Timeline** panel. In the **Effect Controls** panel, the applied **Reverb** effect is displayed.

39. Expand the **Reverb** effect by clicking on the arrow on its left, if not already expanded; the **Custom Setup** and **Individual Parameters** properties are displayed.

40. Expand the **Individual Parameters** property; the parameters corresponding to this property are displayed, as shown in Figure 10-11.

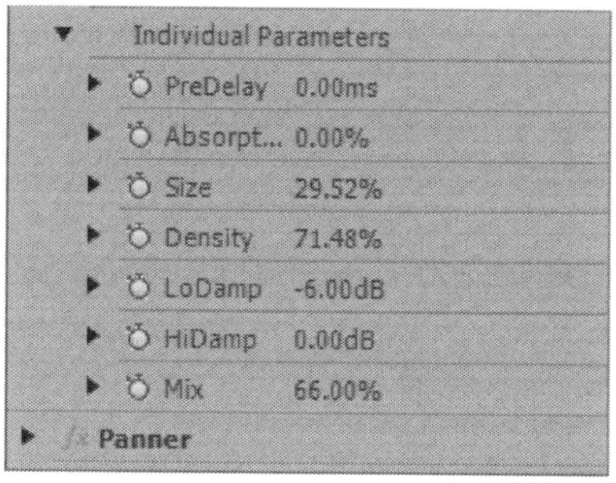

*Figure 10-11 The parameters of the **Reverb** effect*

You can adjust the values of the **Reverb** effect either by using the graphical controls in the **Custom Setup** property or by modifying parameters in the **Individual Parameters** property. In the following steps, you will adjust the parameters of the **Reverb** effect by using the parameters in the **Individual Parameters** property.

41. Expand various properties such as **PreDelay**, **Absorption**, **Size**, **Density**, and so on in **Individual Parameters**; the corresponding sliders are displayed, as shown in Figure 10-12.

    The **PreDelay** property is used to specify the distance the sound travels from source to listener via the reflecting walls in a live environment. The **Absorption** property specifies how much of the sound would be absorbed in terms of percentage. The **Size** property is used to specify the apparent relative size of the room. The **Density** property specifies the space between the first and subsequent reflections of the reverbs. The higher the size value, the greater will be the density range. The **LoDamp** property specifies the amount of dampening for low frequencies. The **HiDamp** property specifies the amount of dampening for high frequencies. The **Mix** property is used to control the amount of reverb.

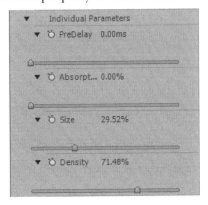

*Figure 10-12 Partial view of **Reverb** parameters*

42. Move the CTI to the beginning of the sequence in the **Timeline** panel. Press the SPACEBAR key to play the clip.

43. Drag the sliders corresponding to different properties and notice the effect on the **audio_speech.wma** clip.

44. Choose the **Edit** button next to **Custom Setup**; the **Clip Fx Editor** dialog box is displayed, as shown in Figure 10-13.

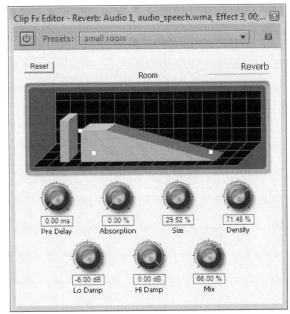

*Figure 10-13 The **Clip Fx Editor** dialog box*

45. Choose the **Reset** button available on the top left in this dialog box, refer to Figure   Reset
10-13; the parameters are set to their default values.

Next, you will adjust the parameters of the **Reverb** effect by using the **Custom Setup** property.

46. Play the **audio_speech.wma** clip and drag the three white handles, refer to Figure 10-14, and notice the effect in the sound of the audio clip.

You can also use some of the presets available for modifying the sound of the audio clip.

47. Choose the **Reset** button available on the left in this dialog box. Now, close this dialog box.

48. Choose the **Presets** button located on the right of the **Reverb** effect in the **Effect**   🕑
Controls panel; a flyout is displayed with a list of available presets, as shown in Figure 10-15.

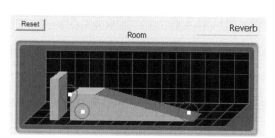

Figure 10-14 *The highlighted white handles*

Figure 10-15 *The flyout after choosing the Presets button*

49. Select one of the presets from the flyout. Note that the parameters in the **Custom Setup** and **Individual Parameters** properties change accordingly.

50. Play the clip and notice the difference in the pitch after applying the preset.

Now, you will apply the **Balance** effect to the **audio_speech.wma** audio clip. This effect is used to control the relative volumes of the left and right channels. This effect is available only for stereo clips.

51. Delete the **Reverb** audio effect from the **Effect Controls** panel.

52. Select the **Balance** audio effect in the **Effects** panel. Press and hold the left mouse button on it and drag it to the **audio_speech.wma** clip in the **Timeline** panel. Release the left mouse button; the **Balance** effect is applied to the clip.

53. Make sure the **audio_speech.wma** clip is selected in the **Timeline** panel. In the **Effect Controls** panel, the **Balance** effect that you have applied is displayed.

54. Expand the **Balance** effect by clicking on the arrow on its left, if not already expanded; the **Bypass** and **Balance** properties are displayed.

55. Expand the **Balance** property; its slider is displayed, as shown in Figure 10-16.

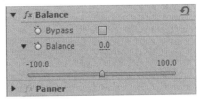

*Figure 10-16 The properties of the **Balance** effect*

The positive value for the **Balance** property signifies the increment in proportion of the right channel and the negative value for the **Balance** property signifies the increment in proportion of the left channel.

56. Move the CTI to the beginning of the sequence in the **Timeline** panel. Press the SPACEBAR key to play the clip.

57. In the **Effect Controls** panel, move the slider to left or right. While moving the slider, notice the difference in the relative volume of the left and right channel clips.

58. Press CTRL+S to save the file.

Tutorial 2

In this tutorial, you will edit multiple audio tracks by using Audio Mixer.
(Expected Time: 25 min)

The following steps are required to complete this tutorial:

a.   Open the project file.
b.   Edit audio using Audio Mixer.

Opening the Project File

In this section, you will open the project file.

1. First, open the *chapter10_audio mixer.prproj* file that you have downloaded from the CADCIM website.

2. Save the *chapter10_audio mixer.prproj* file to the location *\Documents\Adobe Premiere Tutorials\c10_premiere_cc_tut* with the name *chapter10_audio mixer_02.prproj*. The *chapter10_audio mixer_02* file is displayed, as shown in Figure 10-17.

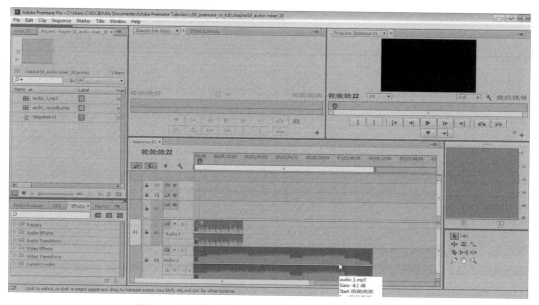

Figure 10-17 *The chapter10_audio mixer_02 file*

Editing Audio Using Audio Track Mixer

You may need to expand the audio tracks to view the audio clips properly. To work with the Audio Mixer, first you need to change the current workspace to the Audio workspace.

1. Choose **Window > Workspace > Audio** from the menu bar; the **Audio Track Mixer** panel is displayed on the screen, as shown in Figure 10-18.

    In the **Audio Track Mixer** panel, each Audio Mixer track corresponds to a track in the current sequence in the **Timeline** panel. Each track is labeled at the bottom of the Audio Mixer with the same name that the track has in the **Timeline** panel, refer to Figure 10-18. By default, the Audio Mixer tracks are named as Audio 1, Audio 2, Audio 3, Audio 4, and Master. You can modify the default names based on your requirement.

    Next, you will modify the names of the Audio 1 and Audio 2 tracks.

2. Select the **Audio 1** name in the **Audio Track Mixer** panel; it is highlighted, as shown in Figure 10-19.

3. Next, enter the name **audio_speech** in it and press the ENTER key; the name of the track is changed. Note that the track name in the **Timeline** panel is also changed accordingly, refer to Figure 10-20.

4. Modify the name of the **Audio 2** track as **audio_music**.

5. Make sure the CTI is placed at the beginning of the sequence and play the sequence. The VU (volume unit) meters in the **Audio Track Mixer** panel show the volume levels, as shown in Figure 10-21.

Figure 10-18 The **Audio Track Mixer** panel in the **Audio** workspace

Figure 10-19 The track
name highlighted

Figure 10-20 The track name changed in the **Timeline** panel

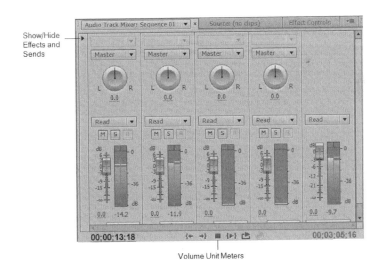

Show/Hide
Effects and
Sends

Volume Unit Meters

Figure 10-21 The volume levels in the VU meters

You will notice that the volume level of the **audio_music** track is very high and you cannot hear the audio of the **audio_speech** track properly. Therefore, you need to adjust the volume level of both the tracks using the **Audio Track Mixer** panel so that both tracks are clearly audible.

6. In the **Audio Track Mixer** panel, click over the edit box located below the VU meter of the **audio_music** track; the value is highlighted in the edit box.

7. Enter **-18** in the edit box and press the ENTER key; the volume level of the **audio_music** track is lowered. Note that the slider of the VU meter also moves down as you enter the new value in the edit box.

   You can also adjust the volume level of the audio tracks by dragging the slider of the VU meter up or down.

8. In the **Audio Track Mixer** panel, press and hold the left mouse button over the slider of the VU meter of the **audio_speech** track and drag it upward till the edit box displays the value 3.0. Alternatively, you can enter this value in the edit box given below the slider. It is recommended that you watch the VU meter of the **Master** track while adjusting the volume level of other tracks.

9. Move the CTI to the beginning of the sequence and play the sequence. The volume level of both the tracks are adjusted and you can hear the audio of both the tracks properly.

   Next, you will apply an audio effect to the audio track using the **Audio Track Mixer** panel.

10. In the **Audio Track Mixer** panel, choose the **Show/Hide Effects and Sends** arrow, refer to Figure 10-21; it expands and displays the empty panels, as shown in Figure 10-22.

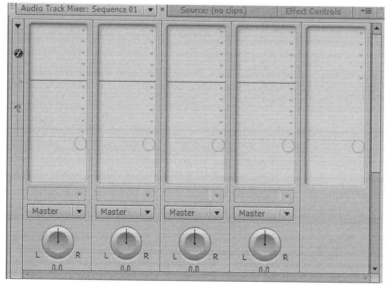

*Figure 10-22 The empty panels in the **Audio Track Mixer** panel*

11. Move the cursor over the **Effect Selection** button for the **audio_speech** track; it is activated now, refer to Figure 10-23.

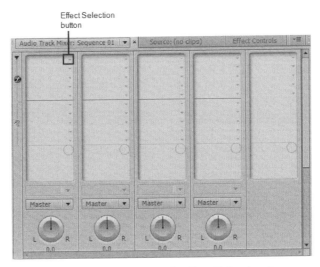

*Figure 10-23 The activated **Effect Selection** button*

12. Choose the **Effect Selection** button; a flyout is displayed with a list of audio effects. Next, choose **Trim and Pitch > PitchShifter** from the flyout, as shown in Figure 10-24; the selected effect is applied to the **audio_speech** track and is displayed on the track, as shown in Figure 10-25.

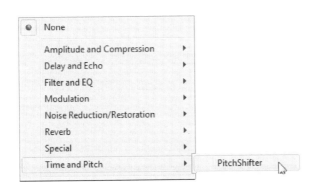

*Figure 10-24 Choosing **PitchShifter** from the flyout*

*Figure 10-25 The **PitchShifter** effect applied on the **audio_speech** track*

13. Choose the **Solo Track** button located above the VU meter of the **audio_speech** track. The **Solo Track** button is used to isolate the track corresponding to it. Also, it mutes the other tracks simultaneously. Note that when you choose the **Solo Track** button, the **Mute Track** button for the other tracks is chosen automatically.

Note
*You can choose the **Solo Track** button for more than one track to listen to a group of tracks.*

By default, the **Pitch** property is displayed at the bottom of the track for the **PitchShifter** effect, refer to Figure 10-25.

14. Move the CTI to the beginning of the track and choose the **Play-Stop Toggle** button located at the bottom of the **Audio Track Mixer** panel. Note that only the **audio_speech** track starts playing.

15. Next, press and hold the **Set the value for the selected parameter** icon on the circle above the **Pitch** property and drag the cursor to modify the pitch of the audio based on your requirement.

16. Click on the arrow on the right of **Pitch**; a flyout is displayed, as shown in Figure 10-26.

*Figure 10-26 The flyout displayed by clicking on the arrow located on the right of **Pitch***

Next, choose the required option to modify the audio of the **audio_speech** track.

17. Choose the **Effect Selection** button; a flyout is displayed. Choose the **None** option from the flyout; the **PitchShifter** effect is removed.

18. Choose the **Show/Hide Effects and Sends** arrow to collapse the panels.

19. Press CTRL+S to save the file.

Tutorial 3

In this tutorial, you will use various automation modes. **(Expected Time: 20 min)**

The following steps are required to complete this tutorial:

a. Open the project file.
b. Automate changes in audio tracks by using audio mixer.

Opening the Project File

In this section, you will open the project file.

1. Open the *chapter10_audio mixer_02.prproj* file that is created in Tutorial 2.

2. Save the file at the location *Documents\Adobe Premiere Tutorials\c10_premiere_cc_tut* with the name *chapter10_automatechanges*. The *chapter10_automatechanges.prproj* file is displayed.

Using Audio Track Mixer to Automate Changes in Audio Tracks

First, you will set new volume levels for the **audio_speech** track by lowering and raising its volume at different intervals in the sequence. In this section, you will automate changes in audio track by using audio mixer.

1. In the **Audio Track Mixer** panel, select the **Write** option from the **Automation Mode** drop-down list, as shown in Figure 10-27.

*Figure 10-27 Selecting the **Write** option from the
Automation Mode drop-down list*

By default, the **Read** automation mode is selected for the **audio_speech** track. The **Read** automation mode is used to adjust the track volume and other audio properties for the entire track uniformly. On selecting the **Write** option from the **Automation Mode** drop-down list, you will notice that the VU meter slider is currently at 3.0, refer to Figure 10-28.

Figure 10-28 The VU meter slider

In the **Write** automation mode, the adjustments made while playing the sequence are recorded as keyframes.

2.   Choose the **Solo Track** button for the **audio_speech** track, if it is not chosen.

3.   Make sure the CTI is set to the beginning of the sequence in the **Timeline** panel and play the sequence.

4.   In the **Audio Mixer** panel, drag the VU meter slider up and down for raising and lowering the volume of the **audio_speech** track. Next, press the SPACEBAR key to pause the playback. Note that the automation mode in the drop-down list is automatically changed to **Touch**. Now, if you again play the sequence, then the VU meter slider will jump back to its original value 3.0.

5.   Choose the button on the top right of the **Audio Track Mixer** panel; a flyout is displayed, as shown in Figure 10-29.

By default, the **Switch to Touch after Write** option is chosen in this flyout. This option is used to automatically switch from **Write** to **Touch** when you pause the playback. The **Touch** automation mode specifies that if you change the volume of an audio and then stop changing it and release the mouse button, then the audio will go back to its original volume in a certain period of time. Usually, in the **Touch** animation mode, a keyframe is recorded when you pause a playback and that keyframe always return to its original value.

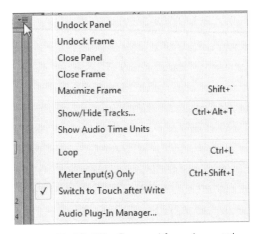

Figure 10-29 The flyout with various options

6. Choose the **Switch to Touch after Write** option from the flyout to disable it.

7. Next, set the automation mode to **Write** and play the sequence. Also, drag the VU meter slider to increase and decrease the volume. Now, pause the playback and play it again. Notice that the VU meter slider does not jump back to its original position.

Note
*It is recommended that you switch back to the **Read** automation mode immediately after making the adjustments. By doing so, the changes to the volume will not be recorded accidentally.*

Note that while working with the **Audio Track Mixer** panel, the changes made do not affect the clip but affect the track of the clip. The changes made in the track in the **Write** automation mode are displayed as keyframes in the **Timeline** panel. To view those keyframes, you need to follow the steps given below:

8. Choose the **Show Keyframes** button from the **audio_speech** track in the **Timeline** panel; a flyout is displayed, as shown in Figure 10-30. Choose the **Track Keyframes** option from the flyout; the **Add-Remove Keyframe** button gets activated. Now, click on this button to insert the keyframes one by one on the **audio_speech** track in the **Timeline** panel, as shown in Figure 10-31.

*Figure 10-30 The flyout displayed on choosing the **Show Keyframes** button*

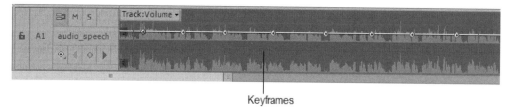

Keyframes

*Figure 10-31 The keyframes on the **audio_speech** track*

You may need to zoom in the sequence to view the keyframes properly.

Next, you will record the keyframes in the **Touch** automation mode.

9. Invoke the **Pen Tool** from the **Tools** panel and select all the keyframes in the **Timeline**
    panel by dragging a selection box around them, refer to Figure 10-32.

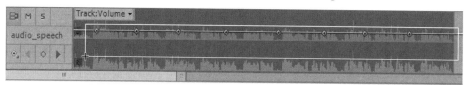

*Figure 10-32 The keyframes selected using the **Pen** tool*

10. Press the DELETE button; the selected keyframes are deleted.

11. In the **Audio Track Mixer** panel, select the **Touch** automation mode for the **audio_speech**
    track.

12. Move the CTI to the beginning of the track in the **Timeline** panel and play the sequence.

13. In the **Audio Track Mixer** panel, drag the VU meter slider down and then release the
    left mouse button. Again, drag the VU meter slider down and release the left mouse
    button. Next, pause the playback.

    Note that after releasing the left mouse button, the VU meter slider goes back to the value
    that was set when you started recording. You can ascertain this time. To do so, choose **Edit
    > Preferences > Audio** from the menu bar; the **Preferences** dialog box is displayed with
    the **Audio** option selected in it.

    On the right of the **Preferences** dialog box, the default value 1.0 is displayed in the
    Automatch Time edit box. This value indicates the time VU meter slider will take in going
    back to the value that was set when recording was started, refer to Figure 10-33. You can
    change this time based on your requirement. Choose the **OK** button to close this dialog
    box.

    Next, you will record the keyframes in the **Latch** automation mode. In the **Latch** automation
    mode, if you pause the playback and release the left mouse button, then the VU meter
    slider will stay at the last set value.

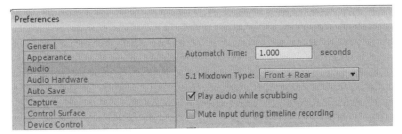

*Figure 10-33 The **Automatch Time** edit box in the **Preferences** dialog box*

14. In the **Audio Track Mixer** panel, select the **Latch** automation mode for the **audio_speech** track.

15. Move the CTI to the beginning of the track in the **Timeline** panel and play the sequence.

16. In the **Audio Track Mixer** panel, drag the VU meter slider down and then release the left mouse button.

    Note that after releasing the left mouse button, the VU meter slider stays at the value that you had set last.

Note
In the Touch automation mode, when you pause the playback, the VU meter slider goes back to the value that was set when you started making adjustments. On the other hand, in the Latch automation mode, the VU meter slider stays at the value that you adjusted last.

If you want to hear the sound of the audio track before making adjustments in it using various automation modes, then follow the steps given below:

17. In the **Audio Track Mixer** panel, select the **Off** automation mode for the **audio_speech** track.

18. Move the CTI to the beginning of the track in the **Timeline** panel and play the sequence to hear the sound of the original audio track.

19. Press CTRL+S to save the file.

Tutorial 4

In this tutorial, you will use the **Time Remapping** effect to vary the speed of the video portion of a clip.   **(Expected Time: 20 min)**

The following steps are required to complete this tutorial:

a. Open the project file.
b. Apply time remapping effect.

Opening the Project File

In this section, you will open the project file.

1. First, open the *chapter10_time_remapping.prproj* file that you have downloaded from the CADCIM website.

2. Save the *chapter10_time_remapping.prproj* file with the name *chapter10_time_remapping_02.prproj* at the location *\Documents\Adobe Premiere Tutorials\c10_premiere_cc_tut*.

Applying the Time Remapping Effect

The **Time Remapping** effect is used to change the frame rate at which the video is playing. Therefore, it changes the speed of the video portion of a clip. You can create the slow motion and fast motion effects in a video using the **Time Remapping** effects in which the rate of speed varies.

1. In the **Timeline** panel, click on the icon on the top of the **beach clip (7).mov** in the V1 track; a flyout is displayed, as shown in Figure 10-34.

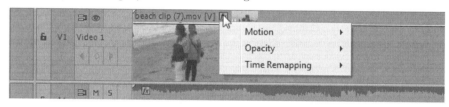

Figure 10-34 The flyout displayed

2. Choose the **Time Remapping > Speed** option from the flyout; a horizontal line on this track specifies the time remapping speed, as shown in Figure 10-35.

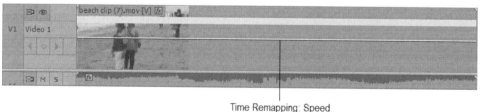

*Figure 10-35 The V1 track after selecting the **Time Remapping** effect*

Next, you will change the speed of the video between 00:00:05.08 and 00:00:14:05 frames.

3. Click on the **Playhead Position** just below the **Sequence 01** label in the **Timeline** panel; it is converted into an edit box. Enter **5.08** in it and press the ENTER key; the CTI moves to the specified frame.

Next, you will create a keyframe on that frame.

4. Move the cursor over a point where the CTI and the horizontal line intersect each other, refer to Figure 10-36.

Figure 10-36 The cursor at the intersection

5. Press and hold the CTRL key; the cursor is changed to an arrow cursor with a little plus sign with it. Next, click on the specified point; a keyframe is created, as shown in Figure 10-37.

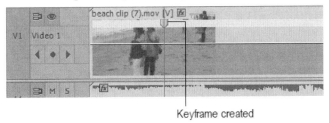

Figure 10-37 The keyframe at 00:00:05:08 frame

6. Create another keyframe at 00:00:14:05 frame by using the same method as discussed previously. The two keyframes are displayed in Figure 10-38.

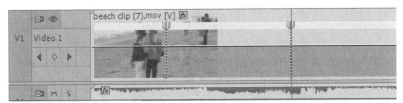

Figure 10-38 Two keyframes on the video clip

7. Move the cursor over the horizontal line between the two keyframes. Press and hold the left mouse button and drag it upward till the tooltip displays 170%, refer to Figure 10-39. Notice that it is not affecting the audio of the clip.

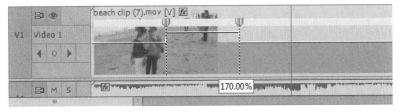

Figure 10-39 The horizontal line displayed on dragging the cursor upward

By dragging the cursor upward, you can increase the speed of the video. Also, the tooltip displays the change in the speed as a percentage of the original speed.

8. Move the CTI to the beginning of the sequence and play it. Notice the difference in the speed of the clip between the two keyframes.

    Next, you will decrease the speed between those two keyframes.

9. Move the cursor over the horizontal line between the two keyframes. Press and hold the left mouse button and drag the cursor downward till the tooltip displays 50.00%, refer to Figure 10-40.

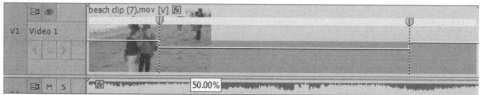

Figure 10-40 The horizontal line displayed on dragging the cursor downward

10. Move the CTI to the beginning of the sequence and play the sequence.

    Notice the difference in the speed of the clip between the two keyframes. Also, note that the change in the speed is instantaneous. To avoid the instantaneous change, you need to split the keyframes using the steps given below.

11. Move the cursor over the 00:00:05:08 keyframe. Press and hold the left mouse button and drag the keyframe toward left slightly; the keyframe is split into two halves, acting as two separate keyframes for the beginning and end of the speed change, as shown in Figure 10-41.

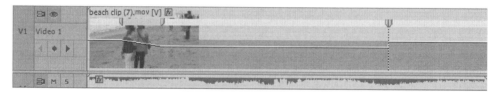

Figure 10-41 The separated keyframes

12. Make sure the CTI is at the beginning of the sequence and play it. You will notice a gradual change in the speed of the video clip.

    The process of separating keyframes to avoid the instantaneous change is known as speed ramping. You can perform the same process for the keyframe at 00:00:14:05 frame.

    The gray area between the halves of the keyframes specifies the length of the speed transition. If you click on the gray area, a blue colored curve control will appear, as shown in Figure 10-42.

13. To change the acceleration or deceleration of the speed, drag the handles of the blue colored curve control based on your requirement, refer to Figure 10-43. On doing so, the change of speed eases in or eases out based on the curve of the speed ramp.

Figure 10-42 The blue colored curve control displayed on the gray area

Figure 10-43 The curve control modified

 Note

On changing the speed of a clip, the duration of the clip will change. On increasing the speed, the total duration will decrease. Similarly, on decreasing the speed, the duration of the clip will increase.

Next, you will move the split and unsplit keyframes in the **Timeline** panel to show the **Time Remapping** effect.

14. To move the split keyframes in the **Timeline** panel, move the cursor over the gray area between the split keyframes; the shape of the cursor is changed, as shown in Figure 10-44.

Figure 10-44 The shape of the cursor changed on moving to gray area

15. Press and hold the left mouse button and drag it toward left or right based on your requirement.

16. To move the unsplit keyframe in the **Timeline** panel, press and hold the ALT key and move the cursor over the unsplit keyframe; the cursor is changed, as shown in Figure 10-45.

Figure 10-45 The cursor after moving it to an unsplit frame

17. Press and hold the left mouse button and drag it toward left or right based on your requirement.

Next, you will play a clip backward and forward using the **Time Remapping** effect.

18. Import the **road drive (5).AVI** clip from the location *Documents\Adobe Premiere Tutorials\ c10_premiere_cc_tut\Media Files\Video\Norway*. Next, add it to the sequence in the **V1** track just after the existing clip.

19. Next, zoom in the sequence to view the **road drive (5).AVI** clip properly.

20. In the **Timeline** panel, click on the icon on the top of the **road drive(5).AVI** clip in the **V1** track; a flyout is displayed.

21. Choose the **Time Remapping > Speed** option from the flyout; the video clip now displays the text **Time Remapping: Speed**. The horizontal line on the track indicates the time remapping.

22. Press and hold the CTRL key and click on the horizontal line to create a keyframe on the **road drive (5).AVI** clip on any frame.

23. Again, press and hold the CTRL key, click on the keyframe and drag it to the place where you want the backward motion to end. Two keyframes are added for the forward playback of the clip, refer to Figure 10-46. Next, release the CTRL key.

*Figure 10-46 The keyframes on the **road drive (5)** clip*

While dragging the keyframe, a tooltip is displayed showing the speed as a negative percentage of original speed. This negative speed indicates backward motion. The video clip between the first two keyframes shows arrows pointing toward left indicating backward motion. The video clip between the last two keyframes is played forward.

24. Move the CTI to the beginning of the **road drive (5).AVI** clip and play the sequence to view the backward and forward motions.

The video clip plays backward at full speed from the first keyframe to second. Then, it plays forward at full speed from the second to third keyframe. Finally, it returns to the frame at which the backward motion began. This effect is known as the **Palindrome Reverse** effect.

Next, you will freeze the video portion using the **Time Remapping** effect.

25. Add the **road drive (5).AVI** clip again in the **V1** track to create an instance of it.

26. In the **Timeline** panel, click on the icon on the top of the instance of the **road drive(5). AVI** clip; a flyout is displayed.

27. Choose the **Time Remapping > Speed** option from the flyout; the video clip now displays the **Time Remapping: Speed** text. Also, a horizontal line is displayed on the track indicating the time remapping.

28. Press and hold the CTRL key and click on the horizontal line to create a keyframe on the **road drive (5).AVI** clip at any frame as required.

29. Press and hold the CTRL+ALT key, and then click on the keyframe and drag it to the place where you want the frozen video portion to end. Release the CTRL+ALT keys. You will notice vertical lines displayed between the two keyframes indicating a frozen video clip, refer to Figure 10-47.

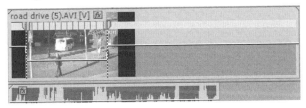

Figure 10-47 *The vertical lines indicating the frozen video clip*

30. Move the CTI to the beginning of the instance of the **road drive (5).AVI** clip and play the sequence to view the frozen video portion between the two keyframes.

31. Press the CTRL+S keys to save the file.

Tutorial 5

In this tutorial, you will keyout the green background from a clip and then composite it with another clip using the **Ultra Key** effect. The output of the sequence at frame 00:00:01:11 is shown in Figure 10-48. **(Expected Time:20 min)**

Figure 10-48 *The output of the sequence at frame 00:00:01:11*

The following steps are required to complete this tutorial:

a.   Create a new project.
b.   Import clips
c.   Apply ultra key effect.

Creating a New Project

In this section, you will create a new project.

1.   Open Adobe Premiere Pro CC; the **Welcome to Adobe Premiere Pro** window is displayed. Next, choose the **New Project** button; the **New Project** dialog box is displayed.

2.   In the **General** tab, type **chapter10_ultrakey** in the **Name** text box.

3.   In the **Location** area, make sure the location is *\Documents\Adobe Premiere Tutorials\ c10_premiere_cc_tut*.

4.   Choose the **Scratch Disks** tab and select the **Same as Project** option from the drop-down list corresponding to the **Captured Video**, **Captured Audio**, **Video Previews**, and **Audio Previews** areas.

5.   Choose the **OK** button in the **New Project** dialog box; the new project is displayed with various panels. Also, the file is saved with the name *chapter10_ultrakey.prproj* at the location *\Documents\Adobe Premiere Tutorials\c10_premiere_cc_tut*.

    You will create a sequence for this file after importing the media files in it. Next, you will import the media files in it.

Importing the Clips

In this section, you will import the clips.

1.   Press the CTRL+I keys; the **Import** dialog box is displayed.

2.   In this dialog box, browse to the location *\Documents\Adobe Premiere Tutorials\c10_premiere_cc_tut\ Media Files\Video\Locked Backdrop*; the PNG files are displayed in it.

3.   Select the **hcw_locked_backdrop.00000.png** file from the **Import** dialog box.

4.   Select the **Image Sequence** check box and choose the **Open** button; the image sequence including all the *png* images is displayed in the **Project** panel with the name **hcw_locked_backdrop.00000.png**.

 Note
You can download the green screen plates used in this chapter from the following link:
http://www.hollywoodcamerawork.us/greenscreenplates.html
Footage Courtesy: *Hollywood Camera Work*

5. Click on the name of the video clip in the **Project** panel; it is converted into a text box. Type **green screen** as the new name for this clip and press the ENTER key.

6. Next, import the **beach clip (2).mov** clip from the *\Documents\Adobe Premiere Tutorials\ c10_premiere_cc_tut\Media Files\Video\Beach clips* folder that you have downloaded from the CADCIM website. Then, superimpose the **green screen** clip on the **beach clip (2).mov** clip.

    Next, you will create a sequence for the project.

7. Choose the **New Item** button at the bottom of the **Project** panel; a flyout is displayed. Choose the **Sequence** option from the flyout; the **New Sequence** dialog box is displayed.

8. In the **Available Presets** area of the **Sequence Presets** tab, expand the **DV-PAL** option, if not already expanded. Now, select the **Widescreen 48kHz** preset; the settings of this preset are displayed on the right in the **Preset Description** area.

    Note that the settings of the **Widescreen 48KHz** preset are very similar to the settings of the **beach clip (2).mov** clip in the **Project** panel.

9. In the **Sequence Name** text box, make sure that the **Sequence 01** is displayed. Next, choose the **OK** button in this dialog box; the new sequence is displayed in the **Timeline** and **Project** panels.

    Next, you will add the imported clips to the **Sequence 01** in the **Timeline** panel.

Applying the Ultra Key Effect

In this section, you will apply the ultra key effect.

1. Add the **beach clip (2).mov** clip in the **V1** track. Also, add the **green screen** video clip in the **V2** track. Press the BACKSLASH key to view both the clips properly. The clips are displayed in the sequence and Program Monitor, as shown in Figure 10-49.

  Note
*If the **Clip Mismatch Warning** message box is displayed, choose **Keep existing settings** from the message box.*

    Notice that the size of the **green screen** video clip is too large to fit properly on the screen in the Program Monitor. So, you need to adjust its size.

2. Select the **green screen** video clip in the **Timeline** panel and then select the **Effect Controls** panel; the properties of the **green screen** video clip are displayed.

3. Expand the **Motion** property and set the value **55.0** in the **Scale** edit box; the **green screen** video clip is scaled, as shown in Figure 10-50.

Next, you will apply the **Ultra Key** effect to the **green screen** clip to make its green background transparent.

4. Select the **Effects** panel, if it is not already selected.

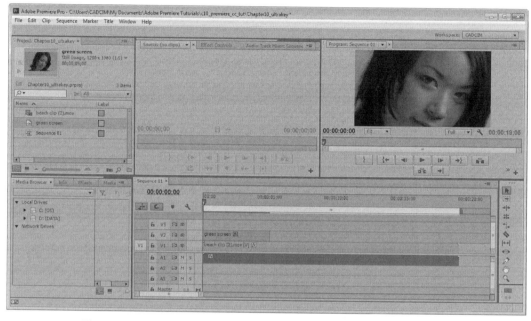

Figure 10-49 The video clips in the sequence and the Program Monitor

*Figure 10-50 The modified **green screen** clip*

5. Expand **Video Effects** by clicking on the arrow on its left; various video effects are displayed.

6. Next, expand the **Keying** bin by clicking on the arrow on its left; various keying effects such as **Alpha Adjust**, **Blue Screen Key**, and so on are displayed.

7. Select the **Ultra Key** effect and drag it from the **Effects** panel to the **Timeline** panel over the **green screen** video clip in the **V2** track; the **Ultra Key** effect is applied to the green screen video clip. Also, its properties are displayed in the **Effect Controls** panel.

8. Make sure the **green screen** clip is selected in the **Timeline** panel. Then, expand the **Ultra Key** effect in the **Effect Controls** panel, if not already expanded; the properties of the **Ultra Key** effect are displayed, as shown in Figure 10-51. Make sure that **Composite** is selected in the **Output** drop-down list.

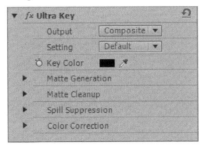

Figure 10-51 The properties of the **Ultra Key** effect in the **Effect Controls** panel

9. In the **Effect Controls** panel, choose the button similar to an eyedropper on the right of the **Key Color** property; the shape of the cursor is changed.

10. Move the cursor over the **green screen** clip in the Program Monitor and click on the green color to choose it; the chosen color becomes transparent. Therefore, you can view the **beach clip (2).mov** video clip in the background, refer to Figure 10-52. Notice that the color swatch on the right of the **Key Color** property displays the color that you have chosen using the eyedropper button.

Figure 10-52 The **beach clip (2).mov** as background in the Program Monitor

Note
You can also adjust the size and position of the **green screen** *video clip using the parameters in the* **Motion** *property.*

11. Press CTRL+S to save the file. Next, press the ENTER key to view the output of the sequence in the Program Monitor. The output of the sequence at frame 00:00:01:11 is displayed, as shown in Figure 10-53.

Figure 10-53 *The output of the sequence at frame 00:00:01:11*

Self-Evaluation Test

Answer the following questions and then compare them to those given at the end of this chapter:

1. Which of the following audio effects is used to increase or decrease the frequencies that are below or equal to 200 Hz?

    (a) **Bass**   (b) **PitchShifter**
    (c) **Delay**   (d) All of these

2. Which of the following effects is used to adjust the pitch of the incoming signal?

    (a) **Reverb**   (b) **Bass**
    (c) **PitchShifter**   (d) **Delay**

3. Which of the following effects is used to add an effect similar to the sound of an audio being played in a room?

    (a) **Delay**   (b) **Treble**
    (c) **Bass**   (d) **Reverb**

4. Which of the following properties determines the time lapse occurred before the echo starts playing?

    (a) **Bypass**   (b) **Mix**
    (c) **Delay**   (d) **Boost**

5. In the properties of the **Reverb** effect in the **Effect Controls** panel, the _____ property is used to specify the distance the sound would travel through reflecting wall and back to the listener in a live setting.

6. The _____ effect is used to control the relative volumes of the left and right channels of a stereo clip.

7. In Premiere, _____ is used to adjust volume levels and other characteristics for multiple audio tracks.

8. The **Pitch** parameter is used to specify the change in pitch in semitone steps. (T/F)

9. You can apply an audio effect to an audio clip using the **Audio Track Mixer** panel. (T/F)

10. The **Latch** automation mode is used to adjust the track volume and other audio properties for the entire track uniformly. (T/F)

Review Questions

Answer the following questions:

1. Which of the following effects is used to add echo to the sound of an audio clip for a specific time interval?

   (a) **Bass**   (b) **PitchShifter**
   (c) **Delay**   (d) **Reverb**

2. Which of the following effects is used to increase or decrease the higher frequencies equal or above 4000 Hz?

   (a) **Bass**   (b) **Treble**
   (c) **Reverb**   (d) Both (a) and (b)

3. Which of the following properties is used to specify the percentage of echo added to an audio to create multiple decaying echoes?

   (a) **FormantPreserve**   (b) **Feedback**
   (c) **FineTune**   (d) **Pitch**

4. The _____ button in the **Audio Mixer** panel is used to isolate the corresponding track and mute the other tracks.

5. The _____ animation mode records a keyframe when you pause the playback and that keyframe always returns the property to its original value.

6. The **Write** automation mode is used to record the adjustments you make as keyframes while playing the sequence. (T/F)

7. You can make the green background of a video clip transparent using the **Time Remapping** effect. (T/F)

8. The **Ultra Key** effect is used to change the frame rate at which the video is played. (T/F)

9. The **Pitch** parameter ranges between -12 and +12 semitones. (T/F)

EXERCISE

Exercise 1

Create a new project in Premiere as per the settings of your clips. Add some of your audio clips to the sequence. Try to apply various audio effects to the clips in the sequence and notice the difference. Use the **Audio Mixer** panel to modify the properties of multiple clips simultaneously. Also, use the **Ultra Key** effect and modify its properties in the **Effect Controls** panel to view the difference.

Answers to Self-Evaluation Test
1. a, **2.** c, **3.** d, **4.** c, **5. PreDelay**, **6. Balance**, **7. Audio Track Mixer**, **8.** T, **9.** T, **10.** F

Chapter *11*

Animating the Motion and Other Effects

Learning Objectives

After completing this chapter, you will be able to:

- *Animate the position of a clip*
- *Add keyframes to scale a clip*
- *Add keyframes to rotate a clip*
- *Copy keyframes*
- *Interpolate keyframes*
- *Apply the interpolation methods*
- *Create picture-in-picture effect*
- *Animate the Basic 3D effect*
- *Apply and animate the Camera View effect*

INTRODUCTION

In Chapter 9, you learned how to position, scale, and rotate a clip using the parameters in the **Motion** effect in the **Effect Controls** panel. Also, you learned about the anchor point of a clip and how the position and anchor point are related to each other. In this chapter, you will learn to animate the **Motion** effects, copy keyframes, interpolate keyframes, work with keyframes, use **PiPs Presets** effects, and animate the **Basic 3D** and **Camera View** effects.

KEYFRAME INTERPOLATION

In Premiere, interpolation means generating new values between two keyframes. When you move a clip from left to right by creating the two position keyframes, then the frames between these two keyframes get interpolated to make the movement appear smooth. Usually, there are two types of interpolation, Temporal Interpolation and Spatial Interpolation. The Temporal Interpolation refers to the changes over time. It determines the changes in velocity of an object moving across a motion path. The Spatial Interpolation refers to the changes in shape. The Spatial Interpolation is used to determine whether the corners will be rounded or angular. There are various types of Spatial and Temporal Interpolation.

TUTORIALS

Before you start the tutorials, you need to download the *c11_premiere_cc_tut.zip* file from *www.cadcim.com*. The path of the file is as follows: *Textbooks > Animation and Visual Effects > Adobe Premiere Pro > Adobe Premiere Pro CC: A Tutorial Approach*

Next, extract the contents of the zip file at *\Documents\Adobe Premiere Tutorials*.

Tutorial 1

In this tutorial, you will animate the **Motion** effect using keyframes. The output of the sequence at frame 00:00:06:13 is shown in Figure 11-1.   **(Expected Time: 25 min)**

Figure 11-1 The output of the sequence at frame 00:00:06:13

The following steps are required to complete this tutorial:

a.   Open the project file.
b.   Animate the position of clip.
c.   Animate the scale of clip.
d.   Animate the rotation of clip.

Opening the Project File

In this section, you will open the project file.

1. Open the *chapter11.prproj* file that you have downloaded from the CADCIM website.

2. Save the *chapter11.prproj* file with the name *chapter11_02.prproj* to the location *\Documents\Adobe Premiere Tutorials\c11_premiere_cc_tut*. The *chapter11_02.prproj* file is displayed.

Animating the Position of the Clip

In this section, you will animate the position of the clip.

1. Choose **Window > Workspace > Effects** from the menu bar; the interface is changed, as shown in Figure 11-2.

*Figure 11-2 The interface displayed on choosing the **Effects** workspace*

2. In the Program Monitor, click on the **Select Zoom Level** button; a drop-down list is displayed. Select the **25%** option from the drop-down list; the clip is zoomed out in the Program Monitor, as shown in Figure 11-3.

    By adjusting the zoom level, you will be able to view and work with the bounding box of the **Motion** effects easily. Next, you will move the clip in the Program Monitor from left to right.

3. Double-click on the clip in the Program Monitor to select it; a bounding box with handles and a crosshair is displayed around the clip, as shown in Figure 11-4.

Figure 11-3   *Clip zoomed out in the Program Monitor*

Figure 11-4   *A bounding box around the clip*

When you select the clip in the Program Monitor, it also gets selected in the **Timeline** panel. Also, various effects such as **Motion**, **Opacity**, **Time Remapping**, and so on are displayed in the **Effect Controls** panel.

4. In the **Effect Controls** panel, expand the **Motion** effect to view its properties such as **Position**, **Scale**, **Rotation**, and so on.

   To move the clip from left to right in the Program Monitor, you need to work with the **Position** property.

5. Make sure the clip is selected in the Program Monitor and then drag it completely off the screen toward left, refer to Figure 11-5. Alternatively, modify the **Position** coordinate values to **-360, 288** in the **Effect Controls** panel to make the clip completely off the screen.

Figure 11-5   *The clip after dragging it off the screen*

You may need to increase the size of the Program Monitor to view the entire clip at the new position.

6. Press the HOME key to move the CTI to the beginning of the sequence, if it is not at the beginning. You will notice that the CTI also moves in the timeline view of the **Effect Controls** panel.

Next, you will add a keyframe for the current position of the clip.

7. In the **Effect Controls** panel, choose the **Toggle animation** button on the left of the **Position** property; a keyframe is added in the Timeline view for the **Position** property, as shown in Figure 11-6.

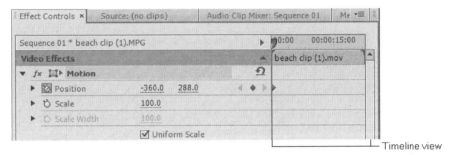

Figure 11-6 *A new keyframe in the timeline view*

8. Move the CTI to the frame 00:00:09:06 in the **Timeline** panel. The CTI also moves in the timeline view of the **Effect Controls** panel.

9. Modify the **Position** coordinate values to **1080, 288** in the **Effect Controls** panel; the clip is moved completely off the screen to the right, as shown in Figure 11-7. Also, another keyframe is created in the Timeline view for the **Position** property, where the CTI is placed, refer to Figure 11-8.

Figure 11-7 *The clip at the new position*

Figure 11-8 *The new keyframe for the new position of the clip*

Notice that when as you add keyframes to the timeline, a path is automatically created and displayed as a white colored curve in the Program Monitor, refer to Figure 11-7.

10. Press the HOME key to move the CTI to the beginning of the sequence and play the sequence to view the movement of the clip from left to right.

Animating the Scale of the Clip
In this section, you will animate the scale of the clip.

1. Choose the **Go to Previous Keyframe** button located on the right of the **Position** property in the **Effect Controls** panel to move the CTI to the first keyframe.

   You might need to choose the **Go to Previous Keyframe** button twice if the CTI was at the last keyframe.

2. Choose the **Toggle animation** button located on the left of the **Scale** property; a new keyframe is created in the Timeline view for the **Scale** property. Note that the value for the **Scale** property is **100** at this keyframe.

3. Move the CTI to the frame 00:00:04:15 in the **Effect Controls** panel to add a keyframe.

4. Modify the **Scale** value to **40**; another keyframe is created in the Timeline view for the **Scale** property.

5. Choose the **Go to Next Keyframe** button located on the right of the **Position** property to move the CTI to the second keyframe.

6. Modify the **Scale** value to **100**; another keyframe is created for the **Scale** property. Now, there are total three keyframes for the **Scale** property, refer to Figure 11-9.

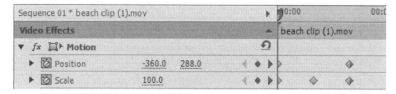

*Figure 11-9 Three keyframes for the **Scale** property*

7. Move the CTI to the beginning of the sequence and play it. Note that the position and scaling values of the clip keep on changing over time, based on the keyframes you have created.

 Note
You can also make the rate of change slow by moving the keyframes apart.

Animating the Rotation of the Clip

In this section, you will animate the rotation of the clip.

1. Press the HOME key to move the CTI to the first frame. Next, choose the **Toggle animation** button located on the left of the **Rotation** property; a new keyframe is created in the Timeline view for the **Rotation** property.

   The value for the **Rotation** Property is **0** at this keyframe.

2. Choose the **Go to Next Keyframe** button located on the right of the **Scale** property to move the CTI to the second keyframe.

3. Modify the **Rotation** value to **40**; another keyframe is created for the **Rotation** property.

4. Choose the **Go to Next Keyframe** button located on the right of the **Position** or **Scale** property to move the CTI to the third keyframe.

5. Modify the **Rotation** value to **0**; another keyframe is created for the **Rotation** property.

   Now, there is one keyframe each for the **Rotation**, **Position** and **Scale** properties, refer to Figure 11-10.

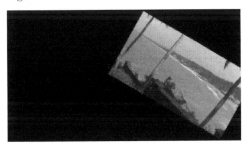

Figure 11-10 *The keyframes for the* ***Position****,* ***Scale****,
and* ***Rotation*** *properties*

6. Move the CTI to the beginning of the sequence and play it. Notice that the position, scaling, and rotation values of the clip keep on changing over time, based on the keyframes you have created, refer to Figure 11-11.

Figure 11-11 *The position of the clip at 00:00:05:19 frame*

Next, you will copy the existing keyframes in the **Effect Controls** panel.

7. In the **Effect Controls** panel, select the second keyframe of both the **Scale** and **Rotation** properties by dragging a selection box around them, refer to Figure 11-12.

8. Press and hold the ALT key and drag the keyframes toward right just after the third column of keyframes to the frame 00:00:12:21, refer to Figure 11-13. The keyframes are copied.

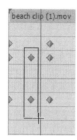 

Figure 11-12 The selection box   *Figure 11-13* The copied keyframes
around the keyframes

9. Similarly, copy the first column of keyframes of the **Position**, **Scale**, and **Rotation** properties and place them next to the fourth column of keyframes to the frame 00:00:15:00.

10. Move the CTI to the beginning of the sequence and play to the sequence view the animated effect.

11. Press CTRL+S to save the file. The output of the sequence at frame 00:00:06:13 is shown in Figure 11-14.

Figure 11-14 The output of the sequence at frame 00:00:06:13

Tutorial 2

In this tutorial, you will generate new values between two keyframes using the interpolation methods. The output of the sequence at frame 00:00:03:19 is shown in Figure 11-15.

(Expected Time: 20 min)

The following steps are required to complete this tutorial:

a. Open the project file.
b. Apply interpolation methods.

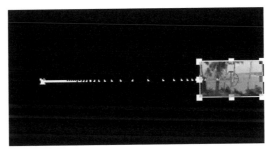

Figure 11-15 *The output of the sequence at frame 00:00:03:19*

Opening the Project File

In this section, you will open the project file.

1. Open the *chapter11_interpolation.prproj* file that you have downloaded from the CADCIM website. The opened file is shown in Figure 11-16.

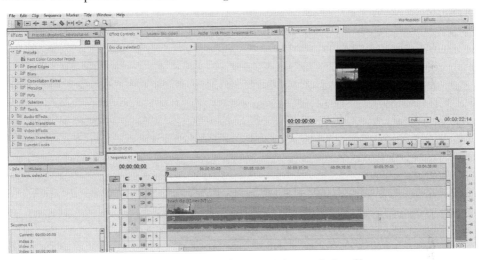

Figure 11-16 *The chapter11_interpolation file*

2. Save the *chapter11_interpolation.prproj* file to the location *\Documents\Adobe Premiere Tutorials\c11_premiere_cc_tut* with the name *chapter11_interpolation_02.prproj*.

Applying the Interpolation Methods

In this section, you will apply the interpolation methods.

1. Double-click on the clip in the Program Monitor; the path of the movement is displayed, as shown in Figure 11-17. Notice that there is a straight path for the movement of the clip.

2. Play the sequence; the clip starts moving from left to right in a straight line. This is known as the **Linear Spatial** interpolation.

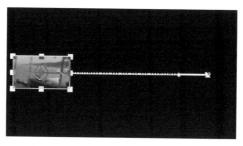

Figure 11-17 *The straight path for the movement of the clip*

3. In the **Effect Controls** panel, choose the **Go to Previous Keyframe** button located on the right of the **Position** properties; the clip is moved to the first keyframe.

4. Move the cursor over the clip handle; the shape of the cursor is changed, refer to Figure 11-18. Now, press and hold the left mouse button and move it to the top left corner to get a curved path, as shown in Figure 11-19.

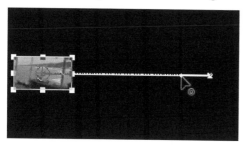

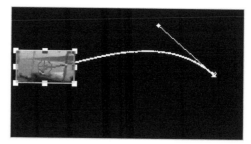

Figure 11-18   *The changed cursor after moving it to the clip handle*

Figure 11-19 *The curved path*

5. Play the sequence; the clip starts moving on the curved path. This is known as the **Bezier Spatial** interpolation.

6. Move the CTI to 00:00:01:14 frame. In the **Effect Controls** panel, modify the parameters for **Position** to **300.9, 462.1**; the curved path is changed, as shown in Figure 11-20. Also, a handle is created at the frame 00:00:01:14.

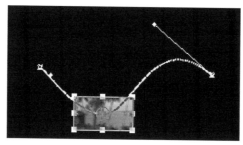

Figure 11-20 *The modified curve after changing the parameters*

7. Choose the **Go to Next Keyframe** button located on the right of the **Position** properties; the clip is moved to the last keyframe and a handle at the frame 00:00:01:14 is displayed in the Program Monitor.

    If you change the curve of the path by changing the parameters without adjusting the clip handles, then it is known as **Auto Bezier Interpolation**.

8. Modify the shape of the path by adjusting the clip handles, refer to Figure 11-21. While adjusting the handles, when you move one handle up, the other handle automatically moves down. This indicates that there is a relationship between the incoming and outgoing curves. This is known as **Continuous Bezier Interpolation**.

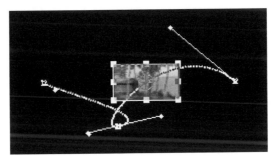

Figure 11-21 *The modified curve after moving the clip handles*

9. Move the cursor over one of the clip handles; the cursor is changed into a different shape. Next, press and hold the CTRL key and move the clip handle up, refer to Figure 11-22.

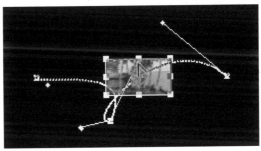

Figure 11-22 *The modified curve after moving one of the clip handles*

Next, you will change the current keyframe interpolation to **Linear Spatial Interpolation**.

10. In the timeline view of the **Effect Controls** panel, select the keyframe created between the first and last keyframes.

11. Press the DELETE key to delete the selected keyframe. Now, there are only two keyframes in the timeline view.

12. Select both the keyframes in the timeline view and right-click on them; a shortcut menu is displayed. Choose the **Spatial Interpolation** from the shortcut menu; a cascading menu is displayed, refer to Figure 11-23. Choose the **Linear** option from the cascading menu; the interpolation between the selected keyframes is changed to **Linear Spatial Interpolation**.

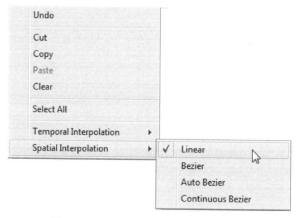

Figure 11-23 *The cascading menu*

Also, the path of the curve becomes straight in the Program Monitor, as shown in Figure 11-24. Now, when you play the sequence, the clip will move in a straight line.

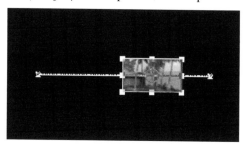

Figure 11-24 *The straight path*

In the **Temporal** interpolation, the rate of change between keyframes is affected. Next, you will create the gradual acceleration or deceleration between the two keyframes using the **Ease In** and **Ease Out** temporal interpolation methods. The **Ease Out** method is used to create a gradual acceleration out of a keyframe and **Ease In** method is used to create a gradual deceleration in a keyframe.

Before moving ahead, expand the **Position** property in the **Effect Controls** panel. Notice that in the Timeline view of the **Effect Controls** panel, a straight curve is displayed between the two keyframes, refer to Figure 11-25.

Figure 11-25 The straight curve in the timeline view

13. Make sure both the keyframes in the timeline view is selected and right-click on them; a shortcut menu is displayed. Choose the **Temporal Interpolation** option from the shortcut menu; a cascading menu is displayed. Choose the **Ease In** option from the cascading menu; the shape of the keyframes is changed in the timeline view, refer to Figure 11-26.

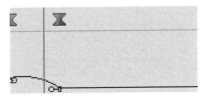

Figure 11-26 The changed shape of the keyframes

14. Make sure the keyframes are selected and then right-click on them; a shortcut menu is displayed. Choose the **Temporal Interpolation** option from the shortcut menu; a cascading menu is displayed. Next, choose the **Ease Out** option from the cascading menu; the shape of the keyframes is changed.

15. Press the HOME key and play the sequence; there is a gradual acceleration and deceleration in the speed of clip between the two keyframes.

    Notice that the shape of the curve between the two keyframes is changed in the timeline view, refer to Figure 11-27. This curve indicates the rate of change in the speed between two keyframes. Also, the curve goes up first and then comes down gradually indicating the gradual acceleration and deceleration.

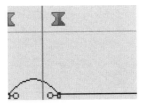

Figure 11-27 The changed shape of the curve

In the Program Monitor, the path or curve includes little dots. Each of these dots represents a frame. If the dots are closer, then the rate of change of speed will be slower. However, if the dots are apart, the rate of change will be faster.

16. Zoom in the timeline view to see the curve and keyframes properly using the slider at the bottom of the **Effect Controls** panel, refer to Figure 11-28.

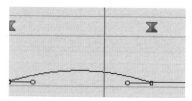

Figure 11-28 The timeline view zoomed in

17. Make sure the keyframes are selected in the timeline view. Move the cursor over one of the clip handles, refer to Figure 11-29. Next, press and hold the left mouse button and drag it toward right; the shape of the curve is changed, as shown in Figure 11-30. Also, the dots on the path move apart in the Program Monitor, refer to Figure 11-31.

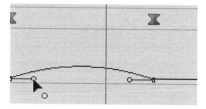

Figure 11-29 The cursor moved to one of the clip handles

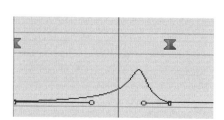   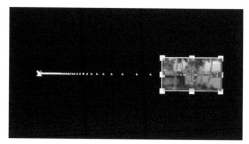

Figure 11-30   The changed shape of the curve   *Figure 11-31 The dots on the path moved apart*

18. Move the clip handles of another keyframe toward left; the shape of the curve is changed, as shown in Figure 11-32.

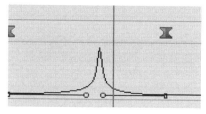

Figure 11-32 The shape of the curve after moving both clip handles

19. Press the HOME key and play the sequence. You will notice that speed of the clip slows down.

20. Press CTRL+S to save the file. The output of the sequence at frame 00:00:03:19 is shown in Figure 11-33.

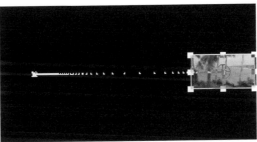

Figure 11-33 *The output of the sequence at frame 00:00:03:19*

Tutorial 3

In this tutorial, you will modify the properties of the **Motion** effects to reposition the graphics using the **PiPs** effects. The output of the sequence at frame 00:00:01:19 is shown in Figure 11-34. **(Expected Time: 25 min)**

Figure 11-34 *The output of the sequence at frame 00:00:01:19*

The following steps are required to complete this tutorial:

a. Open the project file.
b. Create picture-in picture effect.

Opening the Project File

In this section, you will open the project file.

1. Open the *chapter11_PIP.prproj* file that you have downloaded from the CADCIM website.

2. Save the *chapter11_PIP.prproj* file to the location *\Documents\Adobe Premiere Tutorials\ c11_premiere_cc_tut* with the new name *chapter11_PIP_02.prproj*. The *chapter11_PIP_02. prproj* file is displayed, as shown in Figure 11-35.

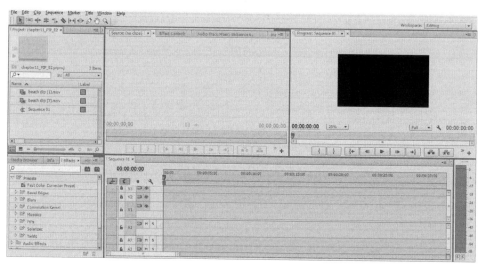

Figure 11-35 *The chapter11_PIP_02.prproj file opened*

Creating Picture-in-Picture Effect

In this section, you will create picture-in-picture effect.

1. In the **Project** panel, double-click on the **beach clip (1).mov**; it is opened in the Source Monitor.

2. Move the cursor over the **Drag Video Only** button at the bottom of the Source Monitor; the shape of the cursor is changed. Next, press and hold the left mouse button on it and drag it to the beginning of the **V1** track in the **Timeline** panel; the video portion of the **beach clip (1).mov** is placed in the **V1** track, as shown in Figure 11-36.

Figure 11-36 *The video portion of the **beach clip (1).mov** in the V1 track*

Note
*If the **Clip Mismatch Warning** message box is displayed, choose the **Change sequence settings** option from the message box.*

3. In the **Project** panel, double-click on the **beach clip (7).mov**; it is opened in the Source Monitor.

   Next, you will set the In and Out points for the **beach clip (7).mov** in the Source Monitor.

4. In the Source Monitor, enter **00:00:19:19** in the **Playhead Position** to move the **Playhead** to this frame. Next, choose the **Mark In** button to set the In point at this frame.

5. Again, move the CTI to **00:00:22:21** frame in the Source Monitor and then choose the **Mark Out** button to set the Out point at this frame.

Next, you will add the trimmed clip to the sequence in the **Timeline** panel.

6. Move the cursor over the **Drag Video Only** button at the bottom of the Source Monitor; the shape of the cursor is changed. Next, press and hold the left mouse button on it and drag it to the beginning of the **V2** track in the **Timeline** panel; the video portion of the **beach clip (7).mov** is placed in the **Timeline** panel.

7. Expand the **V2** track by double-clicking on the blank area at the right side of the **Toggle Track Output** button; the **beach clip (1).mov** and **beach clip (7).mov** are displayed in the **Timeline** panel, as shown in Figure 11-37.

*Figure 11-37 The **beach clip (1).mov** and **beach clip (7).mov** displayed in the **Timeline** panel*

If you play the sequence, you will only be able to see the **beach clip (7).mov** in the Program Monitor, which is located on the top track (**V2**). It covers the **beach clip (1).mov** beneath it in the sequence. To view both the clips simultaneously, you need to modify the parameters of the **Motion** effect for the **beach clip (7).mov**. You can modify the parameters manually using the **Effect Controls** panel. But in this section, you will apply the **PiPs** effect in the **Presets** node to apply the presets of the **Motion** parameters.

8. Select the **beach clip (7).mov** in the **Timeline** panel.

Next, you will apply a preset of the **Motion** effect from the **Effects** panel.

9. Select the **Effects** panel; various effects are displayed. Next, expand the **Presets** node; various effects such as **Bevel Edges**, **Blurs**, **Mosaic**, **PiPs**, and so on are displayed.

10. Expand the **PiPs** node; the **25% PiPs** node is displayed. Expand the **25% PiPs** node; various effects such as **25% LL**, **25% LR**, **25% Motion**, and so on are displayed. Next, expand the **25% UR** node; various effects are displayed, refer to Figure 11-38.

11. Select the **PiP 25% UR** effect and drag it from the **Effects** panel to the **beach clip (7).mov** in the **Timeline** panel. The size of **beach clip (7).mov** is reduced in the Program Monitor, refer to Figure 11-39. Also, in the **Effect**

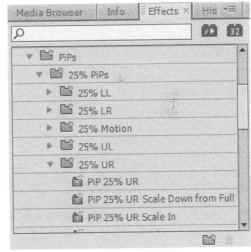

*Figure 11-38 Various effects displayed on expanding the **25% UL** node*

Controls panel, the parameters for the **Position** and **Scale** properties are changed based on the effect you applied to the clip. You can also modify the parameters for the applied effect by using the **Effect Controls** panel, if required.

*Figure 11-39 The reduced size of the **beach clip (7).mov** after applying the effect*

12. Make sure the CTI is at the beginning of the sequence and play the sequence to view the effect applied to the clip. Next, move back the CTI to the beginning of the sequence.

    Next, you will apply the bevel effect to apply a small border to the **beach clip (7).mov** to make it look attractive.

13. In the **Effects** panel, expand the **Presets** node, if it is not expanded. Next, expand the **Bevel Edges** node; the **Bevel Edges Thick** and **Bevel Edges Thin** effects are displayed.

14. Select the **Bevel Edges Thin** effect and drag it from the **Effects** panel to the **beach clip (7).mov** in the **Timeline** panel. On doing so, the effect is displayed on the clip in the Program Monitor, as shown in Figure 11-40.

    Next, you will modify the parameters of the **Bevel Edges Thin** effect.

15. Make sure the clip is selected in the **Timeline** panel. Select the **Effect Controls** panel, if it is not already selected. The **Bevel Edges** effect is displayed in this panel. Expand the **Bevel Edges** effect, if not already expanded; its parameters are displayed, as shown in Figure 11-41.

*Figure 11-40 The **beach clip (7).mov** in the Program Monitor after applying the **Bevel Edges Thin** effect*

*Figure 11-41 The **Bevel Edges** effect in the **Effect Controls** panel*

16. Modify the parameters of the **Bevel Edges** effect as given below:

    Light Angle: **-81.0**   Light Intensity: **1.0**

17. Choose the color swatch located on the right of the **Light Color** option; the **Color Picker** dialog box is displayed. In this dialog box, set the following parameters and then choose the **OK** button:

R: **189**   G: **95**   B: **76**

After modifying the parameters, the **beach clip (7).mov** is displayed in the Program Monitor, as shown in Figure 11-42.

Figure 11-42 The **beach clip (7).mov** *after modifying the parameters*

Next, you will add a drop shadow to the **beach clip (7).mov** clip.

18. In the **Effects** panel, expand the **Video Effects** node; various video effects are displayed. Next, expand the **Perspective** node; various effects are displayed, as shown in Figure 11-43.

Figure 11-43 *The effects in the* **Perspective** *bin*

19. Select the **Drop Shadow** effect and drag it to the **beach clip (7).mov** in the **Timeline** panel; the **Drop Shadow** effect is displayed in the **Effect Controls** panel.

Next, you will modify the parameters of the **Drop Shadow** effect in the **Effect Controls** panel.

20. Modify the parameters of the **Drop Shadow** effect as given below:

Direction: **-135**   Distance: **23**

After modifying the values, the **beach clip (7).mov** is displayed with the drop shadow in the Program Monitor, as shown in Figure 11-44.

Figure 11-44 *The **beach clip (7).mov** with the **Drop Shadow** effect*

21. Press CTRL+S to save the file. Next, press the ENTER key to view the output of the sequence in the Program Monitor. The output of the sequence at frame 00:00:01:19 is shown in Figure 11-45.

Figure 11-45 *The output of the sequence at frame 00:00:01:19*

Tutorial 4

In this tutorial, you will apply the **Basic 3D** effect. The output of the sequence at frame 00:00:03:01 is shown in Figure 11-46.   **(Expected Time: 15 min)**

Figure 11-46 *The output of the sequence at frame 00:00:03:01*

The following steps are required to complete this tutorial:

a. Open the project file.
b. Animate the basic 3D effect.

Opening the Project File

In this section, you will open a project file.

1. Open the *chapter11_PIP.prproj* file that you have downloaded from the CADCIM website.

2. Save the *chapter11_PIP.prproj file* to the location *\Documents\Adobe Premiere Tutorials\ c11_premiere_cc_tut* with the name *chapter11_Basic 3D.prproj*. As a result, the *chapter11_Basic 3D.prproj* file is displayed.

Animating the Basic 3D Effect

In this section, you will animate the basic 3D effect.

1. In the **Project** panel, select the **beach clip (1).mov** clip and add it to the sequence in the **Timeline** panel, as shown in Figure 11-47.

*Figure 11-47 The **beach clip (1).mov** in the **Timeline** panel*

2. In the **Effects** panel, choose **Video Effects > Perspective**; various effects are displayed in the **Perspective** node.

3. Select the **Basic 3D** effect and drag it to the **beach clip (1).mov** in the **Timeline** panel.

    The **Basic 3D** effect is used to manipulate a clip in 3D space. It is used to rotate a clip around the horizontal or vertical axis and to move it toward and away from you. It is also used to create a specular highlight to give the appearance of light reflecting from a rotated surface.

    Next, you will modify the parameters of the **Basic 3D** effect in the **Effect Controls** panel.

4. Select the **Effect Controls** panel; various effects for the **beach clip (1).mov** are displayed.

    Next, expand the **Basic 3D** effect, if not already expanded; its parameters are displayed, as shown in Figure 11-48.

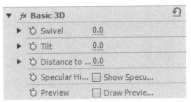

*Figure 11-48 The parameters of the **Basic 3D** effect*

The **Swivel** option is used to control the rotation of a clip about its vertical axis. The **Tilt** option is used to control the rotation of a clip about its horizontal axis. The **Distance to Image** option is used to specify the distance of the clip from the viewer. As you increase the value in the **Distance to Image** edit box, the size of the image gets reduced. The **Specular Highlight** option is used to add a glint of light that reflects off the surface of the rotated image. The **Preview** option is used to draw a wireframe outline of the 3D image that is used to perform the render process quickly.

5. Move the cursor over the value field corresponding to the **Swivel** parameter; the shape of the cursor is changed. Next, press and hold the left mouse button and drag the cursor to modify the value based on your requirement. On doing so, the clip in the Program Monitor is rotated accordingly, refer to Figure 11-49.

6. Move the cursor over the value field corresponding to the **Tilt** parameter; the shape of the cursor is changed. Next, click on it; an edit box is displayed at its place. Enter a value based on your requirement in the edit box and press the ENTER key; the clip in the Program Monitor is rotated accordingly, refer to Figure 11-50.

Next, you will apply the **Basic 3D** effect to create animation.

Figure 11-49 *The clip rotated around the vertical axis*

Figure 11-50 *The clip rotated around the horizontal axis*

7. Select the **beach clip (1).mov** clip in the sequence and press the DELETE key to delete it.

8. Add only the video portion of **beach clip (1).mov** to the sequence in the **V1** track, as discussed earlier.

9. Similarly, add only the video portion of **beach clip (7).mov** to the sequence in the **V2** track, refer to Figure 11-51.

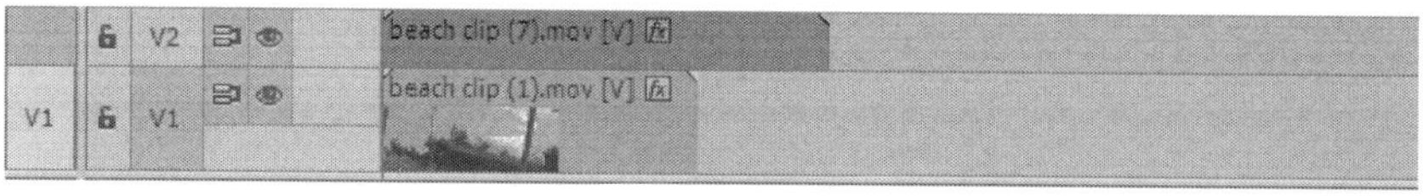

Figure 11-51 *The **beach clip (7).mov** and **beach clip (1).mov** added in the sequence*

10. Next, add the **Basic 3D** effect to the **beach clip (7).mov**, as discussed earlier. Next, you will create some animation by adding keyframes for various properties in the **Effect Controls** panel.

11. Make sure the **beach clip (7).mov** is selected in the **Timeline** panel. Next, select the **Effect Controls** panel; various effects are displayed.

12. Make sure the CTI is at the beginning of the sequence.

13. Expand the **Motion** effect and modify the value for the **Scale** property to **0**.

14. Next, choose the **Toggle animation** button located on the left of the **Scale** property; a keyframe is created for the value you entered.

15. Move the CTI to 00:00:03:18 frame. Modify the value for the **Scale** property to **100**; another keyframe is created for the new value.

Next, you will create keyframes for the **Basic 3D** effect.

16. Expand the **Basic 3D** effect in the **Effect Controls** panel, if not already expanded.

17. Choose the **Go to Previous Keyframe** button located on the right of the **Scale** property; the CTI is moved to the first keyframe.

18. Choose the **Toggle animation** button on the left of the **Swivel** property; a keyframe is created for the current value of the **Swivel** property, which is 0.

19. Choose the **Go to Next Keyframe** button on the right of the **Scale** property; the CTI is moved to the second keyframe.

20. Next, modify the value for the **Swivel** property to **180**; another keyframe is created for the new value. Now there are two keyframes for the **Scale** property and two keyframes for the **Swivel** property, refer to Figure 11-52.

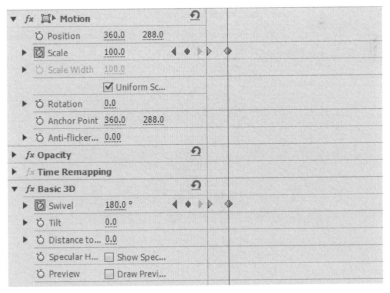

*Figure 11-52 The keyframes for the **Scale** and **Swivel** properties*

21. Move the CTI to the beginning of the sequence and play the sequence to view the animation effect; the **beach clip (7).mov** starts scaling as well as rotating around its vertical axis based on the values entered for the keyframes, refer to Figure 11-53.

Figure 11-53   *The animated **beach clip (7).mov** at one of the frames*

22. Press CTRL+S to save the file. Next, press the ENTER key to view the output of the sequence in the Program Monitor. The output of the sequence at frame 00:00:03:01 is shown in Figure 11-54.

Figure 11-54   *The output of the sequence at frame 00:00:03:01*

Tutorial 5

In this tutorial, you will create the **Camera View** effect. The output of the sequence at frame 00:00:00:05 is shown in Figure 11-55.   **(Expected Time: 20 min)**

Figure 11-55   *The output of the sequence at frame 00:00:00:05*

The following steps are required to complete this tutorial:

a. Open the project file.
b. Apply and animate the camera view effect.

Opening the Project File
In this section, you will open the project file.

1. Open the *chapter11_PIP.prproj* file that you have downloaded from the CADCIM website.

2. Save the *chapter11_PIP.prproj* file with the name *chapter11_Camera_View.prproj* to the location *\Documents\Adobe Premiere Tutorials\c11_premiere_cc_tut*. The *chapter11_Camera_View.prproj* file is displayed.

Applying and Animating the Camera View Effect
In this section, you will apply and animate the camera view effect.

1. In the **Project** panel, select the **beach clip (1).mov** clip and add only the video portion to the sequence in the **V1** track.

2. Add the video portion of the **beach clip (7).mov** to the **V2** track in the **Timeline** panel. Also, expand the **V2** track to view the clip properly.

3. From the **Effects** panel, choose **Video Effects > Transform**; various effects are displayed.

4. Select the **Camera View** effect and drag it to the **beach clip (7).mov** in the **Timeline** panel.

    The **Camera View** effect is used to distort a clip by simulating a camera viewing the subject from different angles.

    Next, you will modify the parameters of the **Camera View** effect in the **Effect Controls** panel.

5. Make sure the **beach clip (7).mov** is selected in the **Timeline** panel and select the **Effect Controls** panel; various effects including the **Camera View** effect are displayed.

6. Expand the **Camera View** effect, if not already expanded; various parameters such as **Longitude**, **Latitude**, **Roll**, and so on are displayed, refer to Figure 11-56.

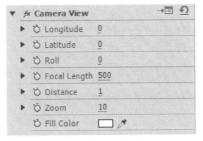

Figure 11-56 *The parameters of the **Camera View** effect*

7. Set the value **35** for the **Longitude** parameter; the **beach clip (7).mov** flips horizontally, as shown in Figure 11-57.

8. Choose the **Reset** button on the right of the **Camera View** effect; the **beach clip (7).mov** is set to its original position.

9. Next, set the value **45** for the **Latitude** parameter; the **beach clip (7).mov** flips vertically, as shown in Figure 11-58.

*Figure 11-57 The **beach clip** (7).mov after*   *Figure 11-58 The **beach clip** (7).mov after*
*modifying the **Longitude** parameter*   *modifying the **Latitude** parameter*

10. Choose the **Reset** button on the right of the **Camera View** effect; the **beach clip (7).mov** is again set to its original position.

11. Set the value **45** for the **Roll** parameter; the **beach clip (7).mov** is rotated, as shown in Figure 11-59.

12. Set the value **1** for the **Focal Length** parameter.

    The **Focal Length** parameter is used to give an effect that is similar to changing the focal length of the camera. The clip after changing the value is shown in Figure 11-60.

*Figure 11-59 The **beach clip** (7).mov after*   *Figure 11-60 The **beach clip** (7).mov after*
*modifying the **Roll** parameter*   *modifying the **Focal Length** parameter*

  Note
*The smaller value in the **Focal Length** edit box result in wider views, whereas the larger value result in narrower but closer views of the clip.*

13. Set the value **3** for the **Distance** parameter; the distance between the center of the clip and the camera is increased, and the clip is displayed, as shown in Figure 11-61.

14. Set the value **5** for the **Zoom** parameter; the view of the clip gets enlarged, as shown in Figure 11-62.

*Figure 11-61 The **beach clip** (7).mov after modifying the **Distance** parameter*

*Figure 11-62 The **beach clip** (7).mov after modifying the **Zoom** parameter*

15. Choose the color swatch on the right of the **Fill Color** option; the **Color Picker** dialog box is displayed. By default, the white color is chosen in it. You can choose a color of your choice and then choose the **OK** button; the chosen color is displayed as the background color of the clip, refer to Figure 11-63.

*Figure 11-63 The **beach clip** (7).mov after modifying the background color*

16. Choose the **Reset** button located on the right of the **Camera View** effect to reset its parameters to their original values.

Next, you will animate some of the properties of the **Camera View** effect to add a special effect by using the keyframes.

17. Make sure the CTI is at the beginning of the sequence.

18. Choose the **Toggle animation** button on the left of the **Zoom** option; a keyframe is created for the current value in the **Zoom** edit box. Next, set the new value **40** for the **Zoom** parameter for the created keyframe. After modifying the value, the zoom level of the clip is reduced, as shown in Figure 11-64.

*Figure 11-64   The **beach clip (7).mov** after*
*modifying the value in the **Zoom** edit box*

19. Choose the **Toggle animation** button on the left of the **Roll** option; a keyframe is created for the current value in the **Roll** edit box.

20. Move the CTI to 00:00:01:22 frame. Next, enter the value **360** in the **Roll** edit box; another keyframe is created for the new value. Next, set the value **10** for the **Zoom** parameter; a new keyframe is created for the new value of the **Zoom** option. Now, there are two keyframes for the **Zoom** and **Roll** options, as shown in Figure 11-65.

▼ *fx* Camera View		→▭ ↩
► ☉ Longitude	0	
► ☉ Latitude	0	
► ▧ Roll	360	◄ ♦ ▷ ♦
► ☉ Focal Length	500	
► ☉ Distance	1	
► ▧ Zoom	10	◄ ♦ ▷ ♦
☉ Fill Color	▭ ⁄	

*Figure 11-65   The keyframes created for the **Zoom***
*and **Roll** options*

21. Move the CTI to the beginning of the sequence and play the sequence; the **beach clip (7).mov** starts animating based on the values entered for the keyframes, refer to Figure 11-66.

*Figure 11-66   The **beach clip (7).mov** at one*
of the frames during animation

While playing the sequence, you will notice that there is a white colored background for the **beach clip (7).mov**. To remove this background, you need to follow the steps given below:

22. Choose the **Go to Previous Keyframe** button to move the CTI to the first keyframe.

23. Choose the **Setup** button on the right of the **Camera View** effect; the **Camera View**
    Settings dialog box is displayed, as shown in Figure 11-67.

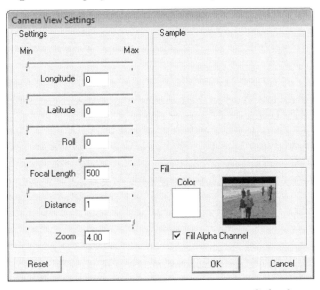

*Figure 11-67 The **Camera View Settings** dialog box*

24. In the **Camera View Settings** dialog box, clear the **Fill Alpha Channel** check box and choose
    the **OK** button; the white background of the **beach clip (7).mov** becomes transparent.
    Also, the **beach clip (1).mov** becomes visible at the back of the **beach clip (7).mov**, refer
    to Figure 11-68.

*Figure 11-68 The **beach clip (1).mov** visible with the **beach clip (7).mov***

The **Fill Alpha Channel** check box is used to make the background transparent.

25. Play the sequence to view the effect in the Program Monitor.

Note

*You can also set the **Latitude**, **Longitude**, and other settings of the **Camera View** effect using the **Camera View Settings** dialog box.*

26. Press CTRL+S to save the file. The output of the sequence at frame 00:00:00:05 is shown in Figure 11-69.

Figure 11-69 The output of the sequence at frame 00:00:00:05

Self-Evaluation Test

Answer the following questions and then compare them to those given at the end of this chapter:

1. Which of the following buttons in the **Effect Controls** panel is used to activate the keyframing process?

    (a) **Add/Remove Keyframe**   (b) **Reset**
    (c) **Toggle animation**   (d) None of these

2. Which of the following keys is used to move the CTI to the beginning of the sequence?

    (a) END   (b) HOME+left arrow keys
    (c) Page Down   (d) HOME

3. If you modify the shape of a clip by adjusting the handles of the clip and there is a relationship between the incoming and outgoing curves, then it is known as the _____ interpolation.

4. In the _____ interpolation, clip moves on a curved path.

5. The _____ option in the **Camera View** effect is used to flip the clip horizontally.

6. The _____ option in the **Basic 3D** effect is used to control the rotation of a clip around its vertical axis.

7. If you want to change the position, scale, and other properties of the clip over time, then you need to use keyframes. (T/F)

8. The **Temporal Interpolation** type determines the changes in the velocity of an object that moves across a motion path. (T/F)

Review Questions

Answer the following questions:

1. Which of the following buttons is used to move the CTI from one keyframe to another?

    (a) **Go to Previous Keyframe**   (b) **Go to Next Keyframe**
    (c) Both (a) and (b)   (d) **Add/Remove Keyframe**

2. Which of the following keys is used to select multiple keyframes?

    (a) ALT   (b) CTRL
    (c) SHIFT+ALT   (d) ALT+CTRL

3. Which of the following effects is used to manipulate a clip in 3D space?

    (a) **PiPs**   (b) **Basic 3D**
    (c) **Camera View**   (d) None of these

4. The _____ interpolation refers to the changes in shape. It is used to determine whether the corners will be rounded or angular.

5. The **Camera View** effect is used to distort a clip by simulating a camera viewing the subject from different angles. (T/F)

6. If you change the curve of the path by changing the parameters without adjusting the clip handles, then it is known as **Temporal Interpolation**. (T/F)

7. The **Basic 3D** effect is used to rotate a clip about the horizontal and vertical axes. (T/F)

EXERCISE

Exercise 1

Create a new project in Premiere. Add video clips to the sequence. Next, apply various video effects to the clips in the sequence. Try to animate various parameters of the effects using keyframes in the **Effect Controls** panel and notice the difference. Also, change the mode of interpolation for the added keyframes to view the difference.

Answers to Self-Evaluation Test
1. c, **2.** d, **3. Continuous Bezier Spatial**, **4. Bezier Spatial**, **5. Longitude**, **6. Swivel**, **7.** T, **8.** T

Chapter 12

Learning Compositing Techniques

Learning Objectives

After completing this chapter, you will be able to:

• *Apply the Opacity effect*
• *Apply the Blend Modes*
• *Apply the Alpha Channel effects*
• *Apply the Garbage Matte Key Effects*
• *Apply the Image Matte Key Effect*
• *Apply the Track Matte Key Effect*

INTRODUCTION

In Premiere, if clips are placed in higher video tracks, then they cover up the clips placed in lower video tracks. You can combine the content of various video tracks. The method of combining the content from various tracks is known as compositing. In Chapter 10, you learned about the **Ultra Key** effect, which is one of the compositing techniques. In this chapter, you will learn in detail about other compositing methods such as blend modes, **Opacity** effect, alpha channels, and matte keys.

MATTE KEY EFFECTS

Generally, there are two types of matte key effects, **Garbage** and **Graphic**. The **Garbage** matte key effects are used to remove the unwanted portion of a clip. There are two types of **Garbage** matte key effects, namely **Four-Point Garbage Matte** and **Eight-Point Garbage Matte**.

The **Graphic** matte key effects are used to key out or key in another clip or graphics. There are four types of **Graphic** matte key effects, namely **Difference Matte**, **Image Matte Key**, **Track Matte Key**, and **Remove Matte**.

The matte key effects such as **Difference Matte**, **Image Matte Key**, **Track Matte Key**, **Four-Point Garbage Matte** are used to create a hole in one clip such that the portions of another clip beneath it can be seen through. Also, they are used to crop the clips to place them on the top of other clips. In this section, you will learn to use some of the matte key effects.

TUTORIALS

Before you start the tutorials, you need to download the *c12_premiere_cc_tut.zip* file from *www.cadcim.com*. The path of the file is as follows: *Textbooks > Animation and Visual Effects > Adobe Premiere Pro > Adobe Premiere Pro CC: A Tutorial Approach*

Next, extract the contents of the zip file at *\Documents\Adobe Premiere Tutorials*.

Tutorial 1

In this tutorial, you will use the opacity effect, alpha channels, and blend modes on the video clip. The output of the sequence at frame 00:00:09:14 is shown in Figure 12-1.

(Expected Time: 20 min)

Figure 12-1 The output of the sequence at frame 00:00:09:14

The following steps are required to complete this tutorial:

a.   Apply the Opacity effect.
b.   Apply the blend modes.
c.   Apply the Alpha Channel effects.

Applying the Opacity Effect

One of the easiest compositing methods is to place the entire clip uniformly transparent or semi-transparent on the higher track to make the clip placed on the lower track visible. To do so, you need to use the **Opacity** effect. In this section, you will apply the **Opacity** effect.

1.   Open the *chapter12.prproj* file that you have downloaded from the CADCIM website.

2.   Save the *chapter12.prproj* file to *\Documents\Adobe Premiere Tutorials\c12_premiere_cc_tut* with the name *chapter12_opacity.prproj*. The *chapter12_opacity.prproj* file is displayed, refer to Figure 12-2.

Figure 12-2 The chapter12_opacity.prproj file displayed

Next, you will create some background graphics using the Titler window to superimpose the existing clip on the **Timeline** panel.

3.   In the **Project** panel, choose the **New Item** button; a flyout is displayed. Next, choose the **Title** option from the flyout; the **New Title** dialog box is displayed.

4.   In the **New Title** dialog box, type **BG01** in the **Name** text box and choose the **OK** button; the Titler window is displayed, as shown in Figure 12-3. Also, the **BG01** file is added to the **Project** panel.

Figure 12-3 *The Titler window for* ***BG01*** *background*

5. In the **Title Properties** panel of the Titler window, select the **Background** check box; the Titler screen is filled with default black colored solid background, refer to Figure 12-4.

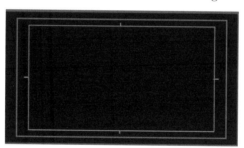

Figure 12-4 *The Titler screen with default*
black colored background

6. In the **Background** area, make sure the **Solid** option is selected in the **Fill Type** drop-down list. Next, choose the color swatch on the right of the **Color** option; the **Color Picker** dialog box is displayed. In this dialog box, set the parameters as follows:

R: **118**   G: **45**   B: **19**

After setting the values, choose the **OK** button in the **Color Picker** dialog box; the chosen color is displayed as the background color in the Titler window.

7. Close the Titler window. The background created is displayed with the name **BG01** in the **Project** panel.

Next, you will add the **BG01** background to the sequence in the **Timeline** panel.

8. Select **BG01** in the **Project** panel and drag it to the **Timeline** panel in the **V2** track. Also, expand the **V2** track by double-clicking on the empty area to the right of the **Toggle Track Output** button, if it is not expanded, refer to Figure 12-5.

Figure 12-5 The BG01 background in the V2 track

9. Place the cursor at the end of the **BG01** background and drag it toward right to increase its length upto the same size as the length of the clip in the **V1** track, refer to Figure 12-6.

Figure 12-6 The BG01 background stretched in the V2 track

If you notice the Program Monitor, you will find that the **BG01** background is completely covering the clip in the **V1** track, refer to Figure 12-7. Therefore, you cannot view the video clip in the **V1** track. To make the clip visible, you need to apply the **Opacity** effect to the **BG01** background in the **V2** track.

Figure 12-7 The BG01 background in the Program Monitor

10. Make sure the **BG01** background is selected in the **Timeline** panel and various effects are displayed in the **Effect Controls** panel. Next, expand the **fx Opacity** node; its properties are displayed. Now, expand the **Opacity** node, if it is not expanded, to display its parameters. refer to Figure 12-8.

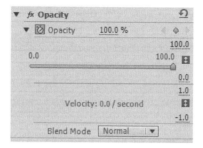

Figure 12-8 The parameters of the Opacity node

Notice that the default value for the **Opacity** effect is 100%. As a result, the **BG01** background is totally opaque. Next, you will set new values for the **Opacity** effect using keyframes.

11. Make sure the CTI is at the beginning of the sequence. Choose the **Add/Remove** **Keyframe** button on the right of the **Opacity** property; a keyframe is set for the default value of the **Opacity** effect.

12. Move the CTI to the frame 00:00:04:21. Modify the value of the **Opacity** effect to **0** percent; another keyframe is created for the newly entered value. As a result, the graph for the entire effect is displayed in the timeline view of the **Effect Controls** panel, as shown in Figure 12-9. Also, the horizontal line specifying the opacity in the **Timeline** panel will become slanting, as shown in Figure 12-10.

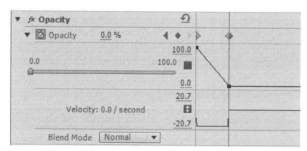

Figure 12-9 The graph for the Opacity effect in the Effect Controls panel

Figure 12-10 The curve of the horizontal line changed after creating keyframes

 Note
*If the horizontal line is not visible in the **Timeline** panel, choose the **Timeline Display** **Settings** button in the **Timeline** panel; a flyout is displayed. Choose **Show Video Keyframes** from this flyout.*

13. Move the CTI to the beginning of the sequence and play it. You will notice that gradually the **BG01** background starts becoming less opaque, refer to Figure 12-11, and finally it becomes transparent. Now, you can view the video clip placed in the **V1** track clearly, refer to Figure 12-12.

*Figure 12-11 The **BG01** in the Program Monitor showing the less opaque effect*

*Figure 12-12 The totally transparent **BG01** in the Program Monitor*

Next, you will use a gradient background in the **V2** track. Also, you will copy the **Opacity** effect and paste it to the new gradient background.

14. Follow the steps 3 and 4 and create a new background with the name **BG02**. Next, in the **Title Properties** panel of the Titler window, make sure the **Background** check box is selected.

15. Select the **Linear Gradient** option from the **Fill Type** drop-down list. Adjust the gradient handles as shown in Figure 12-13. Also, set the color for the first and second handle as white and black respectively by double clicking on it, refer to Figure 12-13.

16. Close the Titler window. The **BG02** background is displayed in the **Project** panel.

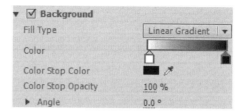

Figure 12-13 *Gradient handles adjusted*

Next, you will copy the **Opacity** effect from the **BG01** background in the **Timeline** panel.

17. Select the **BG01** background in the **Timeline** panel and right-click on it; a shortcut menu is displayed. Choose the **Copy** option from the shortcut menu; the effects of the **BG01** are copied.

18. Press the DELETE key to delete the **BG01** background from the **Timeline** panel.

Next, you will add the **BG02** background to the sequence.

19. Select the **BG02** background in the **Project** panel and drag it above the clip in the **V1** track in the **Timeline** panel. On doing so, the **BG02** background is displayed in the Program Monitor, as shown in Figure 12-14.

Figure 12-14 *The **BG02** background in the Program Monitor*

20. Right-click on the **BG02** in the **Timeline** panel; a shortcut menu is displayed. Choose the **Paste Attributes** option; the **Paste Attributes** dialog box is displayed. Now, choose the **OK** button; the copied effects are pasted on the **BG02** background including the keyframes that you had set for the **BG01** background.

21. Move the CTI to the beginning of the sequence and play it. The **BG02** background will display the same effect in the Program Monitor that you had applied to the **BG01** background, refer to Figure 12-15.

22. Press the ENTER key to view the output of the sequence in the Program Monitor.

Figure 12-15 The **BG02** *background at one of the frames after pasting the effects*

Applying the Blend Modes

In this section, you will apply the blend modes.

1. Make sure the *chapter12_opacity.prproj* file is opened. Next, select the **BG02** background in the **V2** track, if it is not selected and press the DELETE key; the **BG02** background is deleted from the **Timeline** panel.

2. Make sure the **BG02** background in the **Project** panel is selected and then add it to the beginning of the sequence in the **V2** track.

3. Select the **BG02** background in the **Timeline** panel; various effects are displayed in the **Effect Controls** panel.

4. Expand the **Opacity** node; its properties are displayed. Notice that there is a **Blend Mode** drop-down list at the bottom of the **Opacity** node, refer to Figure 12-16.

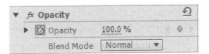

Figure 12-16 The **Blend Mode** *drop-down list*

By default, the **Normal** option is selected in the **Blend Mode** drop-down list. As a result, the resulting color of the clips will be the source color and the underlying color will be ignored, refer to Figure 12-17.

Note
*The source color is the color of the layer to which you applied the Blend Mode. The underlying color is the color of the layers placed below the source layer in the **Timeline** panel. The resulting color is the output of the blending mode.*

Figure 12-17 *The clips in the **Normal** blend mode*

5. Select the **Soft Light** option from the **Blend Mode** drop-down list; the layers are blended and displayed in the Program Monitor, as shown in Figure 12-18.

Figure 12-18 *The clips in the **Soft Light** blend mode*

The **Soft Light** blend mode darkens or lightens the color channel values of the underlying layer depending on the source color.

  Tip. *You can try other options in the **Blend Mode** drop-down list to create different types of effects.*

Applying the Alpha Channel Effects

Generally, the color information of an image contains three channels, namely red, green, and blue. It may also contain an additional channel known as alpha channel. The alpha channel contains the transparency information. In this section, you will apply the alpha channel effects.

1. Make sure the *chapter12_opacity.prproj* file is opened. Next, select the **BG02** background in the **V2** track and delete it.

2. In the **Project** panel, import the **alpha channel.psd** clip from \Documents\Adobe Premiere Tutorials\c12_premiere_cc_tut\Media\psd.

3. Add the **alpha channel.psd** clip to the beginning of the sequence in the **V2** track.

Note
The alpha channel.psd is a Photoshop file that consists of a graphic with an alpha channel. When you add it to the sequence, alpha channel becomes opaque, thus displaying the graphic available beneath this channel, refer to Figure 12-19.

Figure 12-19 The alpha channel.psd file in the Program Monitor after adding it to the sequence

4. Move the cursor at the end of the **alpha channel.psd** clip and then drag it towards right to make its length similar to the clip in the **V1** track.

    Next, you will apply the **Alpha Adjust** effect to the **alpha channel.psd** clip to view the alpha channel and other effects. Generally, the **Alpha Adjust** effect is used in place of the **Opacity** fixed effect to change the default render order of the fixed effects.

5. In the **Effects** panel, expand **Video Effects > Keying**; various effects are displayed, as shown in Figure 12-20.

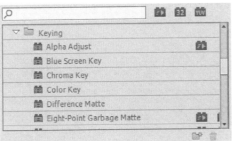

Figure 12-20 The effects in the Keying bin

6. Select the **Alpha Adjust** effect and drag it to the **alpha channel.psd** clip in the **Timeline** panel

7. In the **Effect Controls** panel, expand the **Alpha Adjust** node, if not already expanded to display its various properties, as shown in Figure 12-21.

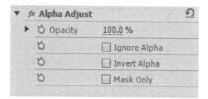

Figure 12-21 *The properties of the* ***Alpha Adjust*** *node*

By default, the value for the **Opacity** property is 100 percent. You can change this value to create different levels of transparency. Next, you will select the required options from the **Alpha Adjust** node to interpret the alpha channel in the **alpha channel.psd** clip.

8. Select the **Ignore Alpha** check box; the alpha channel of the **alpha channel.psd** clip is ignored. Also, the **alpha channel.psd** clip is displayed in the Program Monitor, as shown in Figure 12-22. Next, clear the **Ignore Alpha** check box.

Figure 12-22 *The* ***alpha channel.psd*** *clip displayed in the Program Monitor*

9. Select the **Invert Alpha** check box; the transparent and opaque areas of the **alpha channel.psd** clips are reversed, as shown in Figure 12-23. Next, clear the **Invert Alpha** check box.

10. Select the **Mask Only** check box; the **Alpha Adjust** node is applied only to the masked area, as shown in Figure 12-24. Next, clear the **Mask Only** check box.

Figure 12-23 *The* ***alpha channel.psd*** *clip after selecting the* ***Invert Alpha*** *check box*

Figure 12-24 *The* ***alpha channel.psd*** *clip after selecting the* ***Mask Only*** *check box*

11. In the **Effect Controls** panel, select the **Alpha Adjust** effect and then delete it.

    Next, you will use some of the video effects that work with the alpha channel graphic file, **alpha channel.psd**.

12. In the **Effects** panel, expand the **Video Effects > Perspective**, if not already expanded; various effects are displayed.

13. Select the **Bevel Alpha** effect and drag it to the **alpha channel.psd** clip in the **Timeline** panel.

14. In the **Effect Controls** panel, expand the **Bevel Alpha** node, if not already expanded; the properties in this node are displayed, as shown in Figure 12-25. Also, the **alpha channel.psd** clip is displayed in the Program Monitor, as shown in Figure 12-26.

Figure 12-25 *The properties of the Bevel Alpha effect*

Figure 12-26 *The **alpha channel.psd** file after applying the **Bevel Alpha** effect*

15. Modify the value of the **Edge Thickness** property to **5.00**; the clip is displayed in the Program Monitor with a thick edge, as shown in Figure 12-27.

Figure 12-27 *The clip after modifying the value of the **Edge Thickness** property*

Next, you will apply the **Alpha Glow** effect to the **alpha channel.psd** clip. The **Alpha Glow** effect is used to add colors or glow around the edge of the masked alpha channel.

16. In the **Effects** panel, expand **Video Effects > Stylize,** if not already expanded; various effects are displayed.

17. Select the **Alpha Glow** effect and drag it to the **alpha channel.psd** clip in the **Timeline** panel.

18. In the **Effect Controls** panel, expand the **Alpha Glow** node, if not already expanded; the properties in this node are displayed, as shown in Figure 12-28. Also, note that the **Alpha Glow** effect is applied to the **alpha channel.psd** clip, as shown in Figure 12-29.

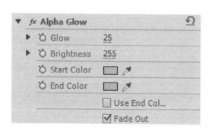

Figure 12-28 The properties of the Alpha Glow effect

Figure 12-29 The clip after applying the Alpha Glow effect

The **Glow** property in the **Alpha** effect is used to control the limit up to which the color extends from the alpha channel edge. The **Brightness** property is used to set the initial opacity of the glow. The **Start Color** property is used to specify the color of the glow. The **End Color** property is used to add an additional color at the outer edge of the glow. You will be able to use the end color in the glow only if the **Use End Color** check box is selected. The **Fade Out** check box is used to specify whether the colors will fade out or stay solid.

19. Modify the values of various properties of the **Alpha Glow** effect in the **Effect Controls** panel, based on your requirement.

20. Delete the **Bevel Alpha** and **Alpha Glow** effects in the **Effect Controls** panel.

    Next, you will apply the **Channel Blur** effect to the **alpha channel.psd** clip. The **Channel Blur** effect is used to blur the red, blue, green, or alpha channel individually.

21. In the **Effects** panel, expand **Video Effects > Blur & Sharpen**, if not already expanded; various blur effects are displayed.

22. Select the **Channel Blur** effect and drag it to the **alpha channel.psd** clip in the **Timeline** panel.

23. In the **Effect Controls** panel, expand the **Channel Blur** node, if not already expanded; the properties in this node are displayed, as shown in Figure 12-30.

    The **Red Blurriness**, **Green Blurriness**, **Blue Blurriness**, and **Alpha Blurriness** properties are used to blur the red, green, blue, and alpha channels, respectively. You can select the **Repeat Edge Pixels** check box to blur the pixels beyond the edge of the clip.

24. Modify the value in the **Green Blurriness** edit box to **50.0**; the clip is modified and displayed in the Program Monitor, as shown in Figure 12-31.

By default, the **Horizontal and Vertical** option is selected in the **Blur Dimensions** drop-down list in the **Channel Blur** effect. This option is used to blur the corresponding channel in the horizontal as well as in the vertical direction, refer to Figure 12-31.

Figure 12-30 The properties of the *Channel Blur* node

Figure 12-31 The clip blurred in horizontal and vertical directions

25. Select the **Vertical** option in the **Blur Dimensions** drop-down list; the clip is blurred only in the vertical direction, as shown in Figure 12-32.

Figure 12-32 The clip blurred in the vertical direction

26. Select the **Horizontal** option in the **Blur Dimensions** drop-down list; the clip is blurred only in the horizontal direction, as shown in Figure 12-33.

Figure 12-33 The clip blurred in the horizontal direction

27. Press CTRL+S to save the file. Next, press the ENTER key to view the output of the sequence in the Program Monitor. The output of the sequence at frame 00:00:09:14 is displayed, as shown in Figure 12-34.

Figure 12-34 *The output of the sequence at frame 00:00:09:14*

Tutorial 2

In this tutorial, you will crop out the unwanted portion by using **Four-Point**, **Eight-Point**, and **Sixteen-Point Garbage Matte Key** effects. The output of the sequence at frame 00:00:03:09 is shown in Figure 12-35.   **(Expected Time: 20 min)**

Figure 12-35 *The output of the sequence at frame 00:00:03:09*

The following steps are required to complete this tutorial:

a. Open the project file.
b. Apply the garbage matte key effects.

Opening the Project File

In this section, you will open the project file.

1. Open the *chapter12.prproj* file that you have downloaded from the CADCIM website; the **beach clip (1).mov** clip is already placed in the **V1** track.

2. Save the *chapter12.prproj* file to *\Documents\Adobe Premiere Tutorials\c12_premiere_cc_tut* with the name *chapter12_matte_key.prproj*.

Applying the Garbage Matte Key Effects

In this section, you will apply the garbage matte key effects.

1. In the **Project** panel, import the **beach clip (9).mov** from *Documents\Adobe Premiere Tutorials* *c12_premiere_cc_tut\Media\Video\Beach Clips* that you have downloaded from the CADCIM website. Next, add it to the **V2** track at the beginning of the sequence in the **Timeline** panel; the Program Monitor shows the **beach clip (9).mov**.

    Next, you will apply the **Four-Point Garbage Matte** effect to the **beach clip (9).mov** to crop a portion of it.

2. In the **Effects** panel, expand **Video Effects > Keying**; various matte key effects are displayed. Select the **Four-Point Garbage Matte** effect and drag it to the **beach clip (9).mov** in the **V2** track.

    The **Garbage** matte key effects such as **Four-Point**, **Eight-Point**, and **Sixteen-Point Garbage Matte** are used to crop out the unwanted portion of a video clip.

3. In the Program Monitor, choose the **Select Zoom Level** button; a flyout is displayed. Select the **25%** option from the flyout, if not already selected to zoom out the screen, refer to Figure 12-36.

Figure 12-36 The screen in the Program Monitor after selecting the 25% zoom level

4. Select the **beach clip (9).mov** in the **Timeline** panel, if it is not selected; the **Four-Point Garbage Matte** effect is displayed with the other effects in the **Effect Controls** panel.

5. Select the **Four-Point Garbage Matte** effect in the **Effect Control** panel; four control points are displayed in the Program Monitor around the screen, refer to Figure 12-37.

6. In the Program Monitor, drag the control points to crop the video clip such that only the girl in the left is visible on the screen, refer to Figures 12-38 and 12-39.

Figure 12-37 *The control points around the clip*

Figure 12-38 *A control point dragged to crop the clip*

Figure 12-39 *All four control points dragged to crop the clip*

Alternatively, you can set the values for the **Top Left**, **Top Right**, **Bottom Right**, and **Bottom Left** properties of the **Four-Point Garbage Matte** effect in the **Effect Controls** panel to crop the clip.

7. Choose the **Select Zoom Level** button; a flyout is displayed. Choose the **Fit** option from the flyout; the clip fits in the Program Monitor.

8. In the Program Monitor, select the **beach clip (9).mov** and drag it to position it at the lower right, as shown in Figure 12-40. Alternatively, you can set the values for the **Position** property in the **Motion** effect of the **Effect Controls** panel to change the position of the **beach clip (9).mov**.

Figure 12-40 The **beach clip (9).mov** *moved to the lower right corner*

9. Make sure the CTI is at the beginning of the clip and view the effect of the **Four-Point Garbage Matte**.

Note
*The **Eight-Point Garbage Matte** and **Sixteen-Point Garbage Matte** effects are similar to the **Four-Point Garbage Matte** effect. The only difference is that instead of four control points, the **Eight-Point Garbage Matte** and **Sixteen-Point Garbage Matte** effects provide eight and sixteen controls points to crop the clip or image, respectively.*

The output of the sequence after applying the effects at frame 00:00:03:09 is shown in Figure 12-41.

Figure 12-41 The output of the sequence at frame 00:00:03:09

Tutorial 3

In this tutorial, you will key out areas of an image based on the luminance values of a still image clip by using the **Image Matte Key** effect. The output of the sequence at frame 00:00:02:22 is displayed, as shown in Figure 12-42.   **(Expected Time:20 min)**

Figure 12-42 The output of the sequence at frame 00:00:02:22

The following steps are required to complete this tutorial:

a.   Open the project file.
b.   Apply the image key effect.

Opening the Project File

In this section, you will open the project file.

1.   Open the *chapter12.prproj* file.

2.   Save the *chapter12.prproj* file to *\Documents\Adobe Premiere Tutorials\c12_premiere_cc_tut* with the name *chapter12_image_matte.prproj*. The *chapter12_image_matte.prproj* file is displayed.

Applying the Image Matte Key Effect

In this section, you will apply the image matte key effect.

1.   In the **Project** panel, import the **child.JPG** image from the location *\Documents\Adobe Premiere Tutorials\c12_premiere_cc_tut\Media Files\Stills*. Next, drag it to the **V2** track at the beginning of the sequence in the **Timeline** panel.

2.   Move the cursor to the endpoint of the image in the **V2** track and drag the clip to match the length of the other clip placed in the **V1** track.

   Notice that the **child.JPG** image clip is not displayed properly in the Program Monitor, refer to Figure 12-43. To display it properly, you need to scale it.

3.   Select the **child.JPG** image clip in the **Timeline** panel, if it is not selected; various effects are displayed the **Effect Controls** panel.

4.   In the **Effect Controls** panel, expand the **Motion** effect and enter the value **43** in the **Scale** edit box. Also, enter the values **360** and **389** in the **Position** edit boxes. After entering the new values, the **child.JPG** image clip is displayed properly in the Program Monitor, as shown in Figure 12-44.

Figure 12-43   *The **child.JPG** image clip in the Program Monitor*   *Figure 12-44*   *The **child.JPG** image clip in the Program Monitor after scaling*

Next, you will apply the **Image Matte Key** effect to the **child.JPG** image clip.

5. In the **Effects** panel, expand **Video Effects > Keying**, if it is not already expanded; various effects are displayed.

6. Select the **Image Matte Key** effect and drag it to the **child.JPG** image clip in the **Timeline** panel; the **Image Matte Key** effect is displayed in the **Effect Controls** panel.
    Next, you will modify the properties of the **Image Matte Key** effect in the **Effect Controls** panel.

7. Expand the **Image Matte Key** node in the **Effect Controls** panel, if it is not expanded; various properties are displayed, as shown in Figure 12-45.

Figure 12-45 Various properties in the Image Matte Key effect

8. Choose the **Setup** button on the right of the **Image Matte Key** effect; the **Select a Matte Image** dialog box is displayed, refer to Figure 12-46.

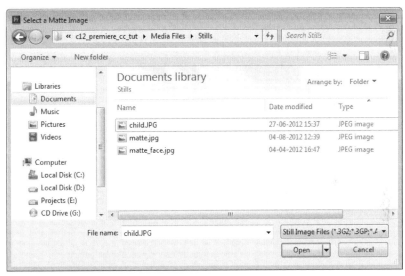

Figure 12-46 The Select a Matte Image dialog box

9. Browse to *\Documents\Adobe Premiere Tutorials\Media Files\Stills* and select the **matte.jpg** image from it. Next, choose the **Open** button in the **Select a Matte Image** dialog box to close it.

    In the **Effect Controls** panel, the **Matte Alpha** option is selected by default in the **Composite Using** drop-down list. As a result, you can composite the clips using the alpha channel values of the image matte that you selected using the **Setup** button.

10. Select the **Matte Luma** option in the **Composite Using** drop-down list; the **child.jpg** image clip is superimposed and displayed in the Program Monitor, as shown in Figure 12-47.

The **Matte Luma** option is used to composite the clips using the luminance values of the image matte that you choose using the **Setup** button.

11. Select the **Reverse** check box; the opaque and transparent areas are swapped in the Program Monitor, as shown in Figure 12-48.

Figure 12-47 *The clips in the Program Monitor after selecting the **Matte Luma** option*

Figure 12-48 *The clips in the Program Monitor after selecting the **Reverse** check box*

12. Select the Reverse check box again and press CTRL+S to save the file. Next, press the ENTER key to view the output of the sequence in the Program Monitor.

The output of the sequence after applying the **Image Matte Key** effect at frame 00:00:02:22 is shown in Figure 12-49.

Figure 12-49 *The output of the sequence at frame 00:00:02:22*

Tutorial 4

In this tutorial, you will use and animate the **Track Matte Key** effect to define the transparency areas in the selected clip and reveal the graphics lying beneath the clip. The output of the sequence at frame 00:00:01:00 is shown in Figure 12-50.   **(Expected Time : 20 min)**

Figure 12-50 *The output of the sequence at frame 00:00:01:00*

The following steps are required to complete this tutorial:

a. Open the project file.
b. Apply the track matte key effect.

Opening the Project File

In this section, you will open the project file.

1. Open the *chapter12_track_matte.prproj* file that you have downloaded from the CADCIM website.

2. Save the *chapter12_track_matte.prproj* file to *\Documents\Adobe Premiere Tutorials* with the new name *chapter12_track_matte02.prproj*. The *chapter12_track_matte02.prproj* file is opened, as shown in Figure 12-51. Notice that the **beach clip (4).mov** clip is placed in the **V1** track as well as in the **V2** track.

Figure 12-51 *The chapter12_track_matte02 file opened*

Applying the Track Matte Key Effect

In this section, you will apply the track matte key effect.

1. Select the **matte_face.psd** image matte clip from the **Project** panel and add it to the **V3** track in the **Timeline** panel. Next, drag the endpoint of the **matte_face.psd** clip to the length of the other clips in the **Timeline** panel, refer to Figure 12-52.

*Figure 12-52 The **matte_face.psd** clip in the **Video 3** track*

Notice that after adding the **matte_face.psd** clip to the **Timeline**, a white circle is displayed on the clip in the Program Monitor, as shown in Figure 12-53. You will position this white circle on the face of the girl with the change in time.

Figure 12-53 The white circle over the clip

2. Make sure the **matte_face.psd** clip is selected in the **Timeline** panel and the CTI is placed at the beginning of the sequence. Next, select the **Effect Controls** panel and expand the **Motion** node.

3. Choose the **Toggle animation** button on the left of the **Position** property; a keyframe is created in the timeline view for the current position of the white circle, as shown in Figure 12-54.

Video Effects		matte_face.psd
▼ *fx* 🖳▸ **Motion**	↩	
▸ 🎬 Position 360.0 288.0 ◂ ◆ ▸		▸
▸ 🕒 Scale 100.0		
▸ 🕒 Scale Width 100.0		

Figure 12-54 The keyframe in the timeline view

Next, you will position the white circle exactly over the face of the girl in the same keyframe.

4. Enter the values **321** and **246** in the **Position** edit boxes; the position of the white circle is changed in the same keyframe, as shown in Figure 12-55.

5. Move the CTI to frame 00:00:00:24. Next, double click on the white circle in the Program Monitor to select it; it is displayed with various control points, as shown in Figure 12-56.

Figure 12-55 *The new position of the white circle*

Figure 12-56 *The control points around the white circle*

6. Move the cursor over the white circle and drag it to cover the face of the girl, refer to Figure 12-57. Notice that as you drag the white circle, the values for **Position** change in the **Effect Controls** panel. Also, a new keyframe is created in the timeline view for the new position.

Figure 12-57 *The white circle dragged to a new position to cover the face of the girl*

7. Similarly, move the CTI to different frames and set new keyframes by changing the position of the white circle to cover the face of the girl at different points of time; various keyframes are created, as shown in Figure 12-58.

Video Effects			matte_face.psd
▼ *fx* ▯▸ Motion		↺	
▸ ◉ Position	304.1	267.4 ◂ ◆ ▸	▷◇◇◇◇ ◇◇ ◀◀◀◇◇◇◀◀◇◇◇◇ ◇ ◀◇ ◀◀
▸ ○ Scale	100.0		
▸ ○ Scale Width	100.0		
	☑ Uniform Sc...		

Figure 12-58 *Various keyframes in the timeline view*

8. Move the CTI to the beginning of the sequence and play it; the white circle starts moving over the face of the girl till the end.

Next, you will apply the **Mosaic** effect to the video clip placed in the **V2** track. The **Mosaic** effect is used to pixelate the clip or image by filling solid colored rectangles.

9. In the **Effects** panel, expand the **Video Effects > Stylize**; various effects are displayed. Next, select the **Mosaic** effect and drag it to the **beach clip (4).mov** clip placed in the **V2** track; the **Mosaic** effect is applied to the **beach clip (4).mov** placed in the **V2** track in the Program Monitor, as shown in Figure 12-59.

*Figure 12-59 The clip after applying the **Mosaic** effect*

Next, you will modify the properties of the **Mosaic** effect.

10. Make sure the **beach clip (4).mov** placed in the **V2** track is selected. In the **Effect Controls** panel, expand the **Mosaic** effect, if it is not expanded; various properties are displayed, as shown in Figure 12-60.

11. Enter the value **40** in both the **Horizontal Blocks** and **Vertical Blocks** edit boxes; you will notice a change in the **Mosaic** effect in the clip, as shown in Figure 12-61.

The **Horizontal Blocks** and **Vertical Blocks** edit boxes are used to specify the number of blocks in each row and column, respectively. The **Sharp Colors** check box is used to provide each rectangle tile the color of the pixel that is at the center of the corresponding region in the original image.

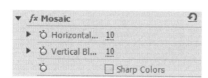

*Figure 12-60 The properties of the
Mosaic effect*

*Figure 12-61   The modified **Mosaic** effect
on the clip*

Next, you will apply the **Track Matte Key** effect such that the **Mosaic** effect appears only over the face of the girl as it moves.

12. In the **Effects** panel, expand **Video Effects > Keying**, if it is not expanded. Next, select the **Track Matte Key** effect in it and drag it to the **beach clip (4).mov** clip placed in the **V2** track.

13. In the **Effect Controls** panel, expand the **Track Matte Key** effect, if it is not expanded; various properties are displayed, as shown in Figure 12-62.

Figure 12-62 The properties of the ***Track Matte Key*** *effect*

14. In the **Matte** drop-down list, select the **Video 3** option. Also, make sure the **Matte Alpha** option is selected in the **Composite Using** drop-down list; the **Mosaic** effect is displayed over the face of the girl. Also, as the face of the girl moves, the effect also moves simultaneously, refer to Figure 12-63.

Figure 12-63 The ***Mosaic*** *effect on the face of the girl at one of the frames in the Program Monitor*

You can also highlight the face instead of giving it the **Mosaic** effect. To do so, follow the steps given next.

15. In the **Effect Controls** panel, choose the **Toggle the effect on or off** button on the left of the **Mosaic** effect to make the effect inactive.

16. In the **Effects** panel, expand **Video Effects > Color Correction**; various effects are displayed. Next, select the **Brightness & Contrast** effect and drag it to the **beach clip (4).mov** placed in the **V2** track; the effect is displayed in the **Effect Controls** panel.

17. Expand the **Brightness & Contrast** effect, if it is not expanded. Enter the value **70** for the **Brightness** parameter and **50** for the **Contrast** parameter. After entering the value, the face of the girl is highlighted, as shown in Figure 12-64. When you will play the sequence, the effect will also move over the face.

18. Press CTRL+S to save the file. Next, press the ENTER key to view the output of the sequence in the Program Monitor. The output of the sequence at frame 00:00:01:00 is shown in Figure 12-65.

Figure 12-64 The face of the girl highlighted at one of the frames

Figure 12-65 The output of the sequence at frame 00:00:01:00

Self-Evaluation Test

Answer the following questions and then compare them to those given at the end of this chapter:

1. Which of the following effects is used to make the entire clip uniformly transparent or semi-transparent?

    (a) **Opacity**   (b) **Brightness & Contrast**
    (c) **Mosaic**   (d) All of these

2. Which of the following effects is used in place of the **Opacity** fixed effect to change the default render order of the fixed effects?

   (a) **Alpha Glow**   (b) **Mosaic**
   (c) **Bevel Alpha**   (d) **Alpha Adjust**

3. The _____ option is used to composite the clips using the luminance values of the image matte.

4. _____ is the process of combining the clips from various tracks in the timeline to generate the final output.

5. In the properties of the **Alpha Glow** node, the _____ check box is used to specify whether the colors fade out or stay solid.

6. The _____ effect is used to blur the red, blue, green, or alpha channel individually.

7. The source color is the color of the layer to which you applied the **Blend** mode. (T/F)

8. The **Graphic** matte key effects are used to remove the unwanted portion of a clip. (T/F)

Review Questions

Answer the following questions:

1. Which of the following effects is used to create a hole in one clip to allow portions of another clip to be seen through?

   (a) **Image Matte Key**   (b) **Four-Point Garbage Matte**
   (c) **Track Matte Key**   (d) All of these

2. Which of the following effects is used to key out areas of an image based on the luminance values of a still image clip that serves as matte?

   (a) **Track Matte Key**   (b) **Difference Matte Key**
   (c) **Image Matte Key**   (d) All of these

3. Which of the following effects is used to pixelate a clip or an image by filling solid colored rectangles?

   (a) **Bevel Alpha**   (b) **Opacity**
   (c) **Brightness & Contrast**   (d) **Mosaic**

4. The _____, _____, and _____ **Garbage Matte Key** effects are used to crop out the unwanted portion of a video clip.

5. If the **Background** check box is selected, the Titler screen is filled with default black colored solid background. (T/F)

6. The underlying color is the color of the layer placed below the source layer in the **Timeline** panel. (T/F)

7. The main difference between the **Image Matte Key** effect and the **Track Matte Key** effect is that in the **Track Matte Key** effect, you need to place the image matte in a separate track whereas in the **Image Matte Key** effect, you need to apply it directly to the clip. (T/F)

EXERCISE

Exercise 1

Create a new project in Premiere and then add video clips to the sequence. Apply various video effects to the clips in the sequence. Try to animate various properties of the effects using keyframes in the **Effect Controls** panel and notice the difference. Also, change the mode of interpolation for the added keyframes to view the difference.

Answers to Self-Evaluation Test
1. a, **2.** d, **3. Matte Luma**, **4.** Compositing, **5. Fade Out**, **6. Channel Blur**, **7.** T, **8.** F

Chapter *13*

Exporting the Sequence

Learning Objectives

After completing this chapter, you will be able to:

- *Export single frame*
- *Export titles of the project*
- *Export a sequence to AVI file format*
- *Export a sequence to JPEG file format*
- *Export the sequence to various formats using the Adobe Media Encoder*
- *Export the project to Final Cut Pro XML*

INTRODUCTION

After compositing the videos in a sequence and completing the video editing part, you may need or convert them into different file formats. You have a number of choices to export the project. You can export a single frame, a series of frames, a clip, or an entire sequence. You can export only audio, video, or full audio/video output. Also, you can set various parameters for exporting the project such as frame size, frame rate, data rate, audio and video compression techniques, and so on. After exporting the project, you can use it for further editing in presentations, or for Internet. In this chapter, you will learn about various techniques used for exporting the final project to different media.

TUTORIALS

Before you start the tutorials, you need to download the *c13_premiere_cc_tut.zip* file from *www.cadcim.com*. The path of the file is as follows: *Textbooks > Animation and Visual Effects > Adobe Premiere Pro > Adobe Premiere Pro CC: A Tutorial Approach*

Next, extract the contents of the zipped file at *\Documents\Adobe Premiere Tutorials*.

Tutorial 1

In this tutorial, you will export a sequence into different file formats. Also, you will export the titles of a sequence.   **(Expected Time: 25 min)**

The following steps are required to complete this tutorial:

a. Open the project file.
b. Export a sequence to avi file format.
c. Export a sequence to jpeg file format.
d. Export title of the project.

Opening the Project File
In this section, you will open the project file.

1. Open the *chapter13.prproj* file that you have downloaded from the CADCIM website.

2. Save the *chapter13.prproj* file with the name *chapter13_export.prproj* to *\Documents\Adobe Premiere Tutorials\c13_premiere_cc_tut*. The *chapter13_export.prproj* file is displayed, as shown in Figure 13-1.

Exporting a Sequence to AVI File Format
In this section, you will export a sequence to the *avi* file format.

1. Make sure the **Sequence 01** tab in the **Timeline** panel is active.

Figure 13-1 *The chapter13_export file displayed*

2. Choose **File > Export** from the menu bar; a cascading menu is displayed, as shown in Figure 13-2.

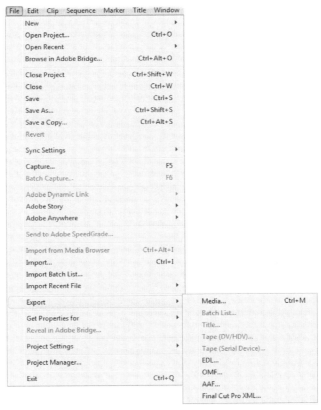

Figure 13-2 *The cascading menu*

There are many options available in this cascading menu for different export techniques.

The **Media** option is used to export the selected sequence to all popular media formats such as AVI, Animated GIF, TIFF, MPEG4, and so on. The **Title** option is used to export only the titles of a project. You can use the exported titles in other projects. By default, this option is inactive. To activate it, select the title to be exported from the **Project** panel. The **Tape** option is used to export a sequence or the entire project to a videotape in a supported camcorder or VTR. The **EDL** option is used to export a file in the edl format and allows you to specify the settings for recreating the file either with related media or by using another editing system. The **OMF** option is used to export active audio tracks from the Premiere sequence to an open media format file. The **AAF** option is used to export an advanced authoring format file that allows you to exchange digital media and metadata between platforms, systems, and applications. The **Final Cut Pro XML** option is used to export an XML file that can be used into Apple Final Cut Pro for further editing.

Next, you will export **Sequence 01** by using the **Media** option from the cascading menu.

3.   Choose the **Media** option from the cascading menu; the **Export Settings** dialog box is displayed, as shown in Figure 13-3. Alternatively, you can press CTRL+M keys to display the **Export Settings** dialog box.

*Figure 13-3 The **Export Settings** dialog box*

The **Export Settings** dialog box is used to set the format for the final output file that you will get after exporting the project.

In the **Export Settings** area of the **Export Settings** dialog box, you can select the **Match Sequence Settings** check box to export the sequence with the same settings that you had specified for the sequence while setting the presets. If you select the **Match Sequence Settings** check box, then other options in this area will become inactive.

The **Format** drop-down list is used to select the format such as AVI, MP3, MPEG4 for the output file. The **Preset** drop-down list is used to specify the preset settings for the output file.

4. Make sure the **Match Sequence Settings** check box is cleared and the **AVI** option is displayed in the **Format** drop-down list.

5. Click on the text on the right of the **Output Name** option; the **Save As** dialog box is displayed, refer to Figure 13-4. Browse to the location where you want to save the final output file. Next, type **chapter13_output** in the **File name** text box. Now, choose the **Save** button; the new file name is displayed in the **Output Name** text box, refer to Figure 13-5.

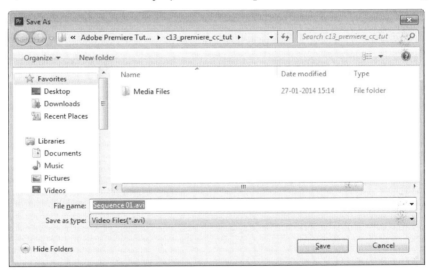

Figure 13-4 The **Save As** dialog box

Figure 13-5 The new file name in the **Output Name** text box

By default, the **Export Video** and **Export Audio** check boxes are selected, refer to Figure 13-5. These check boxes are used to export the video as well as the audio of the sequence. If you do not want to export the video or the audio portion of the sequence, then clear the check box corresponding to that option. The **Summary** area displays the settings of the final output file and the source file, refer to Figure 13-3.

Just below the **Summary** area, there are five tabs in the **Export Settings** dialog box. Note that the number of tabs may vary based on the option selected in the **Format** drop-down list. Choose the **Filters** tab, if not already chosen. In this tab, there is a **Gaussian Blur** check box available for the encoded output and this check box is cleared by default. The **Gaussian Blur** filter is used to reduce the video noise in the final output file by slightly blurring the video. It is recommended not to use this filter. But, if there is too much noise in the final output file, then you can use the **Gaussian Blur** filter by selecting this check box.

The **Video Codec** drop-down list in the **Video** tab is used to set the video compression algorithm. The default values in this tab are set based on the preset you specified for the sequence.

The **Audio** tab is used to adjust the sample rate, channels, sample type, and codec for the audio. The default values in this tab are set based on the preset specified for the sequence.

The **FTP** tab is used to specify the FTP server for uploading the exported video. Retain the default settings in the **Filters**, **Video**, **Audio**, and **FTP** tabs.

At the bottom of the **Export Settings** dialog box, there are four check boxes, namely **Use Maximum Render Quality**, **Use Previews**, **Use Frame Blending**, and **Import into project**. The **Use Maximum Render Quality** check box is used to set the quality of the rendering. If you select this check box, then the rendering process will be slowed down by a factor of four or five. The **Use Previews** check box is used to preview the final rendered file in which all video effects may not be shown properly. The **Use Frame Blending** check box is used to smoothen the motion whenever you change the speed of a source clip in your project or render to a different frame rate. The **Import into project** check box is used to import the final rendered file into the **Project** panel

6. Clear the **Use Maximum Render Quality**, **Use Previews**, **Use Frame Blending**, and **Import into project** check boxes, if they are not cleared.

The **Source Range** drop-down list at the bottom left of the dialog box is used to specify the exporting areas. By default, the **Work Area** option is selected in this drop-down list. As a result, the work area of the sequence is exported. The **Entire Sequence** option in the **Source Range** drop-down list is used to export the entire sequence. The **Sequence In/Out** option in the **Source Range** drop-down list is used to export the area which is set between the In and Out points of the sequence. The **Custom** option in the **Source Range** drop-down list is used to customize the area of the sequence to render. To do so, you need to drag the slider which is just above the **Source Range** drop-down list.

7. Select the **Entire Sequence** option in the **Source Range** drop-down list.

The **Queue** button on the bottom right of the **Export Settings** dialog box is used to send the file to Adobe Media Encoder to queue the sequence for exporting. The **Export** button is used to export the sequence directly from the **Export Settings** dialog box. The **Cancel** button is used to cancel the export process.

8. Choose the **Export** button; the **Encoding Sequence 01** message box is displayed showing the encoding process, refer to Figure 13-6. After completing the encoding process, the **Encoding Sequence 01** message box and the **Export Settings** dialog box are closed. Also, the final output file is saved at the specified location and you can view it anytime.

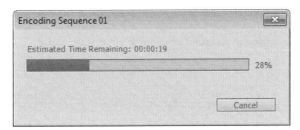

Figure 13-6 *The* **Encoding Sequence 01** *message box*

Exporting a Sequence to JPEG File Format

In Premiere, you can export the single frame instead of exporting the entire sequence or work area bar. In this section, you will export single frame from the sequence.

1. Make sure the *chapter13_export* file is opened. Next, in the Program Monitor, move the CTI to display the frame that you need to export.

2. In the Program Monitor, choose the **Button Editor** button; the **Button Editor** dialog box is displayed. In this dialog box, drag the **Export Frame** button and drop it on the tools available at the bottom of the Program Monitor. Next, choose the **OK** button to close the dialog box. Choose the **Export Frame** button; the **Export Frame** dialog box is displayed, as shown in Figure 13-7.

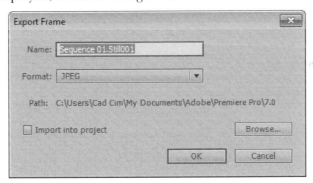

Figure 13-7 *The* **Export Frame** *dialog box*

3. Type a name of your choice in the **Name** text box.

4. Select the **JPEG** option from the **Format** drop-down list, if it is not selected. You can also select any other format of your choice.

5. Specify the location of the output file by using the **Browse** button and then choose the **OK** button; the displayed frame is saved at the specified location with the name you entered in the **Name** text box.

Exporting the Title of the Project

You can also export only the titles of the project and use them later in other projects. In this section, you will export the titles of the project.

1. Make sure the *chapter13_export* file is opened. In the **Project** panel, select the **Title 01** title. Next, choose **File > Export > Title** from the menu bar; the **Save Title** dialog box is displayed, as shown in Figure 13-8.

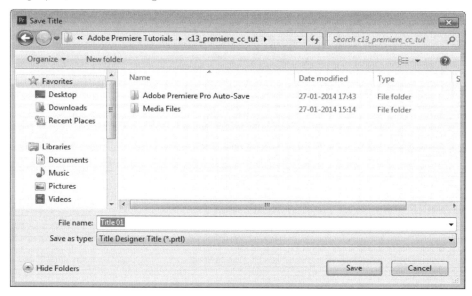

Figure 13-8 The **Save Title** *dialog box*

2. Browse to a location in the **Save Title** dialog box to save the title.

3. Type the name of the title of your choice in the **File name** text box. Also, make sure the **Title Designer Title (*.prtl)** option is selected in the **Save as type** drop-down list. Next, choose the **Save** button; the title is saved at the specified location. Now, you can use the saved title in other projects by importing it in the **Project** panel.

4. Press CTRL+S to save the file.

Tutorial 2

In this tutorial, you will export a project to Final Cut Pro XML and various other file formats using Adobe Media Encoder.   **(Expected Time: 25 min)**

The following steps are required to complete this tutorial:

a. Open the project file.
b. Export the project to Final Cut Pro XML.
c. Export a project file to various formats using the Adobe Media Encoder.

Opening the Project File

In this section, you will open the project file.

1. Open the *chapter13_export_01.prproj* file that you have downloaded from the CADCIM website. Choose the **Sequence 01** tab in the **Timeline** panel.

Exporting the Project to Final Cut Pro XML

In this section, you will export the project to an XML file that can be used in the Apple Final Cut Pro.

1. Choose **File > Export** from the menu bar; a cascading menu is displayed. Choose the **Final Cut Pro XML** option from the cascading menu; the **Save Converted Sequence As - Final Cut Pro XML** dialog box is displayed, as shown in Figure 13-9. Browse to a location of your choice to save the file. Type **chapter13_export_final cut pro** in the **File name** text box. Make sure the **Final Cut Pro XML (*.xml)** is displayed in the **Save as type** drop-down list.

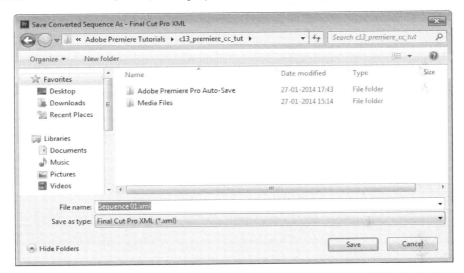

*Figure 13-9 The **Save Converted Sequence As - Final Cut Pro XML** dialog box*

2. Choose the **Save** button; the **Translation Report** message box is displayed, as shown in Figure 13-10. This message box prompts you to check the report of FCP Translation Results for the possible issues encountered during translation. The FCP Translation Report will be saved at the same location as specified for saving the Final Cut Pro XML file. You can now import and use the saved XML file in the Final Cut Pro.

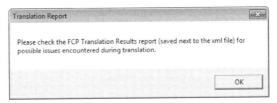

*Figure 13-10 The **Translation Report** message box*

The Premiere and Apple Final Cut Pro have different file compatibilities. Therefore, there may always be some issues while translating the project to the XML format. Next, choose the **OK** button to close the message box.

Exporting a Project File to Various Formats Using Adobe Media Encoder

Adobe Media Encoder can be run from the Windows or can be launched through Premiere. In this section, you will export the project file to various formats using Adobe Media Encoder.

1. Make sure the *chapter13_export_01* file is opened in Premiere and the **Sequence 01** tab in the **Timeline** panel is chosen.

2. Choose **File > Export** from the menu bar; a cascading menu is displayed. Choose the **Media** option from the cascading menu; the **Export Settings** dialog box is displayed.

3. Make sure the **AVI** option is selected in the **Format** drop-down list.

4. Click on the text given on the right of **Output Name**; the **Save As** dialog box is displayed. Browse to the location where you want to save the final output file. Next, type **chapter13_output_02** in the **File name** text box and choose the **Save** button; the new file name is displayed in the **Output Name** text box.

5. Select the **Export Video** and **Export Audio** check boxes, if they are not selected.

6. Retain the default settings in the **Filters**, **Video**, **Audio**, and **FTP** tabs. Choose the **Queue** button at the bottom of the **Export Settings** dialog box; the Adobe Media Encoder is launched, as shown in Figure 13-11.

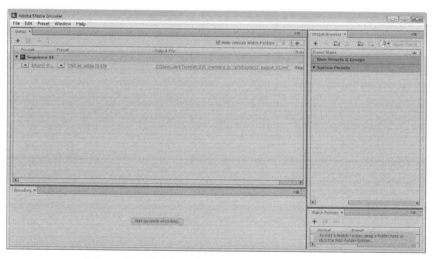

Figure 13-11 *The Adobe Media Encoder launched*

Note that the sequence in the Adobe Media Encoder is displayed as a list. Next, you will duplicate the same sequence to export it in a different format.

7. Right-click on the **Sequence 01** in the Adobe Media Encoder; a shortcut menu is displayed. Next, choose the **Duplicate** option from the shortcut menu; the duplicate sequence is displayed, as shown in Figure 13-12.

Figure 13-12 The duplicate sequence in the Adobe Media Encoder

Note
*You can also add more sequences to export in different formats using the **Add Source*** ✚
*button from the **Queue** area.*

8. Click on the arrow located on the left of the **Format** column in the second row; a 🔽
flyout is displayed, refer to Figure 13-13. Choose a format of your choice. Similarly, you can choose a different preset using the **Preset** column. You can also specify the location for the output file using the **Output File** column.

9. Choose the **Start Queue (Return)** button located on the top right in the **Adobe** ▶
Media Encoder dialog box; the sequences listed in the Adobe Media Encoder start exporting sequentially.

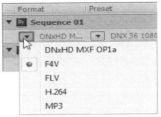

Figure 13-13 Flyout displaying different formats

Self-Evaluation Test

Answer the following questions and then compare them to those given at the end of this chapter:

1. Which of the following options in the **File** menu of the menu bar is used to export a sequence to a videotape in a supported camcorder or VTR?

    (a) **Media**   (b) **EDL**
    (c) **Tape**   (d) **Title**

2. Which of the following options in the **File** menu of the menu bar is used to export a sequence to an XML file?

    (a) **Title**   (b) **Media**
    (c) **OMF**   (d) **Final Cut Pro XML**

3. The _____ filter in the **Export Settings** dialog box is used to reduce the video noise in the final output file by slightly blurring the video.

4. You can press the _____ keys to display the **Export Settings** dialog box.

5. The _____ option is used to export an advanced authoring format file that allows you to exchange digital media and metadata between platforms, systems, and applications.

6. In Premiere, you can export single or multiple frames instead of exporting the entire sequence or Work area bar. (T/F)

7. You can invoke the **Export Settings** dialog box by pressing the CTRL+E key. (T/F)

Review Questions

Answer the following questions:

1. Which of the following options in the menu bar is used to export active audio tracks from a Premiere sequence to an open media format file?

        (a) **AAF**   (b) **OMF**
        (c) **EDL**   (d) All of these

2. The _____ dialog box is used to set the format for the final output file that you will get after exporting the project.

3. The _____, _____ check boxes in the **Export Settings** dialog box are used to export the video as well the audio of the sequence.

4. The **FTP** tab is used to specify the FTP server for uploading on exported video. (T/F)

EXERCISE

Exercise 1

Create a new project in Premiere. Import your video clips and compose them using various effects and transitions. Then, add titles to the project. Next, export the project to various formats using Adobe Encoder.

Answers to Self-Evaluation Test
1. c, **2.** d, **3.** Gaussian Blur, **4.** CTRL+M, **5.** Adobe Encore, **6.** T, **7.** F

Chapter 14

Miscellaneous Effects

Learning Objectives

After completing this chapter, you will be able to:

- *Place light over a part of a clip*
- *Blur a part of a video clip*
- *Create the Split-Screen effect*
- *Zoom and pan a still image*
- *Create the Track Matte Key effect*
- *Highlight a part of an image*
- *Create the ghost effect*

INTRODUCTION

In this chapter, you will create some miscellaneous effects in Premiere using various tools and techniques that you have learned in previous chapters.

TUTORIALS

Before you start the tutorials, you need to download the *c14_premiere_cc_tut.zip* file from *www.cadcim.com*. The path of the file is as follows: *Textbooks > Animation and Visual Effects > Adobe Premiere Pro > Adobe Premiere Pro CC: A Tutorial Approach*

Next, extract the contents of the zipped file at *\Documents\Adobe Premiere Tutorials*.

Tutorial 1

In this tutorial, you will place lights over a part of a video clip. The output of the sequence at frame 00:00:01:02 is shown in Figure 14-1.   (**Expected Time: 20 min**)

Figure 14-1 The output of the sequence at frame 00:00:01:02

The following steps are required to complete this tutorial:

a. Open the project file.
b. Place a light over a part of the clip.

Opening the Project File

In this section, you will open the project file.

1. Open the *chapter14_placing_light.prproj* file that you have downloaded from the CADCIM website. Next, save the *chapter14_placing_light.prproj* file with the name *chapter14_placing_light_02.prproj* to *\Documents\Adobe Premiere Tutorials\c14_premiere_cc_tut*. The *chapter14_placing_light_02.prproj* file is displayed.

    Next, you will add the video portion of the **beach clip (11).mov** clip to the sequence.

Placing a Light Over a Part of a Clip

In this section, you will place a light over the part of a clip.

1. In the **Project** panel, double-click on the **beach clip (11).mov** clip; it is opened in the Source Monitor, as shown in Figure 14-2.

Figure 14-2 The chapter14_placing_light_02 file displayed

2. In the Source Monitor, move the cursor over the **Drag Video Only** button; the shape of the cursor changes into a hand shaped cursor. Next, press and hold the left mouse button and drag the video clip to the beginning of the **V2** track in the **Timeline** panel. Next, double-click on the blank area at the right side of the **Toggle Track Output** button to expand the **V2** track. The clips are displayed in the **Timeline** panel, as shown in Figure 14-3.

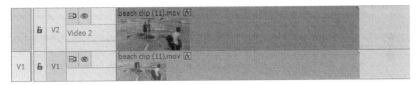

*Figure 14-3 The clips in the **Timeline** panel*

Next, you will apply the **Lighting Effects** effect to the video clip placed in the **V2** track.

3. Make sure the CTI is placed at the beginning of the sequence. In the **Effects** panel, expand **Video Effects > Adjust**; various effects are displayed. Next, select the **Lighting Effects** effect and drag it from the **Effects** panel to the **beach clip (11).mov** clip placed on the **V2** track in the **Timeline** panel. After applying the effect, the clip is displayed in the Program Monitor, as shown in Figure 14-4.

*Figure 14-4 The clip after applying the **Lighting Effects** effect*

Next, you will modify the properties of the **Lighting Effects** effect.

4. Select the **beach clip (11).mov** clip in the **V2** track, if it is not already selected.

5. Select the **Effect Controls** panel; various effects are displayed. Next, expand the **Lighting Effects** effect, if it is not expanded; its properties are displayed. Next, expand the **Light 1** option; various properties of **Light 1** are displayed.

6. Modify the properties of **Light 1** as given next:

    Make sure the **Spotlight** option is selected in the **Light Type** drop-down list.

Center:	**306.0**	**271.0**
Major Radius:	**15.0**	
Minor Radius:	**15.0**	
Intensity:	**25.0**	
Focus:	**86.0**	

    After modifying the properties of **Light 1**, the clip is displayed in the Program Monitor, as shown in Figure 14-5.

*Figure 14-5 The clip after modifying the properties of **Light 1***

7. Play the sequence. You will notice that the light effect is displayed on the entire clip.

    Next, you will trim the clip placed in the **V2** track to make the light effect available only to a part of clip.

8. Move the CTI to the frame 00:00:08:09.

9. Make sure the **Selection Tool** is invoked. Next, move the cursor at the end of the clip placed in the **V2** track; the cursor is changed to a closed bracket with an arrow, refer to Figure 14-6. Next, press and hold the left mouse button and drag the cursor toward left to snap the cursor with the CTI placed at the frame 00:00:08:09, refer to Figure 14-7. Release the left mouse button; the clip is trimmed up to the frame 00:00:08:09 and displayed in the sequence, as shown in Figure 14-8.

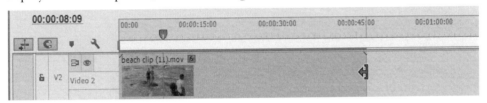

Figure 14-6 The cursor changed to a closed bracket with an arrow

Figure 14-7 The cursor snapped to the CTI while moving toward left

Figure 14-8 The trimmed clip in the V2 track

10. Move the CTI to the beginning of the sequence and play it. You will notice that the light effect is displayed only on a part of the clip. However, the change is very abrupt. To make the change smooth, you need to add transition effects to the clip placed in the **V2** track.

11. In the **Effects** panel, expand **Video Transitions > Dissolve**; various transition effects are displayed. Next, select the **Additive Dissolve** transition effect and drag it to the beginning of the clip placed in the **V2** track. Release the left mouse button; the transition effect is added to the beginning of the clip.

12. Similarly, apply the **Additive Dissolve** transition effect at the end of the clip placed in the **V2** track. After applying the effect, the clip is displayed in the **Timeline** panel, as shown in Figure 14-9.

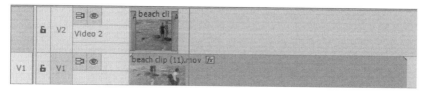

Figure 14-9 *The transition effect at the beginning and end of the clip placed in the V2 track*

13. Move the CTI to the beginning of the sequence and play it. Note that the light effect now appears and disappears smoothly.

14. Press CTRL+S to save the file. The output of the sequence at frame 00:00:01:02 is shown in Figure 14-10.

Figure 14-10 *The output of the sequence at frame 00:00:01:02*

Tutorial 2

In this tutorial, you will blur a part of a video clip. Figure 14-11 displays the output of the sequence at frame 00:00:02:04.   **(Expected Time: 20 min)**

The following steps are required to complete this tutorial:

a. Open the project file.
b. Blur a part of a video clip.

Figure 14-11 *The output of the sequence at frame 00:00:02:04*

Opening the Project File

In this section, you will open the project file.

1. Open the *chapter14_blur.prproj* file that you have downloaded from the CADCIM website.

2. Save the *chapter14_blur.prproj* file with the name *chapter14_blur_02.prproj* to *\Documents\Adobe Premiere Tutorials\c14_premiere_cc_tut*. The *chapter14_blur_02.prproj* file is displayed, as shown in Figure 14-12.

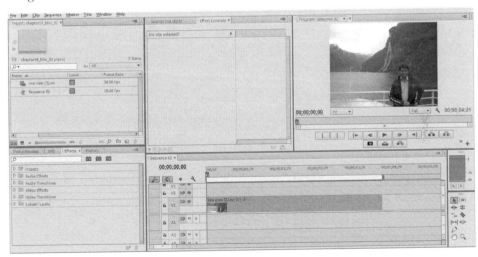

Figure 14-12 *The chapter14_blur_02 file displayed*

Next, you will add the video portion of the **sea view (3).avi** clip to the sequence.

Blurring a Part of a Video Clip

In this section, you will blur a part of a video clip using the **Blur** effect.

1. In the **Project** panel, double-click on the **sea view (3).avi** clip; it is opened in the Source Monitor.

2. In the Source Monitor, move the cursor over the **Drag Video Only** button; the shape of the cursor changes into a hand. Next, press and hold the left mouse button and drag the video clip at the beginning of the **V2** track in the **Timeline** panel. Next, double-click on the blank area at the right side of the **Toggle Track Output** button to expand the **V2** track.

    Next, you need to blur the face of the person in the clip. To do so, first you will apply the blur effect to the video clip placed in **V2** track.

3. In the **Effects** panel, expand **Video Effects > Blur & Sharpen**; various blur effects are displayed. Next, select the **Gaussian Blur** effect and drag it from the **Effects** panel to the clip placed on the **V2** track in the **Timeline** panel.

    Next, you will modify the properties of the **Gaussian Blur** effect.

4. Choose the **Effect Controls** panel; various effects are displayed. Expand the **Gaussian Blur** effect, if it is not expanded; its properties are displayed. Next, enter **35** for the **Blurriness** parameter; the clip is blurred in the Program Monitor, as shown in Figure 14-13.

Figure 14-13 The blurred clip displayed in the Program Monitor

You will notice that the entire clip is blurred. To blur only the face of the clip, you need to follow the steps given next.

5. In the **Effects** panel, expand **Video Effects > Transform**; various effects are displayed. Select the **Crop** effect and drag it to the clip placed in the **V2** track in the **Timeline** panel.

    Next, you will modify the properties of the **Crop** effect in the **Effect Controls** panel.

6. Make sure the CTI is placed at the beginning of the sequence.

7. In the **Effect Controls** panel, expand the **Crop** effect, if it is not expanded and modify the values as given below:

Left: **61.0**   Top: **50.0**
Right: **24.0**   Bottom: **29.0**

After modifying the values of the **Crop** effect, the face of the person in the clip seems blurred and displayed in the Program Monitor, as shown in Figure 14-14.

Figure 14-14 The blurred face in the Program Monitor

8. Play the sequence and you will notice that the blur effect is not overlapping the face of the person in some of the frames, refer to Figure 14-15. To avoid this situation, you need to add keyframes for the **Blur** effect in the **Effect Controls** panel.

Figure 14-15 Part of the face is blurred in some of the frames

9. Move the CTI to the frame 00:00:02:04.

10. In the **Effect Controls** panel, enter the value **40** in the edit box on the right of the **Top** property; the blurred effect is modified, as shown in Figure 14-16.

Figure 14-16 *The blurred face after creating the keyframe*

11. Move the CTI to the beginning of the sequence and play the sequence. Now, the **Blur** effect will protect the identity of the person by hiding his face in the entire clip.

12. Press CTRL+S to save the file. The output of the sequence at frame 00:00:02:04 is shown in Figure 14-17.

Figure 14-17 *The output of the sequence at frame 00:00:02:04*

Tutorial 3

In this tutorial, you will create the split-screen effect using the **Motion** effect. The output of the sequence at frame 00:00:01:06 is shown in Figure 14-18   **(Expected Time: 20 min)**

Figure 14-18 The output of the sequence at frame 00:00:01:06

The following steps are required to complete this tutorial:

a.   Open the project file.
b.   Create split-screen effect.

Opening the Project File

In this section, you will open the project file.

1.   Open the *chapter14_splitscreen.prproj* file that you have downloaded from the CADCIM website.

2.   Save the *chapter14_splitscreen.prproj* file with the name *chapter14_splitscreen_02.prproj* to the *\Documents\Adobe Premiere Tutorials\c14_premiere_cc_tut*. The *chapter14_splitscreen_02.prproj* file is displayed, as shown in Figure 14-19.

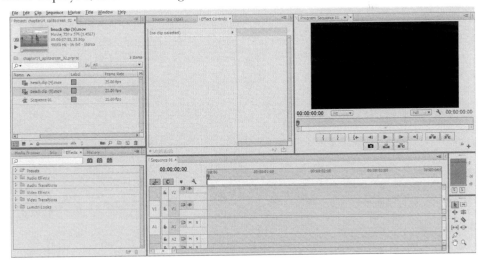

Figure 14-19 The chapter14_splitscreen_02 file displayed

Creating the Split-Screen Effect

In this section, you will create a split-screen effect.

1. In the **Project** panel, double-click on the **beach clip (4).mov** clip; it is opened in the Source Monitor.

    Next, you will create two scenes from the **beach clip (4).mov** clip by setting the In and Out points.

2. In the Source Monitor, move the Playhead to the frame 00:00:00:19 and choose the **Mark In** button; the In point is set for the first scene. Similarly, move the Playhead to the frame 00:00:03:00 and choose the **Mark Out** button; the Out point is set for the first scene, refer to Figure 14-20.

Figure 14-20 The In and Out points for the first scene

Next, you will add the trimmed scene to the sequence in the **Timeline** panel.

3. Move the cursor over the clip in the Source Monitor and drag it to the **V1** track in the **Timeline** panel, as shown in Figure 14-21.

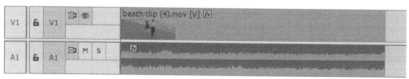

Figure 14-21 The clip added to the sequence

4. Next, in the Source Monitor, move the Playhead to the frame 00:00:11:03 and choose the **Mark In** button; the In point is set for the second scene. Similarly, move the Playhead to the frame 00:00:15:09 and choose the **Mark Out** button; the Out point is set for the second scene.

    Next, you will add only the video portion of the trimmed clip to the sequence in the **Timeline** panel.

5. Move the cursor on the **Drag Video Only** button in the Source Monitor and drag it to the **V2** track in the **Timeline** panel.

    Next, you will create two scenes from the **beach clip (9).mov** clip by setting the In and Out points.

6. In the **Project** panel, double-click on the **beach clip (9).mov** clip; it is opened in the Source Monitor.

7. In the Source Monitor, move the Playhead to the frame 00:00:00:05 and choose the **Mark In** button; the In point is set for the first scene. Similarly, move the Playhead to the frame 00:00:01:16 and choose the **Mark Out** button; the Out point is set for the first scene.

8. Next, add only the video portion of the trimmed clip to the **V3** track in the **Timeline** panel, refer to Figure 14-22.

Figure 14-22 The trimmed clip added to the V3 track

9. Again, in the Source Monitor, move the Playhead to the frame 00:00:03:11 and choose the **Mark In** button; the In point is set for the second scene. Similarly, move the CTI to the frame 00:00:05:14 and choose the **Mark Out** button; the Out point is set for the second scene.

    Note that there are only 3 video tracks and clips are placed in each track. To place the trimmed clip created in step 9, you need to add one more video track to the **Timeline** panel.

10. Right-click on the blank area above **V3** track label in the **Timeline** panel; a shortcut menu is displayed. Choose the **Add Tracks** option from the shortcut menu; the **Add Tracks** dialog box is displayed.

11. In the **Video Tracks** area of the **Add Tracks** dialog box, make sure the **After Video 3** option is selected in the **Placement** drop-down list. Choose the **OK** button; the **V4** track is added to the **Timeline** panel.

 Tip: *You can add one more video track to the **Timeline** panel by dragging the clip on the blank area above **V3** track.*

12. Add only the video portion of the trimmed clip created in step 9 to the **V4** track in the **Timeline** panel. All four clips are placed in a sequence, as shown in Figure 14-23.

*Figure 14-23 The clips in the **Timeline** panel*

13. Move the cursor to the end of the clips placed in **V1**, **V2**, and **V3** tracks one by one and drag them to make their length similar to the clip placed in the **V4** track.

You will notice that in the Program Monitor, you can view only the clip placed in the top track, which is **V4** track. Next, you will create the split screen effect to view all four clips simultaneously.

14. In the **Timeline** panel, select the clip placed in the **V4** track. Next, in the **Effect Controls** panel, expand the **Motion** effect; its properties are displayed. Enter the value **50** for the **Scale** parameter and press the ENTER key; the clip is scaled and displayed in the Program Monitor, as shown in Figure 14-24.

15. Select the scaled clip in the Program Monitor and position it to the top left corner, refer to Figure 14-25.

Figure 14-24 The scaled clip in the Program Monitor

Figure 14-25 The scaled clip at the top left corner in the Program Monitor

16. Scale the clips placed in the **V3**, **V2**, and **V1** tracks by **50** units and place them at the corners of the screen, refer to Figure 14-26.

Figure 14-26 All clips scaled and placed at the corners of the screen

17. Make sure the CTI is placed at the beginning of the sequence and play it to view the split-screen effect.

Note
You can also create the eight-screen, two-screen, or sixteen-screen effects using the same method as discussed above.

18. Press CTRL+S to save the file. The output of the sequence at frame 00:00:01:06 is shown in Figure 14-27.

Figure 14-27 *The output of the sequence at frame 00:00:01:06*

Tutorial 4

In this tutorial, you will zoom in and pan a still image using keyframe animation. The output of the sequence at frame 00:00:02:10 is shown in Figure 14-28.   **(Expected Time: 15 min)**

Figure 14-28 *The output of the sequence at frame 00:00:02:10*

The following steps are required to complete this tutorial:

a. Open the project file.
b. Zoom and pan a still image.

Opening the Project File

In this section, you will open the project file.

1. Open the *chapter14_zoom.prproj* file that you have downloaded from the CADCIM website.

2. Save the *chapter14_zoom.prproj* file with the new name *chapter14_zoom_02.prproj* to the location *\Documents\Adobe Premiere Tutorials\c14_premiere_cc_tut*. The *chapter14_zoom_02. prproj* file is displayed. Notice that there is one still image named as *C2.JPG* in the **Project** panel.

Zooming and Panning a Still Image

In this section, you will zoom and pan a still image.

1. Add the **C2.JPG** image from the **Project** panel to the **Timeline** panel at the beginning of the sequence in **V1** track. Next, press the EQUAL (=) key to view it properly in the sequence, refer to Figure 14-29. The **C2.JPG** image is displayed in the Program Monitor, as shown in Figure 14-30.

*Figure 14-29 The **C2.JPG** image clip in the **Timeline** panel*

*Figure 14-30 The **C2.JPG** image clip in the Program Monitor*

2. Select the **C2.JPG** image clip in the **Timeline** panel, if it is not selected; various effects are displayed in the **Effect Controls** panel.

3. In the **Effect Controls** panel, expand the **Motion** effect; various properties are displayed.

   Next, you will modify the **Position** and **Scale** properties to zoom in and pan the image over time.

4. Make sure the CTI is placed at the beginning of the sequence. Next, choose the **Toggle animation** button on the left of the **Position** and **Scale** properties; a keyframe is created for the current value of each property, refer to Figure 14-31.

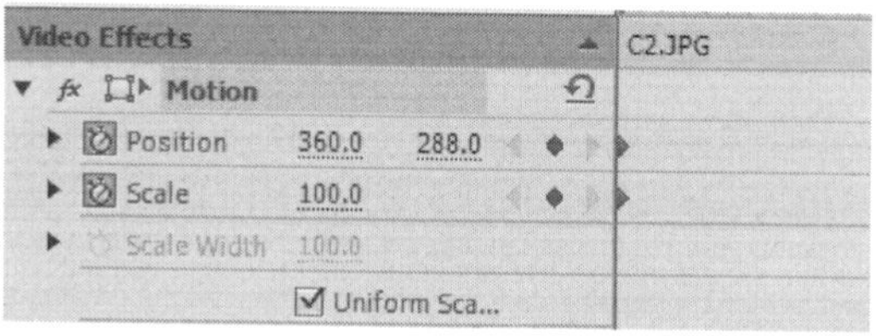

Figure 14-31 Keyframes created for the current values

5. Move the CTI to the frame 00:00:01:18. Next, in the **Effects Controls** panel, specify the values of the parameters as follows:

Position: **150**   **288**
Scale: **50**

After entering the values, the keyframes are created for the modified values. Also, the **C2.JPG** image clip is displayed in the Program Monitor, as shown in Figure 14-32.

Figure 14-32 *The clip in the Program Monitor at the frame 00:00:01:18*

6. Again, move the CTI to the frame 00:00:03:22. Next, specify the values of parameters as follows:

Position: **-148**   **288**
Scale: **131**

After entering the values, other keyframes are created for the modified values. Also, the **C2.JPG** clip image is displayed in the Program Monitor, as shown in Figure 14-33.

Figure 14-33 *The clip in the Program Monitor at the frame 00:00:03:22*

7. Again, move the CTI to the frame 00:00:05:00. Next, specify the parameters as follows:

Position: **-313.7**   **442.6**
Scale: **178**

After entering the values, other keyframes are created based on the modified values. These keyframes are displayed in the **Effect Controls** panel, as shown in Figure 14-34. Also, the **C2.JPG** clip image at 00:00:05:00 frame is displayed in the Program Monitor, as shown in Figure 14-35.

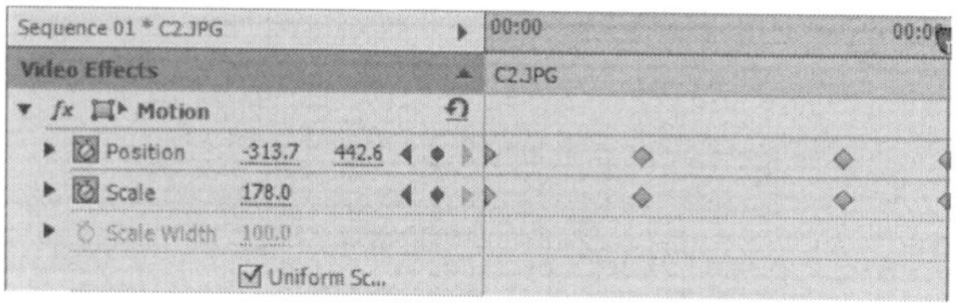

Figure 14-34 *All keyframes in the **Effect Controls** panel*

Figure 14-35 *The clip in the Program Monitor at 00:00:05:00 frame*

8. Move the CTI to the beginning of the sequence and play it; the image displays the zoom and pan effects over time.

9. Press CTRL+S to save the file. The output of the sequence at frame 00:00:02:10 is shown in Figure 14-36.

Figure 14-36 *The output of the sequence at frame 00:00:02:10*

Tutorial 5

In this tutorial, you will create the **Track Matte Key** effect. The output of the sequence at frame 00:00:06:22 is shown in Figure 14-37.   **(Expected Time: 20 min)**

The following steps are required to complete this tutorial:

a. Open the project file.
b. Create the **Track Matte Key** effect.

Figure 14-37 *The output of the sequence at frame 00:00:06:22*

Opening the Project File

In this section, you will open the project file.

1. Open the *chapter14_transporter.prproj* file that you have downloaded from the CADCIM
    website.

2. Save the *chapter14_transporter.prproj* file with the name *chapter14_transporter_02.prproj* to the
    \Documents\Adobe Premiere Tutorials\c14_premiere_cc_tut. The *chapter14_transporter_02.prproj*
    file is displayed, as shown in Figure 14-38. Notice that there are two video clips placed in
    the **V1** track without any audio.

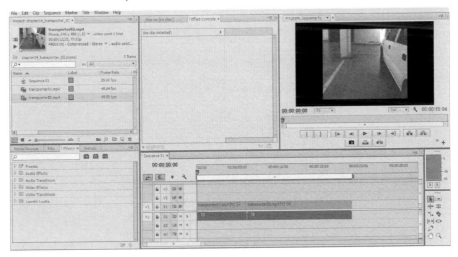

Figure 14-38 *The chapter14_transporter_02 file displayed*

Creating the Track Matte Key Effect

In this section, you will create the **Track Matte Key** effect.

1. Select the **transporter01** clip in the **V1** track and right-click on it; a shortcut menu is displayed. Choose the **Rename** option from the shortcut menu; the **Rename Clip** dialog box is displayed, as shown in Figure 14-39. Type **Start** in the **Clip Name** text box and then choose the **OK** button; the name of the clip is changed. Similarly, rename the **transporter02** clip to **End**.

*Figure 14-39 The **Rename Clip** dialog box*

2. In the **Timeline** panel, add a **V4** track. Next, select the **Start** clip and place it at the beginning of the **V4** track, refer to Figure 14-40.

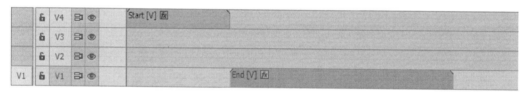

*Figure 14-40 The **Start** clip placed in the **V4** track*

3. Choose the **Toggle Track Output** button on the left of the **V4** track to make this track invisible.

Next, you will copy the **End** clip.

4. Select the **End** clip and right-click on it; a shortcut menu is displayed. Choose the **Copy** option from the shortcut menu to copy the **End** clip.

5. Move the CTI to the end of the **End** clip and press the CTRL+V keys; the copied clip is pasted at the end of the **End** clip in **V1** track, refer to Figure 14-41.

*Figure 14-41 The copied **End** clip in the **V1** track*

6. Rename the first **End** clip in the **V1** track to **Freeze** and then move the **Freeze** and **End** clips at the beginning of the **V1** track, refer to Figure 14-42.

*Figure 14-42 The **Freeze** and **End** clips in the **V1** track*

Next, you will modify the duration of the **Freeze** clip.

7. Select the **Freeze** clip and right-click on it; a shortcut menu is displayed. Choose the **Speed/Duration** option from the shortcut menu; the **Clip Speed / Duration** dialog box is displayed, as shown in Figure 14-43. Next, enter **05.00** in the **Duration** edit box and choose the **OK** button; the duration of **Freeze** clip is now 5 seconds. After modifying the duration of the clip, it is displayed in the sequence, as shown in Figure 14-44.

*Figure 14-43 The **Clip Speed / Duration** dialog box*

*Figure 14-44 The **Freeze** clip in the sequence after modifying its duration*

8. Move the **Freeze** clip toward right to fill the gap between both the clips in the sequence, refer to Figure 14-45.

*Figure 14-45 The **Freeze** clip after it is moved*

Next, you will freeze or hold the **Freeze** clip.

9. Select the **Freeze** clip and right-click on it; a shortcut menu is displayed. Choose the **Frame Hold** option; the **Frame Hold Options** dialog box is displayed, as shown in Figure 14-46.

*Figure 14-46 The **Frame Hold Options** dialog box*

10. In the **Frame Hold Options** dialog box, select the **Hold On** check box, if not already selected. Also, make sure the **In Point** option is selected in the drop-down list on the right of the **Hold On** check box. Next, choose the **OK** button.

11. Move the CTI to the beginning of the **Freeze** clip and play the sequence. You will notice that the **Freeze** clip is frozen.

    Next, you will create a matte to superimpose the sparkles over the freeze.

12. Choose the **Export Frame** button located below the Program Monitor; the **Export Frame** dialog box is displayed. In the **Export Frame** dialog box, type **still image** in the **Name** text box. Make sure the **JPEG** option is selected in the **Format** drop-down list. Also, choose the desired location by choosing the **Browse** button to save the bitmap image. Next, choose the **OK** button; the bitmap image is saved at the specified location.

    Next, you will create a matte in Adobe Photoshop using the saved bitmap image.

13. In Adobe Photoshop, open the bitmap image named as **still image**.

14. Choose the **Lasso Tool** located on the left of the screen. Press and hold the left mouse button and drag to select the subject on the screen, as shown in Figure 14-47.

15. Choose **Select > Inverse** from the menu bar; the selection is displayed, as shown in Figure 14-48.

Figure 14-47 *Subject selected using the **Lasso** tool*   *Figure 14-48* *The inverse selection*

16. Press the DELETE key; the **Fill** dialog box is displayed. In this dialog box, make sure the **Background White** option is selected in the **Use** drop-down list and then choose the **OK** button; everything is deleted from the screen, except the subject, refer to Figure 14-49.

17. Choose the **Set Foreground Color** color swatch on the left of the screen and choose the black color for the foreground.

 Note
Adobe Photoshop CS6 version has been used for the above steps.

18. Press the ALT+BACKSPACE keys to fill the black color in the selection, refer to Figure 14-50.

19. Again, choose **Select > Inverse** from the menu bar; the subject is selected.

20. Choose the **Set Foreground Color** color swatch on the left of the screen and choose the white color for the foreground. Next, press the ALT+BACKSPACE keys to fill the white color in the selection, refer to Figure 14-50.

Figure 14-49 The screen after pressing the DELETE key

Figure 14-50 The black color filled in the selection

21. Press the CTRL+D keys to deselect the subject. Next, save the Photoshop file with the name **matte** at the desired location.

Next, you will add sparkles to the sequence.

22. Switch back to Premiere. In the **Project** panel, import the **sparkles** video clip from *\Documents\Adobe Premiere Tutorials\Media Files\Video* that you have downloaded from the CADCIM website.

23. Make sure the CTI is at the beginning of the **Freeze** clip and add the **sparkles** video clip in the **V2** track just above the **Freeze** clip, refer to Figure 14-51. Also, trim the Out point of the **sparkles** clip to match the duration of the **Freeze** clip, if it is not matching, refer to Figure 14-52.

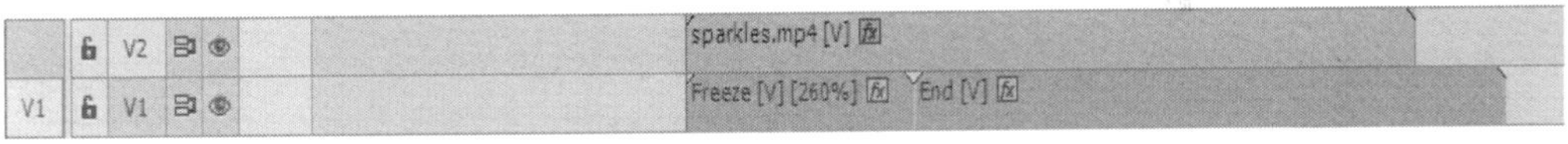

Figure 14-51 The sparkles video clip in the **V2** track

Figure 14-52 The trimmed sparkles clip

Next, you will add the Photoshop file named as **matte** to the sequence that you saved in the earlier steps.

24. In the **Project** panel, import the **matte** file and add it to the **V3** track just above the **sparkles** clip. Also, lengthen the **matte** clip to match with the duration of the **sparkles** clip, if it is not matching, refer to Figure 14-53.

	V3		matte.jpg
	V2		sparkles.mp4 [V]
V1	V1		Freeze [V] [260%] ⚡	End [V] ⚡

Figure 14-53 *The matte clip placed and trimmed in the V3 track*

25. Choose the **Toggle Track Output** button in the **V3** track to make the **matte** clip invisible for now.

    Next, you will apply the **Track Matte Key** effect to the **sparkles** clip so that it can use the **matte** clip as a matte.

26. In the **Effects** panel, expand **Video Effects > Keying**. Next, select the **Track Matte Key** effect and drag it to the **sparkles** clip in the **V2** track. Now, select the **Effect Controls** panel and expand the **Track Matte Key** effect, if it is not expanded; various parameters are displayed. Select the **Video 3** option in the **Matte** drop-down list and select **Matte Luma** from the **Composite Using** drop-down list; the subject is covered with the moving sparkles in the Program Monitor, as shown in Figure 14-54.

Figure 14-54 *The subject covered with the moving sparkles*

27. Make sure the CTI is at the beginning of the **Freeze** clip and play the sequence to view the effect in the Program Monitor.

    Next, you will fade out this effect gradually to reveal the subject.

28. Move the CTI to the beginning of the **sparkles** clip in the **Timeline** panel and make sure the **sparkles** clip is selected.

29. In the **Effect Controls** panel, expand the **Opacity** effect. Next, choose the **Add/Remove Keyframe** button on the right of the **Opacity** property; a keyframe is created for the current value, refer to Figure 14-55. Next, move the CTI to the end of the **sparkles** clip and enter the value **0** in the **Opacity** edit box; a new keyframe is created for the new value, refer to Figure Figure 14-55.

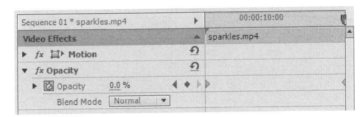

Figure 14-55 Keyframes created

30. Move the CTI to the beginning of the **sparkles** clip in the **Timeline** panel and play the sequence; a gradual fade out effect is created from the start to the end of the clip, refer to Figure 14-56.

Figure 14-56 The fade out effect at one of the frames

Next, you will fade in the entire effect at the starting of the sequence.

31. Choose the **Toggle Track Output** button to make the **V4** track visible.

32. Move the CTI to the frame 00:00:03:14. Select the **matte**, **sparkles**, **Freeze**, and **End** clips together. Next, move them toward the left at the frame 00:00:03:14, refer to Figure 14-57.

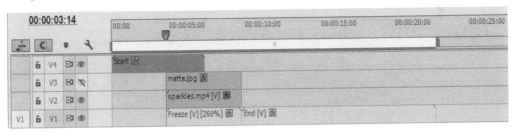

Figure 14-57 The clips moved to the frame 00:00:03:14

33. Select the **Start** clip in the **Timeline** panel and then expand the **Opacity** effect in the **Effect Controls** panel. Next, set three keyframes at the start, middle, and end of the **Start** clip. For the **Opacity** parameter, enter the values **100**, **70**, and **0** for the start, middle, and end keyframes respectively. Figure 14-58 shows the three keyframes added after modifying the values.

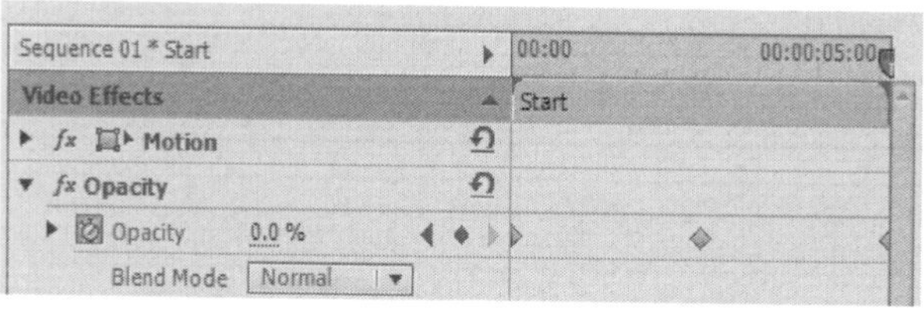

Figure 14-58 *Three keyframes added*

34. Move the CTI to the beginning of the sequence and play it to view the effect.

35. Press CTRL+S to save the file. The output of the sequence at frame 00:00:06:22 is shown in Figure 14-59.

Figure 14-59 *The output of the sequence at frame 00:00:06:22*

Tutorial 6

In this tutorial, you will highlight a part of an image using the Titler window. The output of the sequence is shown in Figure 14-60.   **(Expected Time: 15 min)**

Figure 14-60 *The output of the sequence*

The following steps are required to complete this tutorial:

a.   Open the project file.
b.   Hightlight a part of an image.

Opening the Project File
In this section, you will open the project file.

1.   Open the *chapter14_highlight.prproj* file that you have downloaded from the CADCIM website.

2.   Save the *chapter14_highlight.prproj* file with the name *chapter14_highlight_02.prproj* to *\Documents\Adobe Premiere Tutorials\c14_premiere_cc_tut*. The *chapter14_highlight_02.prproj* file is displayed, as shown in Figure 14-61.

Figure 14-61 The chapter14_highlight_02.prproj file displayed

Highlighting a Part of an Image
In this section, you will highlight a part of an image.

1.   In the **Project** panel, choose the **New Item** button located at its bottom; a flyout is displayed. Choose the **Title** option from the flyout; the **New Title** dialog box is displayed. Type **Image** in the **Name** text box and choose the **OK** button; the Titler window is displayed.

2.   In the Titler window, make sure the **Show Background Video** button is chosen and the image clip is displayed in the background, refer to Figure 14-62.

Figure 14-62 The image clip displayed as background

Next, you will create a shape to overlap the area in the image clip that you want to highlight.

3. Invoke the **Ellipse Tool** from the **Title Tools** panel of the Titler window. Next, create an elliptical shape and overlap the area to highlight, as shown in Figure 14-63.

Figure 14-63 The elliptical shape over the image clip

4. In the **Title Properties** panel of the Titler window, make sure the **Fill** check box is selected. Next, choose the color swatch on the right of the **Color** option; the **Color Picker** dialog box is displayed. Set the following values in the **Color Picker** dialog box as given below and then choose the **OK** button:

R: **0**   G: **0**   B: **255**

After applying the settings, the color of the elliptical shape will become blue. Next, you will create a rectangular shape to cover the entire image clip.

5. Invoke the **Rectangle Tool** from the **Title Tools** panel of the Titler window. Next, create a rectangular shape to overlap the entire image clip. Also, modify its color to black as discussed in the earlier steps.

6. Next, select the black colored shape and right-click on it; a shortcut menu is displayed. Choose the **Arrange > Send to Back** option from the shortcut menu; the image is displayed on the Titler screen, as shown in Figure 14-64. Now, close the Titler window.

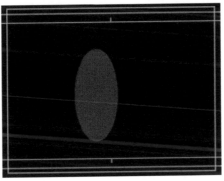

Figure 14-64 The image on the Titler screen

Next, you will add a title to the sequence.

7. Make sure the title created is selected in the **Project** panel and then add it to the **V2** track just above the clip placed in the **V1** track. Also, drag the end point of the title in the **V2** track to match the duration of the clip placed in the **V1** track, refer to Figure 14-65.

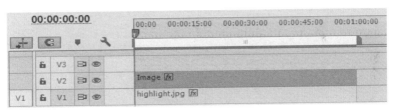

Figure 14-65 The title in the V2 track

8. Select the **Image** placed in the **V2** track and then choose the **Effect Controls** panel; various effects are displayed.

9. Expand the **Opacity** effect and enter the value **60** for the **Opacity** parameter. After modifying the value of **Opacity**, the clips are displayed in the Program Monitor, as shown in Figure 14-66.

Figure 14-66 *The clips in the Program Monitor*

Next, you will apply the **Color Key** effect to the title clip.

10. In the **Effects** panel, expand **Video Effects > Keying**; various effects are displayed. Select the **Color Key** effect and drag it to the **Image** in the **V2** track of the **Timeline** panel.

11. In the **Effect Controls** panel, expand the **Color Key** effect, if it is not expanded and make sure the blue color that you applied to the elliptical shape is selected in the color swatch on the right of the **Key Color** property. The resultant clip is displayed in the Program Monitor, as shown in Figure 14-67.

Figure 14-67 *The clip after applying the* ***Color Key*** *effect*

12. Next, enter the value **10** for the **Edge Feather** parameter; the clip is modified, as shown in Figure 14-68.

13. Press CTRL+S to save the file. The output of the sequence is shown in Figure 14-68.

Figure 14-68 *The clip after modifying the*
Edge Feather *property*

Tutorial 7

In this tutorial, you will customize the **Iris Diamond** transition effect. The output of the sequence at frame 00:00:16:16 is shown in Figure 14-69.   **(Expected Time: 15 min)**

The following steps are required to complete this tutorial:

a. Open the project file.
b. Customize the transition effect.

Figure 14-69 *The output of the sequence at frame 00:00:16:16*

Opening the Project File

In this section, you will open the project file.

1. Open the *chapter14_transition.prproj* file that you have downloaded from the CADCIM website.

2. Save the *chapter14_transition.prproj* file with the new name *chapter14_transition_02.prproj* to *\Documents\Adobe Premiere Tutorials\c14_premiere_cc_tut*. The *chapter14_transition_02.prproj* file is displayed, as shown in Figure 14-70. You will notice that there are two video clips placed in the **V1** track.

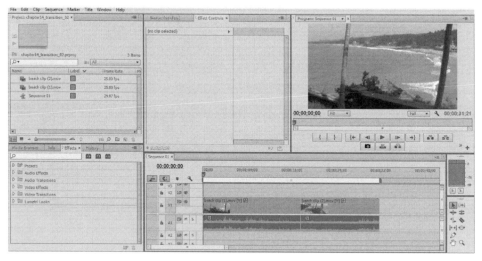

Figure 14-70 The chapter14_transition_02 file displayed

Customizing the Transition Effect

In this section, you will customize the transition effect. Next, you will apply the **Iris Diamond** transition effect between the two video clips.

1. In the **Effects** panel, expand **Video Transitions > Iris**; various transition effects are displayed. Next, select the **Iris Diamond** transition effect and drag it to the **V1** track in the middle of **beach clip (1)** and **beach clip (2)**, refer to Figure 14-71.

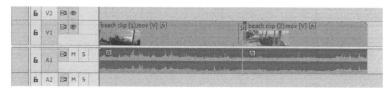

*Figure 14-71 The **Iris Diamond** transition effect between the clips*

2. Make sure the CTI is placed at the beginning of the sequence and play it; the default **Iris Diamond** transition effect is displayed in the Program Monitor at frame **00:00:17:14**, as shown in Figure 14-72.

Figure 14-72 The default **Iris Diamond**
transition effect at frame **00:00:17:14**

Next, you will customize the **Iris Diamond** transition effect.

3. Select the **Iris Diamond** transition effect in the **Timeline** panel; its properties are displayed in the **Effect Controls** panel.

4. In this panel, select the **Show Actual Sources** check box, if not already selected, to display the actual clips on the preview screen, refer to Figure 14-73.

5. By default, the duration of the transition effect is 1 second. To increase its duration, enter the new value **05.00** in the **Duration** edit box.

You can drag the sliders located below the preview screen to modify the start and end times of the transition, refer to Figure 14-73.

Note
Press and hold the SHIFT key to move both start and end sliders simultaneously.

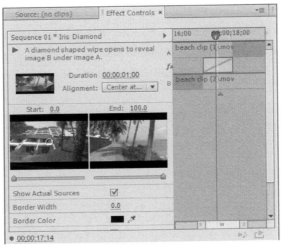

Figure 14-73 Actual clips displayed on the preview screen

6. Enter the value **3.0** in the **Border Width** edit box to display a border around the clip, as shown in Figure 14-74. You can also modify the color of the border by choosing the color swatch on the right of the **Border Color** property. Similarly, you can customize any other transition in Adobe Premiere Pro based on your requirement using the properties in the **Effect Controls** panel.

Figure 14-74 The border around the clip

7. Press CTRL+S to save the file and then press ENTER to view the output of the sequence in the Program Monitor. The output of the sequence at frame 00:00:16:16 shown in Figure 14-75.

Figure 14-75 The output of the sequence at frame 00:00:16:16

Tutorial 8

In this tutorial, you will create the ghost effect. To create a ghost effect, you need two clips, one with the background scene without any actor and another one with the same background along with the ghost actor. Note that the background for both scenes must be still. The output of the sequence at frame 00:00:07:03 is shown in Figure 14-76.   **(Expected Time: 10 min)**

The following steps are required to complete this tutorial:

a. Open the project file.
b. Create the ghost effect.

Figure 14-76 *The output of the sequence at frame 00:00:07:03*

Opening the Project File

In this section, you will open the project file.

1. Open the *chapter14_ghost.prproj* file that you have downloaded from the CADCIM website.

2. Save the *chapter14_ghost.prproj* premiere file with the name *chapter14_ghost_02.prproj* to *\Documents\Adobe Premiere Tutorials\c14_premiere_cc_tut*. The *chapter14_ghost_02.prproj* file is displayed, as shown in Figure 14-77. Notice that there are two video clips in the **Project** panel.

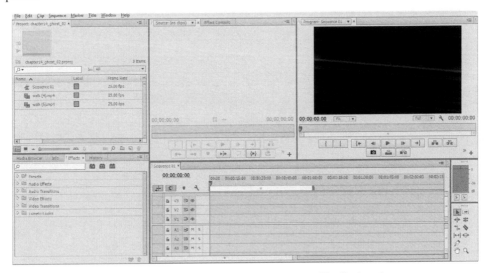

Figure 14-77 *The chapter14_ghost_02 file displayed*

Creating the Ghost Effect

In this section, you will create the ghost effect.

1. In the **Project** panel, select the **walk (5).mp4** clip and add it to the **V1** track in the **Timeline** panel, as shown in Figure 14-78. The **walk (5).mp4** clip has the background scene without any ghost actor, refer to Figure 14-79.

Note
*Press the EQUAL (=) key to zoom in the **walk (5).mp4** file in the **V1** track to view it properly.*

*Figure 14-78 The **walk (5).mp4** clip in the **V1** track*

*Figure 14-79 The **walk (5).mp4** clip*

2. Move the CTI to the frame 00:00:05:10 and add the **walk (4).mp4** clip from the **Project** panel to the **V2** track in the **Timeline** panel, starting from the frame 00:00:05:10, as shown in Figure 14-80. Now, the **walk (4).mp4** clip has the background scene with the ghost actor, as shown in Figure 14-81.

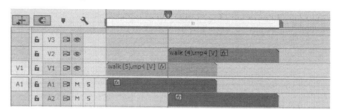

*Figure 14-80 The **walk (4).mp4** clip in the **V2** track*

3. Next, trim the end point of the **walk (4).mp4** clip to match with the end point of **walk (5).mp4** clip, refer to Figure 14-82.

Figure 14-81 The walk (4).mp4 clip

Figure 14-82 The trimmed walk (4).mp4 clip

Next, you will modify the properties of the **walk (4).mp4** clip in the **Effect Controls** panel to create the ghost effect.

4. Select the **walk (4).mp4** clip in the **Timeline** panel and then choose the **Effect Controls** panel; the default effects of the **walk (4).mp4** clip are displayed.

5. In the **Effect Controls** panel, expand the **Opacity** effect; the properties of the **Opacity** effect are displayed.

Next, you will modify the properties of the **Opacity** effect for the **walk (4).mp4** clip.

6. Make sure the CTI is at the frame 00:00:05:10. Next, enter the value **0** for the **Opacity** parameter; a keyframe is created. After modifying the value, the clip becomes totally transparent and the resultant clip is displayed in the Program Monitor, as shown in Figure 14-83.

7. Move the CTI to the frame 00:00:06:04. Next, enter **20** for the **Opacity** parameter; another keyframe is created. The resultant clip is displayed in the Program Monitor, as shown in Figure 14-84.

8. Move the CTI to the frame 00:00:06:23. Again, enter **20** for the **Opacity** parameter; another keyframe is created.

Figure 14-83 *The frame when* ***Opacity=0***

Figure 14-84 *The frame when* ***Opacity=20***

9. Move the CTI to the frame 00:00:07:21. Next, enter the value **0** for the **Opacity** parameter; another keyframe is created. Also, the clip becomes totally transparent.

10. Move the CTI to the beginning of the sequence and play it to view the effect. The ghost actor appears in the scene and then disappears slowly.

The output of the sequence at frame 00:00:07:03 is shown in Figure 14-85.

Figure 14-85 *The output of the sequence at frame 00:00:07:03*

Self-Evaluation Test

Answer the following questions and then compare them to those given at the end of this chapter:

1. Which of the following options is used to place a light in a video clip?

    (a) **SpotLight**   (b) **Directional**
    (c) **Omni**   (d) All of the above

2. You need to press and hold the _____ key to move both start and end sliders simultaneously.

3. The **Opacity** parameter is used to add fade in or fade out effect to the clip. (T/F)

4. The **Scale** parameter is used to zoom in or zoom out the clip. (T/F)

Review Questions

Answer the following questions:

1. Which of the following buttons is used to view the background in the Titler window?

    (a) **Show Background Video**   (b) **Templates**
    (c) **Tab Stops**   (d) None of these

2. The **New Item** button is located at the bottom of the _____ panel.

3. In the **Effects Controls** panel, the **Show Actual Sources** check box is used to display the actual clips on the preview screen. (T/F)

4. The **Title Properties** area is located on the right of the Titler window. (T/F)

EXERCISE

Exercise 1

Create a new project and then import video clips and compose them. Also, add various effects
to the clips.

Index

Other Publications by CADCIM Technologies

The following is the list of some of the publications by CADCIM Technologies. Please visit www.cadcim.com for the complete listing.

Autodesk 3ds Max Design Textbooks
- Autodesk 3ds Max Design 2014: A Tutorial Approach
- Autodesk 3ds Max Design 2013: A Tutorial Approach
- Autodesk 3ds Max Design 2012: A Tutorial Approach

Autodesk 3ds Max Textbooks
- Autodesk 3ds Max 2014: A Comprehensive Guide
- Autodesk 3ds Max 2013: A Comprehensive Guide
- Autodesk 3ds Max 2012: A Comprehensive Guide

Maya Textbooks
- Autodesk Maya 2014: A Comprehensive Guide
- Autodesk Maya 2013: A Comprehensive Guide
- Autodesk Maya 2012: A Comprehensive Guide

Fusion Textbooks
- The eyeon Fusion 6.3: A Tutorial Approach
- The eyeon Fusion 6.2: A Tutorial Approach

Flash Textbooks
- Adobe Flash Professional CC: A Tutorial Approach
- Adobe Flash Professional CS6: A Tutorial Approach

Premiere Textbooks
- Adobe Premiere Professional CS6: A Tutorial Approach
- Adobe Premiere Professional CS5.5: A Tutorial Approach

CINEMA 4D Textbooks
- MAXON CINEMA 4D Studio R15: A Tutorial Approach
- MAXON CINEMA 4D Studio R14: A Tutorial Approach

ZBrush Textbook
• Pixologic ZBrush 4R6: A Comprehensive Guide

NukeX Textbook
• The Foundry NukeX 7 for Compositors

AutoCAD Textbook
• AutoCAD 2014: A Problem Solving Approach

SolidWorks Textbooks
• SolidWorks 2014 for Designers
• SolidWorks 2014: A Tutorial Approach
• SolidWorks 2013 for Designers

Autodesk Inventor Textbooks
• Autodesk Inventor 2014 for Designers
• Autodesk Inventor 2013 for Designers

Solid Edge Textbooks
• Solid Edge ST6 for Designers
• Solid Edge ST5 for Designers
• Solid Edge ST4 for Designers

NX Textbooks
• NX 8.5 for Designers
• NX 8 for Designers
• NX 7 for Designers

EdgeCAM Textbooks
• EdgeCAM 11.0 for Manufacturers
• EdgeCAM 10.0 for Manufacturers

CATIA Textbooks
• CATIA V5-6R2013 for Designers
• CATIA V5-6R2012 for Designers

Pro/ENGINEER / Creo Parametric Textbooks
- Creo Parametric 2.0 for Designers
- Creo Parametric 1.0 for Designers
- Pro/ENGINEER Wildfire 5.0 for Designers

Creo Direct Textbook
- Creo Direct 2.0 and Beyond for Designers

Autodesk Alias Textbooks
- Learning Autodesk Alias Design 2012
- Learning Autodesk Alias Design 2010

ANSYS Textbooks
- ANSYS Workbench 14.0: A Tutorial Approach
- ANSYS 11.0 for Designers

Customizing AutoCAD Textbook
- Customizing AutoCAD 2013

AutoCAD MEP Textbook
- AutoCAD MEP 2014 for Designers

AutoCAD LT Textbooks
- AutoCAD LT 2014 for Designers
- AutoCAD LT 2013 for Designers
- AutoCAD LT 2012 for Designers

AutoCAD Plant 3D Textbook
- AutoCAD Plant 3D 2014 for Designers

AutoCAD Electrical Textbooks
- AutoCAD Electrical 2014 for Electrical Control Designers
- AutoCAD Electrical 2013 for Electrical Control Designers

Autodesk Revit Architecture Textbooks
• Autodesk Revit Architecture 2014 for Architects and Designers
• Autodesk Revit Architecture 2013 for Architects and Designers

Autodesk Revit Structure Textbooks
• Exploring Autodesk Revit Structure 2014
• Exploring Autodesk Revit Structure 2013

AutoCAD Civil 3D Textbooks
• Exploring AutoCAD Civil 3D 2014 for Engineers
• Exploring AutoCAD Civil 3D 2013 for Engineers

AutoCAD Map 3D Textbooks
• Exploring AutoCAD Map 3D 2014
• Exploring AutoCAD Map 3D 2013
• Exploring AutoCAD Map 3D 2012

Paper Craft Book
• Constructing 3-Dimensional Models: A Paper-Craft Workbook

Computer Programming Textbooks
• Learning Oracle 11g
• Learning ASP.NET AJAX
• Learning Java Programming
• Learning Visual Basic.NET 2008
• Learning C++ Programming Concepts
• Learning VB.NET Programming Concepts

AutoCAD Textbooks Authored by Prof. Sham Tickoo and Published by Autodesk Press

• AutoCAD: A Problem-Solving Approach: 2013 and Beyond
• AutoCAD 2012: A Problem-Solving Approach

Textbooks Authored by CADCIM Technologies and Published by Other Publishers

3D Studio MAX and VIZ Textbooks
* Learning 3DS Max: A Tutorial Approach, Release 4
  Goodheart-Wilcox Publishers (USA)
* Learning 3D Studio VIZ: A Tutorial Approach
  Goodheart-Wilcox Publishers (USA)

CADCIM Technologies Textbooks Translated in Other Languages

SolidWorks Textbooks
* SolidWorks 2008 for Designers (Serbian Edition)
  Mikro Knjiga Publishing Company, Serbia
* SolidWorks 2006 for Designers (Russian Edition)
  Piter Publishing Press, Russia

NX Textbook
* NX 6 for Designers (Korean Edition)
  Onsolutions, South Korea

Pro/ENGINEER Textbook
* Pro/ENGINEER Wildfire 4.0 for Designers (Korean Edition)
  HongReung Science Publishing Company, South Korea

Autodesk 3ds Max Textbook
* 3ds Max 2008: A Comprehensive Guide (Serbian Edition)
  Mikro Knjiga Publishing Company, Serbia

AutoCAD Textbooks
* AutoCAD 2006 (Russian Edition)
  Piter Publishing Press, Russia
* AutoCAD 2005 (Russian Edition)
  Piter Publishing Press, Russia
* AutoCAD 2000 Fondamenti (Italian Edition)

Coming Soon from CADCIM Technologies

- Autodesk Maya 2015: A Comprehensive Guide
- Autodesk 3ds Max 2015: A Comprehensive Guide
- Autodesk 3ds Max Design 2015: A Tutorial Approach
- The Foundry NukeX 8 for Compositors
- NX 9.0 for Designers
- NX Nastran 9.0 for Designers
- Autodesk Revit MEP 2015: A Tutorial Approach
- AutoCAD 2015: A Problem Solving Approach
- Autodesk Inventor 2015 for Designers
- Exploring AutoCAD Civil 3D 2015 for Engineers
- Exploring Autodesk Navisworks 2015
- Autodesk Revit Architecture 2015 for Architects and Designers

Online Training Program Offered by CADCIM Technologies

CADCIM Technologies provides effective and affordable virtual online training on various software packages including computer programming languages, Computer Aided Design and Manufacturing (CAD/CAM), animation, architecture, and GIS. The training will be delivered 'live' via Internet at any time, any place, and at any pace to individuals as well as the students of colleges, universities, and CAD/CAM training centers. For more information, please visit the following link: *http://www.cadcim.com*

Made in the USA
San Bernardino, CA
08 August 2014